T0128153

IT'S A LONG WAY FROM FERRYHILL

CLIFF ATKINSON

BALBOA.
PRESS

A DIVISION OF HAY HOUSE

Balboa Press books may be ordered through booksellers or by contacting:

Balboa Press
A Division of Hay House
1663 Liberty Drive
Bloomington, IN 47403
www.balboapress.com.au
1 (877) 407-4847

Because of the dynamic nature of the Internet, any web addresses or links contained in this book may have changed since publication and may no longer be valid. The views expressed in this work are solely those of the author and do not necessarily reflect the views of the publisher, and the publisher hereby disclaims any responsibility for them.

The author of this book does not dispense medical advice or prescribe the use of any technique as a form of treatment for physical, emotional, or medical problems without the advice of a physician, either directly or indirectly. The intent of the author is only to offer information of a general nature to help you in your quest for emotional and spiritual well-being. In the event you use any of the information in this book for yourself, which is your constitutional right, the author and the publisher assume no responsibility for your actions.

Any people depicted in stock imagery provided by Getty Images are models, and such images are being used for illustrative purposes only.
Certain stock imagery © Getty Images.

Print information available on the last page.

ISBN: 978-1-5043-1629-3 (sc)
ISBN: 978-1-5043-1632-3 (e)

Balboa Press rev. date: 01/10/2019

CONTENTS

FOREWORD

Cliff Atkinson started life in the small coal mining village of Ferryhill in the north east of England. The book details the many facets of his life including his childhood which is best described that when asked if he'd read Angela's Ashes, his reply was that not only had he read it he had lived it. Follow his early story through Ferryhill Station, East Howle, The Cragg, Chilton and Chilton Lane. Then higher education and the life changing decision to migrate to Australia.

This is more than a rags to riches story even though that takes up many parts of the book it illustrates how anyone in the world no matter how humble their beginnings can meet and hold court with some of the most wealthy and powerful in the world.

From this small coal mining village Ferryhill, known only as a former mining community of six thousand people that the world by-passes driving along the London - Newcastle motorway.

A working life which begins as a mathematics schoolteacher, then advertising executive, rock concert promoter, television producer/director, record company proprietor, stockbroker and financial advisor on infrastructure projects around the world.

When watching the TV series Madmen he thinks it's a documentary on the advertising industry of the sixties and seventies.

Share his experiences with rock stars including Chuck Berry, Roy Orbison, Billy Connolly, Sandy Denny, John Denver, Dusty Springfield and many others.

Even Elvis and The Eagles get a mention. Not forgetting working with Angelina Jolie, Cate Blanchett, Adrien Brophy, Dermot Mulroney, Brooke Shields, Sam Neill and Robert Redford.

Politicians including Hawke, Keating, Howard, Clinton and numerous West African Presidents.

Religious leaders such as Dr. L. Ron Hubbard.

Sportsmen such as Beckham, Shearer, Maradona, Alan Border. Tony Grieg and George Peponis.

Get an insight on Lindy Chamberlain 'The dingo took my baby' from a slightly drunk sitting High Court judge.

Dealings with three generations of Packers, Australia's most wealthy family dynasty

Being off-loaded from a Pan Am flight in war torn Beirut.

A paper multi-millionaire during the dot-com boom.

Unwittingly getting involved with Mr. Asia, one of the world's major drug lords.

Working with Benny Hill, Sir David Frost and others in television.

This is a fascinating memoir of how high one can fly, and how low one can go if you put yourself out there.

How he broke the major record companies ban on imported music and live recordings in Australia.

Most notable is how a life can change with one phone call which kick started this great adventure in life.

He has played football, soccer, at all levels and continues to do so even at 73 years old for North Sydney over 45's where he carries the nickname Dead Man Walking since his severe heart attack 20 years ago and the recent installation of a heart pacemaker.

Still active and working as CEO of Phoenix Green Capital, advisors on investment in infrastructure in underdeveloped countries predominantly in West Africa and Asia.

CHAPTER 1!

Oops! Wrong Number!

There was the time around July 1973 while working as a researcher for the Victorian Broadcasting Network, a media company that owned and operated a number of regional television stations and radio stations in the state of Victoria in Australia, in the North Sydney sales office, not a very stimulating occupation but it paid the mortgage and could possibly lead to a better position with a major metropolitan TV network. Eating a chicken and salad sandwich for lunch and looking forward to the sticky buttered finger bun with its pink icing sitting on the desk in front of me. Having just finished a year teaching high school girls mathematics at Saint George Girls High School the finger bun had become an essential part of my diet. In those days a balanced diet to me was fish on one side of the plate and chips on the other side. Leaving teaching particularly at this school, had been a difficult decision to make as it was a selective school where only the best and brightest attended. Being a young Englishman one can imagine what it was like, not only embarrassing, when on sports carnival day around eight hundred young girls started singing at the tops of their voices, He's Our Long Haired Lover from Liverpool, as I was making my way to the starting line having been given the task of starter for all the races. Little Jimmy Osmond would have been proud. It had been an interesting posting for a young mathematics teacher at a selective girl's high school where the students would have passed everything with or without my input. However I was very flattered when mothers started to turn up at the school wanting to meet me to discuss what was going on as they had noticed maths homework had become a priority in most homes. At the risk of flattering myself I was one of two male teachers on the staff and the other was looking forward to retirement so I was young, English and driving a flashy sports car.

From my desk at VBN I could look out of the window onto the Sydney Harbour Bridge, maybe that's a bit of an exaggeration, a better description would be a view of the traffic leaving the Harbour Bridge onto the Warringah Expressway.

In those days there were two afternoon newspapers, the Daily Mirror and the Daily Sun, and while reading the Fairfax Sun I noticed a very small article lost in the bowels of the paper, underneath the Vincent's Powders message, and just above the haemorrhoids advertisement announcing that the Sydney Opera House was open for bookings with a phone number 20666 handling enquiries. Only decades later did I appreciate the numbers 666. Probably should remind ourselves that 'The House' as some of us in the current day and age call it, that is the pretentious 'us' who feel we have some spiritual connection with the building, was to be opened by Queen Elizabeth 2 in October 1973 and so far only the construction crews and SOH staff had had access to 'The House'. The only performance so far being on the steps by the American singer Paul Robeson for the workers on the construction site.

Now that we understand its position in the Australian psyche what followed is remarkable.

The thought bubble appeared above my head lit up and it occurred to me to me that it would be a very good idea to get a couple of tickets for any performance at the Sydney Opera House in an effort to please and surprise Patricia, my wife of a few years, and as I've been heard to say many times in the last 50 years, 'to save a marriage'. As time will tell it didn't work.

Putting the finger bun to the side and licking the icing off my fingers I made a life changing phone call. I dialled the number, no push button phones at this office. The number yes, I remember it well, two zero six six six and asked the lady who picked up at the other end how could I make bookings as mentioned in the paper. Put on hold I was then connected and put through to a gentleman called Justin Smith. I mentioned the article in the paper and asked about bookings. He asked me which night I was looking at and I stated the obvious, well it was obvious to me, a Saturday night of course, that was any Saturday night as soon as possible after the Queen had performed the formalities, and if possible and affordable maybe even the opening night. No chance at all! That was for dignitaries, and the programme was close to being finalised. I was then asked which room or hall I was interested in. Which room? What did I know about rooms in the Sydney Opera House? Had no concept of there being more than one venue. No-one had been in it yet. So I replied the big one of course. Not wanting to be thought of as a cheapskate I thought two tickets can't be that expensive, bearing in mind my salary at the time was about a hundred and twenty dollars a week, and when given the good news that Saturdays were available in the Concert Hall I asked how much. My heart skipped not one but a number of beats as I heard seven hundred and fifty dollars guaranteed against 12.5% of takings. A little expensive for a night out I thought, but not wishing to appear a miserly skinflint I queried the 12.5% in my own mind thinking that I'll be able to hang up gracefully and get back to him. But in hindsight I didn't have a clue what he was talking about.

We've all heard about light bulb moments, some but not all of us have had them, I now had a second one within five minutes of the first one. This was my second. I paused and ran things through my befuddled brain and started to think he's offering me the chance to book the hall lock, stock, barrel, stage, lights and everything that went with it. He kept talking but I wasn't hearing the rest of terms and conditions being explained to me, I just knew I had to do this. Whatever 'this' was. Yes, as people have asked me hundreds of times since what was I thinking? The truth is I wasn't. Did I know what I was doing? Not a clue! Had I promoted anything in the entertainment business? Only when I was 13 years old and having taken a dozen guitar lessons with my next door neighbour Eric Haswell we played our only three chord versions of Paul Anka's Diana, Lonnie Donegan's Worried Man and My Old Man's A Dustman in my backyard, and that's a concrete yard in a pitman's terrace house, not a garden as named in other countries, in Ferryhill Station to all the kids in the street. Picture a concrete area five metre by four metres outside the kitchen and in front of the outside toilet. A long zinc bathtub hanging off the wall. Not exactly the Royal Albert Hall. We were a great success and maybe I was destined to be in show business.

One mistake-nobody paid.

Perhaps an omen of things to come.

Back to the Sydney Opera House and if I'd been standing I would have been thinking on my feet, as it was the wheels in my brain were spinning so fast no clear thoughts emerged.

As the conversation went on Justin pointed out that a number of Saturday nights in the Concert Hall were available and could I be interested in them.

So trying to act sophisticated and entrepreneurial, a word I learnt in the coming months, I carried on with the conversation and I dived in.

Some facts and figures should come in handy at this stage. The deposit required for each booking was a hundred and twenty dollars. For the first date deposit due now on signing of contract, other deposits due six weeks before each of the events. EVENTS! WHAT EVENTS? Where am I going to find the first one hundred and twenty dollars never mind the other six for first available 12 Saturday nights I'd booked in the Concert Hall and how was my wife going to react to my foolishness? I passed on my address for postage of the contracts then hung up the phone, took a number of deep breaths and pondered on what I had just done. I convinced myself that they would be a great success, after all I had called up to buy a couple of tickets without knowing what was going to be on the bill. I then got cold feet as I realised that as a researcher and statistician I was breaking a cardinal rule of research by relying on the results of a sample of one respondent. That is me!

However casting doubts aside, first step, how do I get one hundred and twenty dollars? The wife would divorce me if I was to spend a monthly mortgage instalment on such a crazy idea. Just then a work colleague, John Sturzaker, a real gentleman who looked like a debonair David Niven with the smooth moustache and aristocratic bearing, and he had recently moved to Sydney from Melbourne with a history in television advertising sales and marketing, happened to be passing my desk as I put the phone down and after a few minutes I asked him if he was willing to lose sixty dollars on a crazy venture. His reply was along the lines of how crazy? We arranged to meet in the Albert Hotel, our regular after work pub, and after I'd explained what I had done he took a few minutes to think about it, he was a much more conservative person than myself, he actually thought about it, he said yes and a shake of the hand became a life changing moment for both of us.

The contract for the first date arrived in the mail, no email or the like in those days, so off went the cheque for a hundred and twenty dollars and we were in show business. I paid the twenty cents for the stamp on the envelope that I had stolen from the Victorian Broadcasting Network.

Now for the first time we thought about what we would present on the dates booked. But we did have a few months to work it out, or so we thought.............................

CHAPTER 2!

East Howle and more.

How do I remember Ferryhill growing up there?

I have often over dinner asked people what is their earliest memory of their lives. Most people reply that it was the first day they started school. Not very stimulating I would think, surely there would be earlier memories than that. But no not for most people. I remember two incidents from my very early years and I try to remember which one came first. Probably the fairground event as I distinctly remember being carried by my mother into the travelling fairground at the Brewery Field in Spennymoor. Of course I didn't know the name of the field at the time but as I spent all of my grammar school years in Spennymoor I grew to know the place quite well later in life. Even played football on it a couple of times. What I do recall vividly is being carried in my mother's arms and the bright colours of the lights strung around the rides and game stalls along with what appeared to be solid gold mirrors being prizes for the darts or hoopla games. Always strange that I learnt as I grew up no-one ever won the prizes on the top shelves. Barry my older brother was walking alongside with myself resting on my mother's hip. We had with us Mrs Watson, who was married to Alf Watson, dad's best friend and had been his best man, and she was carrying her daughter. As we walked past the tombola stand there was a yell of surprise and it had come from my mother, I remember turning my head to see dad and Alf with two young ladies having the time of their lives. My mother walked straight up to him and saying nothing just thrust me into dad's arms and walked away with Barry in tow. I think that someone's evening was certainly spoilt by mum's reaction. Don't remember going home. Suppose it was on the United number four bus which ran from Spennymoor to Cornforth via East Howle which was the very small village just on the fringe of Ferryhill which was where we were living at the time. East Howle now exists only as a gypsy, apologies, travellers camp as all the old miner's terraces were demolished late last century long after we were living there.

The other early memory is after leaving the doctor's surgery in Ferryhill Village, which is now the Manor House pub, and I was in a push chair. For those who don't know what a push chair is it is the old fashioned equivalent of a stroller. The child now faces forward away from the parent after having spent months facing the mother in the large prams as seen in the Mary Poppins movie. As we were passing the local co-operative store across from the town hall a lady started talking to my mother and telling her what a beautiful girl I was, looking just like Shirley Temple with white curly hair. I can remember mother snapping back that I was a boy and curtly finishing the conversation. This is the only time I can remember her losing her temper.

During a visit to Sydney by my older brother Barry, I asked him his earliest memory and what a laugh we had when he described teaching me to climb trees in the East Howle Little Wood and when he was underneath me pushing me up by my backside I started to laugh which resulted in me peeing all over his head. We never wore underpants in those days.

To put Ferryhill in context it could be the coal mining village in which Billy Elliott is set. Over the years I have returned to Ferryhill as a visitor and remarkably nothing seems to have changed including the people and their whole lifestyle, attitudes and dress appear stuck in a time warp in the middle of the twentieth century. Please don't read this as derogatory it's almost refreshing to hark back to simpler times. I hope the locals on reading this would say 'Why Aye Man'. Translated to 'Of course sir.'

There's more to come ....

CHAPTER 3

Fingers Did The Walking!

So here we are, the Concert Hall of the Sydney Opera House booked for the first 7 available Saturday nights after opening by the Queen in October. Four months seemed like a long time to get our act, or maybe I should say acts, together. With John and I having no experience at all in promoting concerts or events the prospect of selling nearly twenty thousand tickets appeared to be a mammoth task. Fortunately we had our day jobs which had allowed us to pay the first $120 deposit and no worries about the others till six weeks before each performance so maybe we could save up the money in time. As the months passed without worrying too much a small panic set in when a phone call from Justin Smith at the Opera House asking what we had planned and how much were our tickets to be. This galvanised us into action and asking why, Justin let us know that the airlines TAA, Ansett ANA, and Qantas, along with Murrays Coaches and most of the hotels in Sydney were calling up trying to buy packages of tickets for all of the Saturday nights we had booked. This made sense to me as my initial approach had been to get tickets, any tickets, for Saturday night performances in the holiday period. Again having no experience in such matters I asked what were other promoters putting on and what were there tickets going to cost. Fortunately for us Harry M. Miller and Jack Neary, Australia's leading impresarios at the time with productions like Hair, and Jesus Christ Superstar musicals under their belts, had booked the Sunday nights following our Saturdays and they were putting on a series of variety concerts modelled on the English television show, Sunday Night At The London Palladium, which he was going to call, obviously, Sunday Night at the Sydney Opera House, which was to be televised live on the Nine Network. Fishing around I got to know he had booked the likes of Carol Burnett, Glen Campbell, Petula Clark, Dave Allen, Harry Secombe, Des O'Connor, Rod McKuen, David Frost and Diahann Carroll along with many other international acts and he was charging $10.50 a ticket. Quick as a flash and as bold as brass I declared that we were going to use only Australian artists as they were much more deserving of the privilege than these blow ins from overseas. God only knows where the idea sprang from.Worth noting here I had only arrived recently myself from the U.K. What made me say it I had no idea, but it went down very well with the Opera House management and to my horror Lloyd Martin the Deputy Manager called a press conference for a few weeks later for me to announce the series. So much for our four month lead in. I also declared that we would charge only $6.50 a ticket so the Australian public would be able to afford the Sydney Opera House experience. Where these ideas were coming from may I repeat I had no idea, but it gained us a lot of credence and publicity and led to our next bit of good luck. The next call from Justin was to tell me that as one of the Opera House's biggest bookers, surprise, surprise, what is going on here? They were offering us a free evening to put on a performance before the official opening so they could check all the staffing, front of house, catering, bars, backstage etc. with all halls being in use at the same time. The free evening was to be in the Music Room one of the smaller theatres that held just over four hundred patrons. This proved to be a lifesaver as we hadn't got around to working out how we would be able to pay for the other deposits coming due.

We now had to get off our backsides and put some serious thought into what we intended to present. At the time I used to go to a number of pubs in the city that had folk singers performing on Saturday and Sunday nights. The Elizabeth Hotel on the corner of Liverpool and Elizabeth St. the Edinburgh Castle on the corner of Bathurst and Castlereagh there was the PACT folk club in the old Corn Exchange building in Sussex St. and Cellar Folk in the YWCA in Liverpool Street. I approached a number of the performers offering them ten dollars each if they would perform in the Opera House for twenty minutes each and a free meal in the green room. Not a problem, they jumped at the opportunity and all of them also wanted tickets for the performance for their friends and family. The opportunity for people to gain a preview of the Opera House was too good to miss and all tickets were gone in a few days without any publicity or expense needed.

Financial problems solved, two thousand dollars in the bank, we were now off and running. When news got out about this preview performance the next surprise was a telephone call from a Peter Vendrell of ABC television, an executive producer no less, who wanted to record the performance and if things went well would I be interested in helping him produce a folk music television series later that year. My head is spinning now, of course I said yes, partly due to the fact that they were going to pay us a thousand dollars for the right to record and broadcast this concert. Talk about falling on one's feet, I could feel a complete career change coming on. Needless to say the concert was a sell-out success and the ABC decided to go ahead with the television series. I had little to do with it as I now had a major concert series to arrange but the programmes called, Sit Yourself Down Take a Look Around, had a fairly successful season but more importantly I learned that television production is very simple and consists mainly of smoke and mirrors. The next step was to arrange artists and have something to say at the press conference coming up in a few days. If my memory serves me well the acts we booked were John Currie, Marion Henderson, Bernard Bolan, Jeannie Lewis, John J. Francis and the East Neasden Spasm Band. But I'm now feeling a little more confident about putting something together without my boss, John Fink, at the Victorian Broadcasting Network, finding out about my moonlighting and possibly showing me the door. Press conference coming up and no-one booked yet for the concert hall series. We're bound to use only Australian talent because of my earlier statement so let's put something together. John came up with the idea of calling the series 'The Australian Festival of Performing Arts' not a bad idea so let's run with it. We re-booked the folk acts as a reward for the preview performance, which had been an enormous success, and also with the information from the box office that the first night was almost sold out it made sense that probably the least attractive bill should take this date. John being a jazz aficionado suggested jazz for the second date so I wandered up to the Wentworth Hotel in Chifley Square one Saturday night and during a break in the music I introduced myself to Don Burrows. Rather impertinent of me I think he thought at the time.

Don was and probably still is Australia's number one jazz player and so

I asked my now often repeated question, if he and his group would like to play at the Sydney Opera House. It took heavy negotiations of about five minutes, with the main sticking point that even as they would be topping the bill they would need to open the show so they could get back to the supper club for their regular patrons. I bowed to the pressure and even promised two taxis to be waiting to carry them the four hundred metres to the Wentworth. I was starting to get the hang of this promotion business, offering perks. Still hadn't heard of a 'rider' at this stage but that was to come. Who else should we book, no worries, to coin a phrase, Don said he'd get the others for me and we ended up with the best of the best being the Ray Price Quintet, Graeme Bell All Stars, Galapagos Duck and the Col Nolan Trio. I was informed, I had to be as I knew absolutely nothing about jazz, that this was the cream of the crop and they had never ever appeared on the same bill and would probably never do it again.

Next, Country and Western Music, in the immortal words of the Blues Brothers, the two kinds of music we hate. Found out that Reg Lindsay had a saddlery store at Petersham on Parramatta Road so I looked it up in the telephone directory and asked to speak to Reg Lindsay. Reg was famous at the time for his world number one hit A Man Called Armstrong, a tribute to the first moon walk in 1969. Request was refused but his wife Heather McKean came to the phone and I posed my usual question about playing at the Sydney Opera House and got the usual reply 'Of course'. Negotiated a mutually acceptable fee and then I asked if she knew where I could contact Slim Dusty, the country music icon with hits like Pub With No Beer. Things went a little awry at this request and I thought I'd blown the deal as I was pointedly informed that there was no way they would appear on the same bill as Slim Dusty. Vehement is the only word I can think of when given this refusal so I backed down and accepted Reg Lindsay and could they recommend others? Of course they could, and a few days later we had a bill of Reg Lindsay, Johnny Ashcroft, Lee Conway, John Williamson, Gay Kahler, with Smokey Dawson as compere, without Flash the Wonder Horse, as the Opera House management drew the line at a horse on the stage of the concert hall. I found out some months later the Lindsay / Dusty saga had gone back a lot of years with some bad blood involving the fact that Slim was married to Joy McKean the sister of Heather. Bit like the Australian country music's version of King Lear.

Things are coming together now and we're thinking we're unstoppable so I contact the Daly Wilson Big Band who were probably the number one musical act in the country at the time.

Our first rejection, they were planning their own series for early 1974 so thanks but no thanks. However they put me in touch with Kerrie Biddell who was their main vocalist and she in turn put us in touch with another band leader, Peter Lane, who no-one had ever heard of as he worked in the RSL and working men's clubs. A journeyman is probably the best way to describe him, but nevertheless a friendly chap who in the main guided us through the trials and tribulations of dealing with musicians who are more concerned with union rates than performances. Some of the nuances will be explained later.

The Rock n' Roll bill proved the easiest one to organise as during this period we had been approached by a promotional company called Digamae, who it turned out were the programming and promotional arm of the top rock radio stations in the country 2SM and 3XY and a raft of others. Rod Muir the head of Digamae had been a very successful radio DJ and programmer and with others, including Trevor Smith and John Torv who had married into the Murdoch family, he offered to advertise all our shows on their radio stations if we agreed to them being headlined as presenting the first rock show at the Sydney Opera House along with twenty cents for each ticket sold. Again I held out with my tough negotiating skills for about ten seconds before I agreed. So they booked the top acts of the time Brian Cadd, Ross Ryan and Ariel. Ross Ryan was a bit of a one hit wonder having wowed audiences as a support act to international touring acts. Ariel I knew nothing about but accepted Digamae's word they would be crowd pleasers.

Digamae took responsibility for paying the acts, in hindsight probably paying them a small amount plus airplay on their stations or the like in return, so financial success was guaranteed. I was now ready for the looming press conference. When I say ready I was not prepared for the size and scope of it.

Having at this stage dealt with only Justin Smith and Lloyd Martin the assistant General Manager of the house I was surprised and may I say nervous when asked to meet up with the big boss, Frank Barnes the General Manager, and dutifully off I went to have lunch in his office. It was at this lunch that the enormity of what I had done began to sink in. Being a beer and barbeque kind of person the fine dining experience in this magnificent office with north facing views including the Harbour Bridge and Kirribilli and Admiralty houses was unsettling but what threw me the big curve was being introduced to Jack Neary who was Harry M. Miller's partner in the Sunday night presentations, and also as I found out much later a former partner of the same Lloyd Martin, at this time Deputy General Manager. Suffice to say they all made me very welcome and dispelled any impression of competition and in fact Jack Neary applauded me the loudest for having the nerve to take the plunge and wished he'd thought of the Australian concept. It was agreed, I say agreed, as I really had no say that Sunday nights would hold their press conference one week before mine in the next two weeks.

Feeling buoyed and accepted into this rarified company I went away to prepare for a press conference which I thought would only require naming my list of performers which was still under wraps at this stage. Imagine my surprise when I walked into the boardroom to make a simple announcement and set up to meet me were television crews from all stations, microphones from radio stations in a cluster on the lectern and print journalists and photographers flashing away as if I was the President of the United States. Nerves nearly got the better of me as this was a different audience to 30 high school girls, a glass of water wasn't enough to take away the dryness of my throat and when I stood up the trembling in my knees almost gave in but I soldiered on and made my pitch. Then the questions came thick and fast mainly on my own background, my lack of experience, broad northern English accent, but as it went on my confidence grew especially when I announced how the ticket sales were going and then I went out on a limb saying the best facilities in the world would be provided for the Australian talent to display their wares just like Jack Neary was putting together for the overseas visitors.

The Opera House then provided drinks and canapes and for the first time I thought I really am in show business as the press gathered around me mainly asking for complimentary tickets, which I was quick to promise, realising I needed good press.

CHAPTER 4!

Mainsforth Front Row!

Ferryhill itself is a small town situated 7 miles south of Durham City and eleven miles north of Darlington. There is nothing conspicuous or charming about Ferryhill. It existed as a mining village for about 60 years providing the manpower for the three local mines, Dean and Chapter, Mainsforth and Chilton. Times were tough in hindsight but as a child you don't know it you just believe life is like this for everyone. We lived in a small satellite village about two kilometres from the village square called East Howle. There were two parts to the village separated by the coal shunting railway line. The Old Rows and the New Rows. We lived in Grant Street in the New Rows. Old and New probably meant either built in eighteen seventy two when East Howle colliery was opened or eighteen ninety two when another shaft was sunk. Fortunately for everyone East Howle, Old or New doesn't exist anymore as all the houses were condemned and the only life there now is a traveller's encampment on the Old Rows side of the long abandoned railway. Travellers were called Gypsies back then before political correctness reared its ugly head. All the houses were owned by the National Coal Board and were provided to mine workers free of rent. There was a pecking order for allocation of the houses with some algorithm that included factors like years worked at the mine, married or single, number of children and of course seniority in the workplace. East Howle was the lowest rung on the ladder. Reasons being, I assume, because there were only two children in our family at the time but most importantly our father didn't actually work down the mine. When he was seventeen he had an accident at the mine surface which had cost him his right foot and leg halfway up his shin and from then on he had surface work which involved servicing the lamps in what was called the lamp cabin. This involved refilling the Davey lamps with kerosene and re-charging the battery driven helmet lights. This meant we were one of the poorer families as he wasn't in a position to work overtime or receive the production bonuses the underground miners earned. There was a positive side in this in that when the sirens went off at the pithead signalling there had been a fatal accident in the mine our mother never had to panic and run with the other wives to the mine shaft fearing the worst. This was quite a regular occurrence in the fifties. Very reminiscent of the scene from How Green Was My Valley. I could identify with the Roddy McDowall character in the nineteen forty one John Ford film based on the book.

For some reason our mother had a snobbish attitude as to which school we attended. She refused to enrol us in the local East Howle School and by using her father's, our grandfather's, address she sneakily got us into what she considered the better school, Dean Bank. Only she knew why, after all the state school system was undergoing many improvements all over the country. This was fine by us as we knew no better and actually we grew to love it as it required a ten minute bus trip to and from the village on the Martindale's bus. No bus passes in those days. Mum must have scratched and scraped to get the threepence a day for Barry and me to get to school.

One of the memories of those days was when Dad was on night shift. The rotating shift system meant in week one it was day shift, 7am to 3pm. Week two was the back shift 3pm to 11pm and week three was night shift, 11pm to 7am. The night shift week was a nightmare week for us kids as we had to be totally silent while he tried to catch up on his sleep and we would hear the regular call from upstairs to keep those bloody kids quiet. This was the years soon after the Second World War and I recall gas masks hanging in the coal shed and food rationing with small booklets with coupons still in force which allocated small amounts of meat and dairy products to each family depending on their bare needs. I can't ever remember in those days ever having an egg to myself or real butter on the bread. I thought the only meat was in sausages. There was also the fear that if I went to the shop that if I lost the ration book with its stamps in it or dropped any food, in particular eggs, on the way home I could meet a fate worse than death ....

CHAPTER 5!

Quite A Convention!

As we approached the opening night of our series of concerts which we had named, rather pompously, Australian Festival of Performing Arts, everything was going to plan. Two weeks before the opening show, which was sold out, we were given the added bonus of Doug Ashdown returning from America and his manager asking if he could be on the bill. Yes indeed, as he was probably number one in the folk/acoustic field at the time and Mike McLellan had rejected our offer to perform so Doug was more than adequate as a substitute. Then PANIC!!! As I was heading into the city the news came over the radio that a stop-work meeting had halted all activities within the gleaming white sails of the Sydney Opera House with the entire staff threatening to strike over the sacking of an employee. Driving over the Harbour Bridge and on to the Cahill Expressway I could see the meeting being held on the front steps and this was the day before the first of our concerts. The sight of the meeting unleashed a stampede of nerves. With a total feeling of helplessness I managed to find a parking spot and like a man on death row walked slowly to where the meeting was being held. Unable to contribute or even getting down on my knees to beg them to go back to work I listened to the grievances being aired for about an hour. Then the vote was taken and as I listened with my eyes shut they all voted to go back to work. To say I was relieved does no justice to the English language.

The folk concert was an amazing success with standing ovations and every artist had risen to the occasion. We were now promoters. After the show was finished we all retired to the green room backstage where we had arranged drinks and finger food for the artists, musicians and family friends. As the celebrations continued I wanted a quiet moment for myself so I wandered back upstairs to the stage and with a glass of beer in my hand I surveyed the 2670 empty seats spread in front of me and said out loud, 'It's A Long Way From Ferryhill'. This was met with a booming voice over the house public address system ordering me off the stage as they were switching everything off. Sorry! I didn't mind at all as I had tasted show business and I liked it. The series went without a hitch, all sold out, and in the case of the Jazz concert we had to put on an afternoon matinee.

We still had a Saturday night booked at the end of the series for which we hadn't arranged anything and our good fortune continued with a phone call from London and a gentleman on the other end introduced himself as the manager of Fairport Convention, one of the world's top bands of the time. In a conspiratorial manner he swore me to secrecy and let me know that the band was about to break up and they were planning a final world tour and they wanted to record a live album at the Sydney Opera House for their farewell. Guess what! We had the only date booked that fitted into their schedule so would be interested in promoting the Australian leg of the tour. Yes we would be interested but we had no idea how to promote international acts and any costs involved. The problem was solved when he told me they had already confirmed flights and hotels and we could have two concerts, one in Sydney and one in Melbourne for five hundred pounds for each performance, act fully delivered. This was less than what we had paid Australian acts for the first series so we grabbed the offer. It got even better when he told us that along with the band the wife of Trevor Lucas, the Australian leader of the band would be bringing her along who just happened to be Sandy Denny only weeks earlier voted world's number one female singer by the readers of the English New Musical Express, the bible of the music industry.

Things couldn't get any better and with support from the Digamae radio stations we sold out the Festival Hall on the Friday night and had to put on an extra matinee performance at the Opera House on the Saturday. Not only were we international promoters we were now a national touring company all this within a few weeks.

We did not promote the fact that Sandy Denny was performing as their manager told us of a history of substance abuse and unreliability so we were totally hesitant about advertising her as we were afraid of any consequences if she did not appear. It was a relief when on meeting the band at Melbourne airport to see Sandy Denny in the flesh and luckily for us the press picked up on her being in Australia and ticket sales rocketed and even the admission facilitators (ticket touts) got into the act. It was through the touts I learnt that the main source of their tickets were the promoters themselves, the same ones who hypocritically would blast the touts in the press while enjoying the tax free cash bonuses the touts provided. We had not been in the business long enough to take part in this scam. After the Friday performance in Melbourne we flew back to Sydney early Saturday to prepare for the four o'clock performance.

The band went to rest in the hotel and we went directly to the Opera House to check on preparations. Then the second panic situation of our show business career landed on us. The band's manager arrived breathless in the backstage area with the information that the five thousand pound dress Sandy had had made in Paris specially for the Opera House concert had been left in the hotel room in Melbourne and she was in hysterics and threatening not to perform if the dress didn't arrive in time. I called the hotel manager and within ten minutes the dress was discovered hanging in the wardrobe in the hotel room she had occupied. So how could we get the dress to Sydney for the evening's performance?

Only one thing for it. I gave one of my friends and helper George Cliff, a few hundred dollars, told him to get to the airport, fly to Melbourne, pick up the dress and fly back to Sydney. The hotel manager agreed to take the dress himself to Melbourne airport where he met up with George who took the dress and turned around and got back on the same plane.

Nerves were fraying backstage in Sydney and seeing an international star having tantrums and screaming fits is something I'll never forget. It becomes contagious with everyone acting like chickens with no heads. However as soon as the front of house lights went down and the band was introduced, professionalism took over and the matinee was a great success. So much so a lot of the audience were heading direct to the box office trying, without success, to buy tickets for the evening performance.

What a relief it was when George walked into the green room with the dress. After depositing it in the star's dressing room it was only then that George nonchalantly told us he had never been out of Sydney before and this had been his first time on aeroplanes.

It was with some sadness, but little surprise, when Sandy Denny died very young some four years later.

However we were now international promoters so could we continue along this path.

CHAPTER 6!

A Coronation and a Television!

In 1953 television was a new phenomenon at the time and the British government had provided televisions for all schools in the country so no-one had an excuse not to watch the coronation. At seven years old I decided I was going to watch the event at my old school in Dean Bank so without telling anyone I walked the four or five kilometres up the hill through the village and into my old school assembly hall. What a disappointment. About four hundred kids sitting on a hard floor trying to decipher something on a twelve inch screen with what looked like a snowstorm happening in London. I turned around and walked back home thinking to myself I'll see it on the Pathe News at the pictures in a couple of weeks time.

I soon settled in at my new school and I recall coming second in class to Christine Hull at the end of the first term that I attended Ferryhill Station Primary School. I buckled down and she never beat me again.

It turned out the teachers believed I was quite gifted in mathematics and puzzle solving. Somehow the message was never communicated to me till I was in my sixties when my baby sister Sheila told me it was this knowledge that altered the whole lives of my parents.

The headmaster took me aside a few times after school dinners, that's what we called lunch in those days, and taught me how to play chess and my teacher, Miss Cockburn, seemed to revel in the fact that I could help her with the crosswords at my tender age of seven.

As I was now out of the infants school and in junior school it became clear that I was ready to contribute by working to boost the household income and that meant working with my brother Barry either picking potatoes or collecting coal and firewood. In our part of the country schools were closed for two weeks in late Autumn to help the farmers bring in their potato crop and it had a wonderful social atmosphere amongst us kids when the farmer would arrive at a designated meeting place with his tractor pulling a flat trailer and all of us kids jumped on to be taken to the potato fields. It was usually freezing cold at about six in the morning and the work was on no matter what the weather conditions were. It was hard work bending over for hours picking the potatoes out of the mud placing them in buckets then pouring them into sacks. It was seven days a week from dawn till dusk for two weeks but we earned quite a bit of money. Between us Barry and I could earn over ten pounds a week which is only a couple of pounds short of what dad was earning. Then add to that the sacks of potatoes we stole to bring home which were like cattle fodder but for us humans it helped us to get through the winter.

This was a very dark period in our lives but only when I look back on it do I realise the upheavals taking place. Dad had become extremely violent towards our mother and on us boys. This involved a number of beatings for our mother and ourselves. One of our best pieces of luck was that the local policeman lived down the road not a hundred metres from our home. It became a normal event for me to be running to his home / police station while Barry would be doing the best an eleven year old could do to protect our mother. A stark memory I have is the number of times we had to clear up broken crockery, vases etc. that had been thrown during these incidents. The whole thing came to a head when he attacked a neighbour, beating him up and being arrested. He was diagnosed as paranoid schizophrenic and committed to Winterton Psychiatric Hospital.

Of course as kids we weren't aware of this diagnosis and Dad was in hospital and we caught the bus every Sunday to visit him. After six months he was then sent to the miner's benevolent home in Saltburn for convalescence taking another six months. It was during this period that my life was its lowest ebb being on the free school dinner's list and having the teacher reminding everyone every Monday during dinner money collection. The teacher would call out after taking the coins from the rest of the class then announcing the names of the 'Free Dinner' recipients.

In all fairness today it would never happen in such a way but the teachers were not to blame it was a sign of the times so I have forgiven them as I grew older but it didn't help at the time. Today it would be classed as child cruelty. It was even more galling to me as it took away all status gained by being top of the class. As it was and possibly still is in the UK, a free school meal is a school meal provided to a child or young person during a school lunch break and paid for by Government

It was during this period that Barry strode up to the wicket and took charge. For an eleven year old this seemed to be normal to us as he was now the man of the house. I have never ever lost my admiration for Barry and my main regret in life was not telling him so when he was alive..........................

CHAPTER 7

It's A Long Way To The Top!

Then there was the time in 1976 when things took a turn for the worse and when I realised I was not very good as an impresario. We had promoted what we had thought were three good acts, Buffy St. Marie, Chuck Berry and Ralph McTell. All appeared to be quite successful in terms of box office but the people I was dealing with were far too sharp for me. I don't mean the artists themselves but some of the co-promoters had no conscience when it came to distribution of box office takings. I was swimming in the shark tank.

Let's start with Chuck Berry so called father of rock n' roll.

There were stories going the rounds that on a previous Australian tour he had proven impossible to handle by his promoters including refusals to do any media interviews and demanding the most obscure things in his dressing rooms. The main story goes that in the Sydney show which was held outdoors at the Sydney Showground, November 1973, when he saw the crowd of around 25,000 he refused to leave his caravan behind the stage until the promoter produced another $10,000 in cash. The crowd was restless so the promoter, looking at a very handsome profit, agreed and sent a runner to the box office to pick up $10,000 cash from the takings. Chuck was about to go on stage after picking up his brown envelope until he realised these were Australian dollars. He sat down again and refused to go on stage till U.S. dollars were produced. Play money he called the Australian dollars.

Not a chance! 9.30 pm on a Friday evening, banks shut, no hope of getting U.S. dollars. So he closed the caravan door and started to play his guitar to himself with the crowd now baying for blood after waiting close to an hour. The caravan door was opened from the outside and in came a well-known Sydney identity who apparently was a silent partner in the promotion with a pistol in his hand, loaded the story goes, and pointed it at Chuck's head. With that Chuck stood up, walked out of the caravan directly to the stage and saying to the gunman not to worry because Johnny Being Good.

The rumours had it that Tim Bristow one of the hard men of Sydney, legendary private eye, rugby player, bouncer and standover man had been the man. He made his name in the 1950s and '60s in divorce work. Big Tim would come crashing through the bedroom door, photographer close behind, to catch the amorous couple in flagrante delicto.

Now it's 1975 and I've been asked if I'd like Chuck Berry at a bargain price of $5000/show and initially I was hesitant because of the above stories but was convinced when Chuck himself rang me at home one night and made a solemn promise that the bad days were behind him and he would love the chance to make up with his Australian fans and media. The price was too good to pass up on as he only wanted two plane tickets for himself and his daughter and he would use a pick up band when in Australia. Terms as usual, one third on signing of contract, one third on landing in Australia and one third on completion of tour. ie. US$7k. US $7k. and US$6k. That's US $20k payment for four performances.

Everything was going smoothly, simple contract, no extra demands, regular phone calls with my new best friend Chuck, venues arranged, pick up band organised, tickets selling well and advertising scheduled on leading radio stations.

Counting ticket sales up to the day of his arrival we were close to break even and a good press reception with TV interviews would see us make a tidy profit. The media initially were sceptical about working with him but a bit of arm twisting, some free tickets, a few telephone interviews, and the odd lunch had seen us convince them he was going to be available for publicity.

Come the arrival at Sydney airport, into the VIP immigration lounge and about 20 members of the press waiting in the press room, TV radio, magazines, newspapers and a few hangers on. Into the VIP room walks Chuck and his daughter, immigration paperwork completed and ready for the media scrum, not quite! Chuck pulls out his copy of the contract from his inside pocket and points to a paragraph that states a hire car will be available in each of the cities to be visited, not a problem, we have the chauffeur driven hire car waiting outside for when the press conference is over. Here's where different versions of the English language can cause misunderstandings. To him a hire car was a drive yourself Hertz or Avis, not as we in Australia defined it as a chauffeur driven limousine. Off to the Hertz counter we went with some of the press following and some of them berating my off-sider, that's assistant to the non-Australians, George Cliff, small co-incidence, as it appeared that all the previous good work was unravelling. Fifteen minutes later, car booked, contract back in inside pocket, smile on face and let's meet the press. What a half hour that had been but everything appeared to be under control and things were now running smoothly, but for how long?

A very lively and friendly press conference now over it was time to get to the hotel where we had scheduled a number of radio interviews by telephone with the major rock radio stations around the country, priceless publicity, you couldn't buy this type of coverage we'd arranged. Checked into The Sebel Town House, the home in Sydney for all the major rock artists, a very upmarket, discreet, boutique type hotel before boutique hotels were thought of. Did I say things were going well, get ready for the next mood change.

Chuck arrives in the foyer, reaches into his inside pocket, little did I know at the time this single, simple gesture was to be the beginning of the ulceration of my stomach, and it is pointed out to me that US$7000 is now due to be paid and let's get that done before any more publicity chores are taken care of.

The receptionist at the hotel was fielding calls from all over the country for the interviews but no way was Chuck allowing anything to happen before the money was paid. Starting to get the feel of the man I agreed we would go to my bank in North Sydney and arrange the transfer. Chuck drives his hire car with me in the passenger seat and over the Harbour Bridge we go. Into the bank we stride, ask to see George Smith the manager, swan past all the tellers gasping at seeing 'The Chuck Berry' in their bank and over a cup of coffee George arranges a telegraphic transfer to Chuck's bank in Memphis, Tennessee. Smiles all round, for one minute only. How does he know the money is in his bank account? Don't trust telegraphic transfer receipts. Not happy. We point out that it's about 8pm in Memphis yesterday and his bank will see the funds when they open the next day. The discussion went on so long I thought we would still be in George's office till the Memphis bank opened. Talk about long distance information get me Memphis Tennessee! A very grumpy Chuck Berry agreed eventually that he would ring his bank manager to check on the telegraphic transfer as soon as it would be open in Memphis. All this was stomach churning stuff and I blame this day for the ulcer I suffered from years later. Maybe even responsible for my heart attack also, even if it was about thirty years after that.

Not off to a good start so far. The next few hours became a bit more pleasant as we fulfilled the majority of the scheduled radio interviews, had a late lunch. I had a couple of stiff drinks, Chuck didn't drink, I thought it was because he was afraid of spilling something into his pocket where he kept the contract ready to be pulled out in seconds.

We had three TV interviews arranged for the afternoon and he said he didn't have the time as he needed to discuss the contract with me. Boy was this becoming stressful. We sat down for most of the afternoon going through the fine details on equipment, travel, hotels etc. etc. and then his face beaming and to my complete surprise he jumps up and says we can't miss the last TV interview scheduled for the day because it was Flashez on the ABC hosted by Ray Burgess and Michael Meade, and seeing my wife Patricia was one of the production staff on the programme, 'Can't let wives down, it's a family thing you know.' he said. The next few hours went beautifully, one of the most charming people to work with, all broad smiles and nothing too difficult. His daughter proved to be a charmer but I have to say the relief on leaving the Sebel Town House after dinner to seek my own bed was palpable. Couldn't get away fast enough.

But there were 8 more days to go.

The performances in Melbourne and Adelaide came and went with little drama and I had learnt to try to maintain a distance between Chuck and myself in order to keep my sanity and I did this by leaving all duties to the local publicists and I took some sadistic pleasure in seeing how worn out they were after a day or two on the road with Chuck.

Perth was the last city on the tour and I had sold the performance on to a local promoter. This was a common practise in the business and it had worked the other way when southern promoters would sell me the Sydney and Brisbane dates.

The contract between myself and the local promoter was an exact copy of mine with Chuck with the only difference being the number of performances. That meant paragraphs relating to transport and equipment to be supplied were the same as the ones on my contract. On the night of the performance I was in the bar relaxing when up pops the local promoter with a very worried look on his face. Chuck was refusing to perform because he had not supplied the Fender amplifier as the contract stated. He had in fact supplied the world's best equipment and any other performer would have welcomed the chance to use the gear provided. But not Chuck. I took some delight in pulling out of my inside pocket the contract, with the same gestures Chuck had used with me. The promoter was shaking with fear that the performance wasn't going to happen so I went backstage to talk with Chuck and wasn't surprised when he asked for five thousand dollars in cash before he would go on. I passed this on and told the guy he was very fortunate that Chuck now believed in Australian dollars otherwise things could have been very different.

The tour now over we flew back to Sydney so Chuck and his daughter could fly back to Memphis and over breakfast the next morning he explained to me that this had been one of the best organised tours he had done. He then went on to say that he apologised for all the grief he had given me but it was like that because as he said in the early days he had been ripped off by so many promoters he acted the way he did to make sure promoters knew he was the boss. He also believed if he'd been stronger in his youth he would have been a multi- millionaire now instead of not even owning the rights to his compositions.

A cautionary tale....................

CHAPTER 8!

Not Exactly Midsomer!

The first time I realised that we were in the lower echelons of Ferryhill society was on taking home an invitation to Rosamund Orwin's sixth birthday party. Not everyone in the class was invited but as I was on an equal intellectual level with Rosamund and her best friend Anne Gibson, I received the invitation to my first ever party. This put my mother into a state of shock as it turned out the Orwins owned the largest grocery shop in Ferryhill which meant he was not a miner but a class above the coal miners. Also Anne Gibson's father owned a trucking company so I was about to enter the Ferryhill equivalent of the aristocracy. Seems strange to look back now and see the British class system working at all levels of society and how if your dad wasn't a miner in these mining villages that allowed them to look down on the rest of us.

Mum fussed over me for days. Took me to a barber for the first time and not cutting my hair herself. She went to my grandfather's house and borrowed some money to buy me new shorts, shirt and shoes. Come the day of the party I was like Little Lord Fauntleroy and a snappy dresser at that. I received strict instructions on how to behave but what I remember most was the obsequious manner in which my mother approached the Orwins. She thanked them a dozen times before she left for inviting me which only dawned on me years later that maybe she saw a better life than her own. I should point out here that Mum had had to leave school at thirteen to look after her siblings when her mother died, so life had been tough for her.

The best thing about East Howle was the fact that it was unlike the rest of Ferryhill. There were no slag heaps and in fact it appeared to be like an

English country village. Not quite Midsomer but it did possess a certain charm for us kids. It consisted of eight rows of ten terraced houses climbing up a small hill, back yards facing each other across cobbled back lanes and front doors facing each another set of front doors. These front doors were always painted green for some reason with cream trimmings. I only learnt later in life, after our father reversed the colours and painted cream with green trimmings, that this was not allowed as the green was the only colour the National Coal Board allowed on their houses' front doors. Dad had to repaint at his own expense. We were surrounded by farmland and market gardens which were divided into quarter acre allotments and each resident had their own garden allotment to grow vegetables. There were also two woods about a hundred metres away. There was the Big Wood, which all of us younger kids were not allowed into with threats of ogres and various monsters living there. However older brothers always seemed to come out of it alive. Then there was the Little Wood which wasn't so dense or as tall as the trees in the big wood. It also had a clearing in the middle which was used every Sunday afternoon once Sunday dinner was over for an illegal heads or tails school. I learnt years later that in Australia it's a national institution called two up. Almost compulsory on their national remembrance Day Anzac Day.

Barry, my brother, and I had a little job every Sunday keeping look out for the local policeman who would sometimes take a walk into the wood to see what was going on. I had the bottom part and Barry the upper part and we were over the moon with the shilling each we were paid every week. I never told anyone but the local policeman used to arrive about once a month and he'd give me a threepenny bit to hurry along and tell the guys the policeman was on his way. He couldn't be bothered arresting anyone but he was able to report that there were no illegal activities going on whenever he arrived at the clearing in the little wood.

That shilling changed my life. Mum let us keep it so we could go to the cinema Saturday matinee at the Gaiety cinema up in the village. Sixpence admission, tuppence for the bus fare, sometimes we walked it through the fields, and four pence for a Mars bar.

It was the pictures that opened my eyes to the other world outside of Ferryhill ....

29

CHAPTER 9

Johnny Will Be Goode?

So here I am after a sleepless night trying to come to grips with the most harrowing day of my life it was time to renew the Chuck Berry tour, or battle, with a full day ahead of interviews and public relations exercises. Today was also the date of the first performance of the tour at the Hordern Pavilion in Sydney.

On arrival at the hotel to start the day's work we met for breakfast with Chuck and his daughter and by the conversation it was as though yesterday had been a day of bon- hommie and everything was going to plan. We then discussed the day's itinerary which included a few telephone interviews in the morning with interstate radio stations then after lunch time for a sound check and quick rehearsal with the local band we had hired as a backing band. The morning went smoothly then after lunch I headed to the venue to check that everything was going to plan after discussing with Chuck that he should get there around three pm to do be introduced to the band and do the necessaries. I offered to arrange a limousine to pick him up but he insisted he had the hire car, as per his contract, and he would make his own way with his daughter.

At the Hordern Pavilion the roadies from Jands had put everything in place including the P.A. system and the amplifiers as stated in the contract with Chuck, or so we thought!

Three o' clock came and went with no appearance by the Berrys so back to the Sebel I went to see what else could be spoiling my day. At the hotel we found him in the restaurant on his own reading a book and looking as though he didn't have a care in the world. Of course he didn't, I had all those cares for him.

I reminded him about the sound check and the band waiting to meet him and his answer made a lot of sense when considered in hindsight. His reasoning was that if they didn't know Chuck Berry's songs they shouldn't be in a rock n' roll band and he would get himself there in good time, after all he did have his hire car.

This did not fill me with confidence, trust me. But what could I do? I'm at his mercy.

So back to the Hordern Pavilion I go.

I tell the band the story, they are aghast at the news I bring with me. Worth noting at this point the band were a good working band called the Keystone Angels that evolved into one of Australia's top rock bands, The Angels.

Everything appears normal. That is Chaotic! The band nervous as any group of musicians could be as they are about to back up a rock n ' roll legend with no idea about what is going to materialise in the very, very near future. My attention turned to the business part of the promotion in that I went front stage to check on seating, get updated on pre-sales and to have a quick look at the queue forming for roll up ticket sales. We had covered all costs with the pre - sales with a modest profit and the success depended on the tickets to be sold at the door.

I studied the seating plan with all the seats sold crossed off and thought to myself we were in for a successful evening, provided Chuck Berry could find his way to Moore Park and the Hordern Pavilion.

Around seven o' clock the doors were opened and the audience started to find their seats. A friend of mine I remember, Patricia Holloway, was one of the first to arrive and on spotting me asked if I could guide her to her seat that she had purchased at the box office numbered double PP 26. I had the seating plan with me and on looking closely there was no double P row but on inspection of the actual seating we were able to find double O, double P, double Q and double R amounting to two hundred and twenty four seats that were not on the official Royal Agricultural Society seating plan. On closer inspection of the ticket it became obvious that someone was up to no good. The ticket number on the stub was written with a marker pen meaning they were not part of the fully printed and authenticated tickets.

I went to the front entrance where tickets were being sold at the box office then handed to the ushers who tore off the stub and handed it to the buyer. The other halves were being placed in a series of small cardboard boxes which on inspection were one hundred per cent belonging to the mystery double denoted rows. Not only was someone robbing me blind they had put their tickets on sale first without even considering selling some of the authentic tickets. A quick look back inside confirmed my fears as the only rows filling up were the double rows.

To say I was angry does not do any justice to my feelings at the time. I gathered up the cardboard boxes with the RAS security threatening me with all sorts of punishment if I took them and I stormed into the office of the Hordern Pavilion's management. On confrontation they tried to bluff their way out of the situation and only when I threatened to be at the Royal Agricultural Society's office the next day did they soften their position and tried to negotiate a settlement. It was put to me that this was a regular procedure so I hate to think how much money had been misappropriated over the years. Fortunately for me there was another friend of mine in attendance who was a security guard with Metropolitan Security Services so I hired him on the spot to stand over the box office until it was closed and to secure all the cash for me.

With only little arguments from the management lady agreement was reached. I would take all the cash, it was mine legally, and I would not report the incident to the Society.

There was still a concert to be staged so backstage I went. Would you believe it Chuck was already there. However not in his dressing room but sitting in the back seat of his hire car playing his guitar. On being told by his daughter that he wanted to see me the heart palpitations set in again and when I got in the front seat out of his pocket came the dreaded contract. Check the equipment to be supplied paragraph I was told. What we were contacted to supply was a Fender Twin Reverb amplifier and that was not the amplifier that was on the stage and if it wasn't replaced, no show!

Off I went to find Eric Robinson, the head of Jands who were supplying all the equipment and he explained that what was on the stage was the Fender Super Twin Reverb the updated version and the best in Australia. The only difference being the Super Twin was two pieces a speaker cabinet and an amplifier separate while the older version was in the one cabinet.

We went back to Chuck's car and Eric tried to explain the technicalities with little luck as out came the contract again. Panic was starting to set in again and with what had gone on earlier I was not in the mood for any more problems so an offer of five hundred dollars cash was agreed on for Chuck to use the amplifier equipment provided.

Next problem. The backing band were still in diaper mode with only a half hour opening spot from them before they had to provide backing for the great Chuck Berry. They needed to check tuning of the guitars so I had to devise a ruse to get Chuck out of the back of the car so they could grab his guitar and check tuning. I convinced him that he was needed on stage to check positions for the lighting crew and as soon as we walked in through the stage door one of the band took the guitar out of the car, checked the tuning with their equipment, returned it to the car and gave me the thumbs up behind his back and back to the car he went.

The show began with the Keystone Angels delivering a very good warm up set. I was slumped backstage with a few beers to settle my nerves waiting for the next crisis.

It never eventuated!

After a short interval the audience resumed their seats the lights came down and as he walked on stage with the band I remember him shouting to the band, over the chanting of the audience. "Just follow me. I'll shout which key the songs are in as we go."

A resounding success but still three more cities to go..........................

CHAPTER 10!

Saturday Night Is Bath Night!

These were the days before television and the only entertainment was the radio or the pictures. Ferryhill itself with a population of around eight thousand had supported three cinemas, the Pavilion, the Gaiety and the Majestic. To see people in tuxedos drinking champagne in exotic nightclubs on the silver screen was a window on the world to me. That's what I wanted from the age of six. I had determined at that early age I was going to see the world. Casablanca was not just a title of a picture to me it was a place I was going to go to. The Road to Morocco was not just a destination for Bob Hope and Bing Crosby. I was going there no matter what. I was going to be at the top of the Empire State building one day to see where King Kong met his fate. Maybe St. Peter didn't make it to Damascus from Rome in Quo Vadis but I was certain that I would be in both cities one day. There was also the hit song of the time by Joan Stafford 'You Belong to Me' and I'm happy to say I've seen the pyramids along the Nile, I've seen the sun rise on many a tropic isle, I've crossed many oceans in a silver plane and seen the market in old Tangiers. Too many other places to mention. I look back on my life happy that I have done all these things and many more in what I consider a charmed life. Then I got a book as a prize for coming first in class.

Titled 'The Duck Billed Platypus' this book began a lifetime love affair between myself and Australia.

I read about the exotic fauna and flora, the flying doctor, artesian wells. I then found the poetry of Banjo Paterson and Henry Lawson and I could find myself daydreaming about chasing horses near the Snowy River and working with Clancy on the Overflow.

But there was still the boring task of growing up in this small village at the other end of the earth. Survival was first on the list and when Joyce, our sister, was born that meant we were due for a larger house so off we went to what was called Chilton Lane, or The Crag, near Ferryhill Station. The Crag is a misnomer as it refers to a geological formation called the Ferryhill Crack which is a five mile valley which determined the route of the early railway trains. Three Mainsforth Front Row was the address, with three bedrooms upstairs, no hot water, and outside toilets. The bathroom was hung on a large nail on the wall in the back yard and it consisted of a four foot long zinc tub which was brought out once a week for the whole family to have a bath, usually in the same water warmed up by kettles boiling on the coal fire. We soon learnt, that's Barry and I, that most of the kids, boys that is, on Saturday evenings the pit baths were made available for local boys if accompanied by their fathers. Paradise, hot showers with unlimited time to enjoy it. Only one problem. Because our father had lost part of his lower leg in an accident when he was seventeen he was very self-conscious about taking of his prosthetic limb in front of people so we had to devise some subterfuge to enable us to walk into the baths. We just attached ourselves to other fathers and sons and within a couple of weeks we were accepted into the pit baths crowd and our parents and baby sisters could have their bath in the kitchen with us boys out of the way.

The move to Mainsforth Row created a new upheaval as we changed schools leaving Dean Bank and attending Ferryhill Station Primary School which was about 50 metres from our home and it turned out the headmaster Leslie Naylor had also been the headmaster when our father attended the school some years earlier. I have one strong memory of my second day at the school and I can remember the date June 2nd 1953. Yes it was the coronation of Queen Elizabeth the second. ....

CHAPTER 11!

The King Is Dead!

Then there was the Buffy St. Marie tour with performances set for Sydney, Melbourne and Adelaide. Buffy was recognised as a protest/folk singer with her songs predominantly about Native Americans and most people forget she wrote Until It's Time For You To Go, recorded by artists the world over including Elvis Presley.

Nothing very exciting in the first few days apart from my innocence in the bad habits of the co-promoter who would deposit himself in a suite in the Hilton Hotel and hold court over a number of seedy hangers on, racking up the room service bill and appearing stoned for 24 hours a day. Takings were OK, profitable but nothing exciting. The support band had supplied the P.A. system which held down costs and Buffy herself was a lady with no demands and willing to help in any way she could. Melbourne Town Hall was the venue for the second show and during the bump in, that's rock n' roll jargon for loading in the equipment, fate took another twist. The Victorian police arrived and produced an extradition warrant for Vic Hitchcock, one of the road crew, to be taken back to N.S.W. to face living off immoral earnings charges. As he was the only one with a truck driver's licence it created a major problem if he wasn't let out, how could we get the gear to Adelaide?

He was arrested and taken to the Russell St. watch house where we found a duty solicitor who arranged a bail hearing within the hour and after much pleading from myself citing the disappointment that the people of Adelaide would receive if he was not allowed out. The upshot is that he was remanded to my care, which I had to deposit $2000, on the condition that he would appear in a Sydney court four days later. This meant that after reaching Adelaide I bought him a plane ticket to Sydney so he could make the court date. I told him to stay at my house with my wife, who I called to tell her to look after him as two thousand dollars was at stake.

But back to the tour. While my function was tour manager which required me to ensure that all artist's needs were accounted for, equipment was set up and working and all the other minutaie involved with tours, box office was in the hands of the co-promoter, and when it came to settlement back in Sydney, where was the money? Fortunately all bills had been paid so there were no creditors chasing anyone but I needed my share of profits and return of my investment as I had another tour coming through in four weeks time and I had Bryan Nichols to pay back as he had invested in the tour. It was impossible to get any sense, or money, out of the drug frazzled guy and as word passed around we were offered the services of a 'debt collection' company. In good faith we arranged to meet the principal of the company in a bar in Kings Cross, the red light district of Sydney, where we listened to the proposition of retrieving the money less 30% service fee and what else would we like to happen to David X. It was similar to a number of episodes we have seen in Sopranos or Goodfellas. At that point we realised we were in over our head and discretion being the better part of valour we declined the offer. Truth sometimes is stranger than fiction. If he never reads this he doesn't know how close he came to serious harm.

While some people have their brush with fame we had our brush with crime on this most easy going tour I experienced in my short sojourn into the world of Rock n' Roll.

The day after the tour finished I took a phone call in my office from the William Morris Agency Los Angeles' office. Not the best time I remember due to the fact I was chasing for the Buffy money and the guy was making himself invisible, but the call gave me a massive jump in confidence.

How they had contacted me I had no idea as I was still a new boy in the business working from a granny flat behind the house, but it was explained they were looking for other promoters in Australia as they believed other promoters were becoming too difficult to work with. The deal was a three pronged tour schedule for the next year but it was a take one take all three acts for Australia and New Zealand. First up The Who. No problem, stated price seemed OK. Second The Eagles, probably the world's biggest band at the time but the price appeared a little heavy at first glance but I'll do some number crunching on it. I was learning the jargon. Then the biggest surprise, the biggest of them all, could we handle Elvis Presley. Could we? Stated price one million American dollars tax free for each of three shows. We could own television rights for Australia, New Zealand and Pacific Asia. I was certainly playing in the Premier League now. I brought up in the conversation that it was common knowledge that Elvis hated and was afraid of flying. Not true. It was Tom Parker who as an illegal immigrant had pushed that lie for years as he was unable to get a passport to travel and the reason for the tour was that the Colonel believed Elvis had only one year left and this was to be a round the world farewell. I assumed that meant he was going to retire in one year. I asked for a few days to work on the figures and whether I could raise the financing. Fortunately I still had contact with people at the Nine Network and in one phone call to Sam Chisholm, the network managing director, I had a pledge of one million American dollars for the Elvis tour. This was looking good. Costings on The Who showed a good profit which could go towards financing the big one. However The Eagles proved insurmountable as the figures just wouldn't add up. If all stadium shows were sold out at premium prices there was still no way to make money so I had to step aside from the whole deal. I was proven correct in that the New Zealand promoter who picked up on The Eagles went broke in touring them.

I can remember the date of this conversation within a few days because almost one year to the day Elvis died without doing the tour. Maybe that's what the colonel meant when he said he had one year left.

But there's more to come including my final act as a promoter.........

CHAPTER 12

He Ain't Heavy He's My Brother!

My brother's work ethic knew no bounds. With dad in hospital he took on the responsibility of earning as much money as he could, made me take up paper rounds and any other chores that could add income to the small pension, in those days called sick pay, we were receiving. In later years when I had paper rounds, once I had finished my deliveries it was up to me to get myself to the potato fields to help Barry and the two of us could earn double what other kids worked for.

Tatey, or potato to some, picking. We would arrived at the farm for 7am and waited for the tractor and trailer to transport us up to the potato field. Often the mornings were misty and chilly gradually warming up as the day progressed. Everyone took his or her own bucket along. We had no special clothing but everyone wore wellies with knee high woollen socks – mostly of a dismal dark grey colour I remember. Ordinary coats or macs were worn on chilly days and the girls wore pixie hoods (a woollen hat which tied under the chin) and usually hand knitted. Boys wore school caps but these often ended up in their pockets or were deposited on the muddy ground. Our job was to pick up the potatoes turned up by the tractor. Each child had a length of field to work in. It was hard work too, bending down and placing the earthy potatoes into our buckets until it was full and then we emptied these full buckets into sacks then a trailer would pick up the sacks and we began picking all over again. Fine days when the soil was dry, were not too bad, but sometimes the fields were muddy with overnight rain, potatoes were wet and covered in thick earth, our hands became filthy and our wellies clogged and weighted down with mud. On some heavy raining days of course no work could be done at all. We worked until a field was cleared. The farmer then put the potatoes into "clamps", which were long mounds of potatoes which were covered in straw and then earth was piled on the top to form a frost free storage. During the following months, potatoes were put into one hundred weight sacks (112lbs) for sale to the shops during the winter months. Women from the village also joined us in the fields but of course their pay was higher and a useful addition to their household budget. We had a break for lunch and then resumed work in the afternoon. I seem to remember we worked until about 4.30pm. Some children worked harder than others and the boys often had "spud" fights throwing potatoes at each other until reprimanded by the farmer. At the end of the day we climbed onto the trailer and had a ride back to the farm. This was the best part of the day and if possible I liked to ride on the back of the tractor which was very bumpy on the uneven ground. Health and Safety regulations today would not allow it to happen.

Potato picking was only for two weeks in the year so how did we contribute for the other fifty weeks? Living in a mining village the only fuel being used apart from electricity was the coal itself and as part of the perks working for the National Coal Board was free housing and a ton of coal for each household each month. This coal was delivered by a truck and dropped in the back lane under the coal shed's throw hole about two metres off the ground and thus the coal needed to be thrown into the shed. Barry and I would jump on our bikes after school and follow the trucks, then knock on the door offering to 'throw in your coal missus'. We charged half a crown for each load and we could get four loads in a day after school and before dark. I can't recall to this day how we got ourselves clean with the coal dust all over our hands and faces.

Barry, always the mastermind behind money making schemes then came up with the brilliant idea of selling sacks of coal to the people who did not work at the mines including the widows of miners who lost their allowance once the pit worker was dead. But where do we get the coal? Easy for Barry. He had realised when playing on the slag heaps or spoil tips, there was a lot of coal that had missed the screening and there were tons of it there just waiting to be picked up. So on Saturday mornings you could see the pair of us pushing a broken down bicycle along the pit path over the Stell, a small watercourse that took all the water from the mine including the pit baths and flowed into the River Skerne then to the Tees and eventually into the North Sea. We then climbed up the main slag heap called The Blantyre, never ever did find out why it was called this, filled up a sack with lumps of coal bigger than my two hands, in about fifteen minutes then carried it under the crossbar and delivered it to our ever expanding list of customers. We could do about ten sacks a day earning us around three pounds every Saturday. Always thinking, Barry noticed that the Blantyre was also a source of discarded wooden pit props. Ideal to chop up for kindling, again for the widows who didn't have the strength to chop up sticks to get a fire going. We were now offering a package deal. We did this for a few years until our second sister was born. As she was born on Princess Anne's birthday August 15th it seemed to make sense to christen her Anne.

CHAPTER 13!

Take Me By The Hand!

So here I am after the Buffy St. Marie tour which was a disaster financially because of the people we were dealing with.

The travelling was taking its toll on our family life and finances were starting to dry up so it was possibly the last throw of the dice touring Ralph McTell an English singer/songwriter who had had a massive world - wide hit with his song The Streets Of London. His fees were reasonable and there was only two people travelling so this tour looked like it could save the business on only fifty per cent sales.

We created a very successful public relations campaign around the fact that he was the boy next door, no airs and graces, no fancy cars or dressing room riders and his only requirement was to have a bicycle available in each city for him to get around and see the sights and meet the people.

Sydney being my home town and the Opera House my favourite venue we booked the concert hall for a Saturday night and within weeks we had a sell-out. On hearing the news Ralph's brother, also his manager, asked us to arrange a live recording of the concert for a live album they wanted to release using material from the Royal Albert Hall and the Sydney Opera House to be called Ralph, Albert and Sydney. Very clever I thought at the time. I mention that here because with a small claim to fame if you ever hear the album that's me doing the introductions at the start of the first track.

I was approached by the Malvern Star Company who made most of the bicycles sold in Australia at the time, for them to supply the bicycles free of charge and they would create their own mini PR campaign around Ralph and the bicycles.

Couldn't knock back such an offer as they were going to give me one bicycle for free after the tour. However much to my surprise on meeting Ralph at Sydney Airport on his arrival who else had Malvern Star arranged to present the bike, non-other than Dennis Lillee the Australian fast bowler recently retired from the Australian test cricket team. This caused a feeding frenzy amongst the meeting journalists and fellow The Sydney Opera House concert was a sell-out then when we arrived in Melbourne ticket sales were so slow I had to book some television adverts for the two days leading up to the concert. Fortunately I had a friend as sales director at Channel Nine who I'd done a few favours for in a former life. It turned out the guy we had hired to do the publicity for Melbourne and Adelaide was going through a marriage crisis and the Dallas Brooks Hall was left less than half full and Adelaide only got a few hundred. Things were looking bad. Perth just broke even and then New Zealand was a disaster as the local promoter had gone broke hence no money left to pay artists fees and coming so soon after the Buffy St. Marie fiasco I was now broke. I explained my position to Ralph and his manager that I had no funds to pay the last five hundred pounds due. They accepted my word that I would pay as soon as I got back on my feet.

Life got worse. The wife left. She couldn't handle all the creditors knocking on the door, the demand letters, and the fact that I was broke with little hope of getting a job or promoting anyone else in the near future. I don't blame her for leaving me, this wasn't what she had signed up for.

I was now alone in the four bedroom house with a swimming pool in Greenwich on Sydney's lower north shore.

However there were a couple of snags. I couldn't afford to pay the monthly mortgage, my car had two punctures and I couldn't afford the five dollars needed to fix one of them. I had written to all the creditors explaining my destitution and promising to pay as soon as I could get myself together. The final straw was when the electricity company cut off the power. Always the optimist I believed something would turn up to rescue me but when it did it came from a source that I would never ever have contemplated.

Adding to my woes at this time was the death of my father in England at the age of fifty five and how I got the news. The house had no electricity,

I had no telephone switched on and late one night I heard a car horn outside the house. I went out on to the balcony and it was a taxi and the driver, without getting out of his cab, shouted to me that my father had died and my sister had paid him to bring me the news. I went to the motel that backed on to my property and using their yellow public phone rang my mother in England who told me that Dad was still lying on the kitchen floor where he had died after a heart attack brought on by a severe asthma attack. One of my major regrets was that I did not have the money to fly to England to help my mother through the death of my father.

Two nights later sitting alone in the dark one night, freezing cold huddled in a blanket and feeling very sorry for myself there was a knock on the door and standing there was a guy I had met in New Zealand on various tours. I only knew him as Tel or Terry and remembered him always being there to meet the touring acts either at the airports or he'd already checked into the hotels before we arrived. Never thought about him apart from he was maybe a Rock n' Roll groupie with some money to afford the travelling.

To say I was surprised doesn't come near what I was thinking about this nearly perfect stranger that I had probably not exchanged twenty words with over a number of New Zealand tours but I invited him in as I was starving for conversation and any kind of friendship as I felt I had been deserted by all my former friends and employees. Not blaming anyone for their actions as I had brought all this upon myself. Maybe through my trusting nature and far too much self-confidence I had landed in this dark place, both physically and metaphorically.

I was a little embarrassed about my situation but invited him in anyway.

He waved away the taxi he'd arrived in after paying the fare then said we should go for a drink just to talk. Behind my house was the Twin Towers Motel on the Pacific Highway and it had a small cocktail bar. I explained I didn't have any cash to buy drinks but that was no problem he said. Over the drinks he explained he had heard on the grapevine that I had fallen on hard times and on finding out where I lived had made his way to help me out. Was I seeing another soft side of the music industry? Wondering why he felt the need he explained that I had done him a number of favours by making him welcome with the touring parties and he felt he owed me something in return. I didn't have any idea what I could have done but accepted his word for it. After a few more drinks and chewing the fat about some of the artists we had toured and others he had been on it was the first time in weeks I felt relaxed and I opened up to him about all my troubles. It was then he raised his leg and put his boot on the spare stool he reached into his very expensive, highly polished light tan boot and pulled out eight hundred dollars in cash and gave it to me saying it was a loan to get me back on my feet and pay him back when I could. Remember this was the early seventies, eight hundred was a small fortune so I went through the motions of saying I couldn't accept his generosity, half-hearted refusals and feigned pride soon gave way to me accepting the cash and promising to pay him back as soon as I could.

With that we had a couple more drinks, he then said goodnight and got the barman to call a taxi and off went my benefactor into the night. There were no mixed emotions here. I was ecstatic as I could now see the light at the end of the tunnel and this time it wasn't the oncoming train.

I never ever met him again but that eight hundred dollars was a lifesaver. Paid the power bill, what a relief that was. Hooked up the telephone again, now back in touch with the world. How I remember that number 4384906. Isolated no more. Fixed the punctures, now mobile and able to meet people again. Paid a few of the very impatient creditors and made part payments to the others. This actually served me very well as most of them told me they had written off the debts and were surprised to see me paying. Any time I was back in business they would just call they wanted my business. I was now out there in the market place with a very different attitude. Within a couple of weeks I was very fortunate to land a position with McCabe Collins Television Productions who were looking to get programmes on the Ten Network using pop videos as the basis. I was now the producer/director of The Rock n Roll Milkbar Show, three hours of live television every Saturday morning which required me to work in the Sydney office all week then fly to Brisbane with the shows hostess, Kobe Steele, every Friday for production on the Saturday. So I now entered a new phase in my life a very long way from Ferryhill.

There are two postscripts to this episode in my life.

About eighteen months later I read that Ralph McTell was touring Australia once more and in different circumstances. No longer the Opera House but a tour of the colleges and folk clubs. I was now in a good financial position now producing five and a half hours of television a week. Other ideas being pitched and David Frost had taken up a partnership in the business and he took me under his wing so life felt good.

Seeing that Ralph was playing at Macquarie University I went to the bank and drew out the equivalent amount for five hundred and fifty pounds sterling, I was including some interest to assuage my guilt, as Ralph had been a gentleman during my financial crisis and off I went up Epping Road to the university not knowing whether I'd be welcome or not so as I approached the dressing room area I noticed the door was slightly ajar and to my surprise who was there with him looking very comfortable. Yes it was Patricia my wife who had walked out on me eighteen months earlier and we had not exchanged a single word since that day. I jumped to my own conclusion, probably the wrong one, and so to save embarrassment all round I turned around on my heels and walked away without saying a word. Actually had a small laugh to myself because if nothing else I had saved myself five hundred and fifty pounds and had cleared myself of any guilty conscience I may have had for the past eighteen months. The only regret I had was that I missed the concert as I really did like Ralph's performances

The second post script came some thirty years later when I was watching a television documentary about an infamous drug dealer who had been arrested in the United Kingdom, sentenced to life imprisonment and had been died in jail from a heart attack in nineteen eighty three on the Isle Of Wight. It was titled Mr. Asia and told the story of a former New Zealand petty drug dealer who had arranged massive shipments of heroin into Australia and the United Kingdom murdering a few associates on the way and amassing a massive fortune before he was caught. As I was watching it I started to piece together dates and when actual photographs of Mr. Big appeared yes it was one and the same Terry Clarke, Mr. Asia, Mr. Big, my benefactor and only then did I realise what he had meant that I had done him favours. In my naivety I hadn't had any idea that he was the main supplier of drugs to the New Zealand rock circuit in the early days of building his business. Only recently they made a television series on Terry (Tel) Clarke called Underbelly, A Tale of Two Cities and this was the man.

Thank heavens he had never returned to collect repayment.....................

CHAPTER 14!

We're On The Up!

Dad came home and things went back to normal, he was back at work and appeared to be fully recovered with only a few minor losses of temper but the violence seemed to be under control probably because of the medication that he was on.

It was while I was at the doctor's surgery picking up the prescription for this medication that I found out what had been happening in our family. The receptionist at the surgery worked till six pm and when six pm came she packed up her things and handed me the folder containing our family's medical history. Under normal circumstances this folder would be handed to you as you were going into the GP's office. While waiting, as any curious bored nine year old would do, I opened up the folder and read the contents. That was when I saw for the first time the words paranoia and schizophrenia along with police reports citing neighbour's concerns and the hell he was putting our mother through with accusations of infidelity and treachery. I was able to read that doctors thought that all our lives were in danger and that was why he was sectioned. That's the terminology used in the U.K. for forcing people into mental institutions. I recall my feelings at the time were very much in favour of my father and any anger I felt was at what I considered back stabbing and betrayal by everyone, friends, relatives and everyone mentioned in the folder. It was then I decided to become dad's best friend. He was so proud of my scholastic achievements it became absolutely essential that I stayed top of the class every term and in fact I became obsessive about it.

One of the tasks I had to perform twice a year was to catch the forty six bus to Newcastle on my own to pick up his prosthetic limbs. I was able to walk around a big city by myself and every time I took enough money to take in the pictures in the big city as they got the films about eighteen months before the Ferryhill picture houses. I was able to brag about seeing The Robe in Cinemascope months before it ever made The Pavilion. Cinemascope was thought of as a major leap forward in film production as it was the first system to film wide screen which required cinemas to build new wide screens. I became a bit of a novelty at the Newcastle prosthetic premises and they always gave me sandwiches, sweets and soft drink, we called it pop back in those days, because they thought I was so young to be wandering around a major city alone. I also remember that the prosthetic limb in its cardboard carton was as long as I was tall so it was an awkward package to transport on a bus. The other thing was the sandwiches were cut in triangles something I'd never seen before.

Life started to get better and with the extra money we were contributing dad decided we could afford to move into one of the new council houses being built in Chilton. This was a big step in our minds as we believed that actually paying rent made you someone posh. How ironical now when one considers the image of today's chavs, (council housed and violent) who make up most of the government housing population. However this was a major step up for us. Inside toilet, running hot water and everything brand new, with a lawn out front and an allotment out back where we could grow vegetables. This was also the time when my whole world changed. I stayed at Ferryhill Station primary school travelling by bus every day and then came the eleven plus, the examination in mathematics and English every British school kid took at the age of eleven and was used as the filtering system for high school studies. In England, the eleven plus is an examination administered to some students in their last year of primary education, governing admission to various types of secondary school. The name derives from the age group for secondary entry, 11–12 years. In hindsight it was a cruel system that categorised you either as a success or failure at eleven years old, which carried on into your working and adult life. There was never any doubt that I would pass, which I did comprehensively, but I felt sad for my girlfriend of the time if one has proper girlfriends at that age, Christine Hull, who always came second in class behind me failed to make the cut while other less talented people made it. Christine was fortunate in that her family were comparatively well off and they were able to pay for a private education. Some fifty five years later I met up with a former primary schoolmate, Val Pattinson, who after coming third in class for years also missed the cut and had felt resentment all her life about what it meant to feel thrown on to the scrap heap of life at eleven years old.

Coronation Road council house! Spennymoor Grammar Technical school scholarship! England had won the Ashes, Jim Laker had taken nineteen wickets, Auntie Gladys was an usher at the local picture house! Free tickets! Could life be any better?

1956 was a very good year.....................................

CHAPTER 15!

A Pom To Boot!

After the success of the Opera House concerts in seventy three and seventy four we had now moved into the promotion of international acts and we developed a reputation as being well versed in the folk music field which had led to involvement in the tours of Fairport Convention, Steeleye Span, Buffy St. Marie, Sydney Carter, Ewan McColl, Billy Connolly and Ralph McTell. We were also considered as experts on how the Sydney Opera House functioned for pop artists. At one time we had a Saturday night booked in the concert hall without any artist to promote so we were very happy when approached by another promoter to buy the booking off us. Turned out it was for a Roy Orbison tour. Of course it was a sell out and we only made a few hundred dollars for the sale of the date. However we stayed on the Opera House records as the booker of the hall so we had some responsibility for taking care of the venue. This was no major problem but it involved me having to be present at the afternoon's sound check and backstage during the performance. In the afternoon as I got out of the lift backstage I could hear the sound check was underway with the Big O's voice booming out into the empty hall. Imagine my surprise when on looking onto the stage it was the piano player doing the vocals and he was a dead ringer in the vocals department for Roy Orbison himself. It then became no surprise that evening when standing side stage it was plain to see he did all the singing when Roy reverted to miming whenever his voice failed him.

Before the show began Patti Mostyn, the number one publicist in the country and a true lady, asked if I'd like to meet Roy before the performance, as I was still a little star struck I jumped at the opportunity.

On entering the Joan Sutherland dressing room there was a number of people lounging around, drinking and generally chatting with the musical director tickling the ivories on the grand piano that was a permanent fixture in the star's dressing room. Roy Orbison was standing alone with a cigarette in one hand and a glass of wine in the other. To my disappointment he was dressed completely in white not the black one expected of him, and on approaching him the most noticeable feature was the colour of his skin. It looked as though flour had been put on his face giving him the pallor of a corpse. When introduced he put the cigarette in his mouth, moved his drink to his left hand and offered his right hand in a robotic manner for me to shake after which the process was reversed and he stood alone again. Over the years I've always thought of meeting Roy Orbison was like a scene out of the film Westworld in which Yul Brynner and others were robots in a theme park. He may have been walking around but in my mind he was dead inside and understandably so when one takes into account the loss of his wife and children.

It's okay to promote tours on a regular basis but it's such a fickle industry John Sturzaker and myself decided we needed a regular income so we had to come up with something.

Having done very well out of the recordings of Australian folk songs and with my background as a school teacher I approached the Macquarie University Australian Historical Society with the idea of writing a stage production incorporating Australian bush ballads into a short history of Australia beginning with European settlement. Would never get away with that in today's era of political correctness where we must recount on the first forty thousand years of human habitation. We then approached the Opera House management with the idea of promoting the performances to the schools of NSW with letters to history and music teachers. They were very enthusiastic and provided we could use the stage of the concert hall without causing any problems for the Sydney Symphony Orchestra and leave a clean hall before three pm we could have the hall for two hundred and fifty dollars a day.

We went into rehearsals using the musicians from Treasury of Australian Song, a record I had produced for Dyna House records, and attacking the yellow pages section on schools and colleges we posted letters to history and music teachers throughout the state. Working alphabetically we did the schools beginning with the letter A offering a performance for primary schoolchildren at eleven am and for secondary students at two pm. We charged two dollars a seat and made it clear any kids who couldn't afford it were welcome and we would trust the teacher's judgement. Unbelievably the first day's two concerts were sold out in days and we had twenty five letters of the alphabet to go. We had stumbled into something every promoter should aspire to, that is to be able to sell tickets in blocks of thirty or more.

Opening day with my job being to make sure the production went like clockwork because of our time restrictions and John's task to meet the groups, take the money or cheques and basically run front of house. It was interesting after the performance to watch John counting the takings as most of the money came in cash, usually in brown paper bags passed by the supervising teacher who had not sorted it at all. Therefore there were crumpled up one and two dollar notes. For those who don't remember, the one dollar notes were brown and in most cases they wrapped up the coins needed to make up two dollars and the two dollar notes were green. It took John longer to count the money that the performance lasted. The shows were a great success with kids singing along and jumping with fright as Ned Kelly came down the aisles firing his replica gun. If the powers that be had ever heard two thousand children singing Waltzing Matilda as a finale there would have been no doubt as to what the Australian National Anthem should be. It brought tears to the most stoic people who heard it.

We had found Eldorado! We ran the History of Australia schools performances for over a year with overseas and interstate visitors welcomed into the hall as part of their guided tour of the house. We had the soon to be disgraced former Minister for Immigration, Al Grassby as a guest presenter of the gold and platinum discs awarded for Treasury of Australian Song.

We received invitations to take the show to America touring the school summer camps in the Catskills north of New York. We did get a surprise when on the first anniversary of the opening of the Opera House the newspapers afforded us the accolade of being the promoters and performing group that had filled more seats in the first year, beating the Australian Opera, Australian Ballet and the Sydney Symphony Orchestra. As is the usual Australian sense of humour the journalist finished the article with the footnote that the performances were produced, directed and promoted "By a Pom to boot".

CHAPTER 16!

A Grammar School Boy!

As the saying goes 'We were on the up'. Moving into the council house marked a golden era in our lives.

What I can remember is moving in using our Uncle Sam, dad's brother in law who had actually acted as his father, him being married to Aunt Elsie, dad's eldest sister who had brought him up after their parents had died. Sam was the local blacksmith in a time when horses were still part of the transport industry and he had a massive Clydesdale, that's a horse bred for hard haulage work with their massive hooves, which he hitched to his flat cart and then we made the three mile move to Coronation Road with the cart stacked about two metres high. We must have frightened the new neighbours who would have thought it was a gypsy family moving in.

The next task was to get the front and back gardens into shape. Both were about ten metres by ten metres and they needed topsoil about three hundred millimetres deep. That's a huge amount of soil to be carted by wheelbarrow from the communal mound of soil about eight hundred metres away. As it was school holidays Barry and I did it all by ourselves then fertilised it and had it ready for dad to exercise his horticultural skills which involved creating a decorative lawn out front with rose bushes to add colour in the centre with daffodil and tulip bulbs creating a border. The back was transformed into a vegetable patch. Potatoes, brussel sprouts, lettuce, cabbage, radish etc. were planted on a seasonal basis and it was normal practise to pull the vegetables from the ground and directly into the saucepan on the electric stove, a definite change from the saucepan on the coal fire in Mainsforth Front Row.

It soon became time to prepare me for grammar school and the major surprise and financial problem was how to find the money for a school uniform.

The problem was solved as all aunts and uncles contributed to the expense of uniform books, pens, instruments and sports equipment decreed in a letter from the school as essential to a grammar school student's needs. They did this as I was the first Atkinson or Welsh, our mother's maiden name, to have gained a scholarship.

Barry and I both got ourselves a paper round, which isn't too arduous in summer and within a few weeks our youngest sister, Sheila, was born. That's five children now and Sheila was the first one of us not born in the front room. It had been discovered that we as a family had a blood disorder which had not manifested itself on us four but had affected Sheila in the womb hence she had to be born and looked after in the major teaching hospital in Newcastle. Only dad was allowed to visit them as in those days children were not allowed to make visits to a maternity ward.

Things turned out okay and Sheila arrived home just in time for mum to see me on to the school bus, scheduled for us grammar school students, on my first day. I can only imagine how proud she must have been seeing me with all those posh kids.

Being the family we were it was too good to last.

Five children just made life harder and money got tighter. They had never in their lives had rent to pay every week and having the luxury of electric water and home heating along with the electric stove meant more bills than they had ever been used to. I realised at the time that grammar school was another financial burden so I had paper rounds both morning and afternoon. Barry and I still chased the coal delivery trucks.

It was decided that we couldn't afford all this 'luxury' and application was made for a miner's house that could accommodate our large family and we climbed back on to the horse and cart and made our way back to The Crag and 1, Surtees Terrace named after the famous Surtees family who had been involved with coal mining in the Teeside area for centuries. For a grammar school boy this was a disaster. Back to an outside toilet, meaning embarrassment when friends visited, no bathroom, which didn't cause me too much angst as we had showers at school and with physical education every day that meant a compulsory shower every day. Fortunately I didn't suffer from tinea, or athlete's foot as it was called, as those kids weren't allowed in the showers.

CHAPTER 17!

It's Easy Being Green!

Then there was the time in nineteen seventy one when John Hall from RCA records rang me in my office and said that he may have another potential client for me to take into Jackson Wain the advertising agency I worked for at the time. Always looking for ways to ingratiate myself to the masters on the fourth floor I agreed to meet the man who was described to me as an Englishman who was setting up his business in Australia and would need promotion and advertising.

John brought him into the office and he was given the guided tour and a quick precise of our clientele including the major ones such as Qantas, Rothmans, Bushells Coffee and Tea, British Paints etc. Yes I worked on the Rolf Harris 'Trust British Paints' campaign. Suitably impressed he suggested he would like me to meet up with his cousin who was the main player in the potential client's business and invited me for dinner two nights later when his cousin would be in town. Sounded good to me and when he called on the Thursday he asked if I could suggest a restaurant in the city. Not being a fine diner I knew hardly any restaurants in the city or elsewhere, however when we had first arrived in Australia Patricia my wife had taken a second job at the Outrigger, a restaurant on the top floor of the brand new Wynyard Travelodge at number nine York St. I would like to point out at this stage only in the case of fairness that I also took a second job as a cleaner in the ANZ bank in George St. I left because they wouldn't promote me from toilet cleaning to the electrical polishing machines which was top of the mountain in the cleaning business. However I digress and as this was probably the only restaurant I knew I suggested it.

Came the time and I arrive right on time, order a beer at the bar and wait for my hosts, take note, they arrived shortly afterwards and to my surprise the cousin needed no introduction as I recognised him immediately as Simon Dee, a very famous TV and radio personality from the U.K. Unbeknowns to me at the time he had recently been sacked from all his jobs in the U.K. because of his arrogance and demeanour. I remembered him as the face of the sixties driving an E-Type convertible and an Aston Martin, probably the template for Austin Powers in hindsight. He was, I must say, very debonair, smartly dressed and coiffured, smoking Sobranie cigarettes, they were the French ones that came with gold filters and coloured paper. Actually quite an intimidating figure, a good head taller than me and affectations that I'm certain were meant to impress the colonial plebs.

Over dinner, which was quite impressive, with Simon encouraging all to go for all three courses, top of the wine list, reds and whites, the conversation turned to the potential business that they were to be setting up in Australia, with Simon Dee to be the public face of the venture, and would I be interested personally to join up with them as the idea was going to generate millions of dollars for all concerned if we got in on the ground floor. There would be government support, business donations, public contributions etc. etc. Quite heady stuff for an innocent like me to absorb but awe struck by the sheer sales pitch of this English icon. I was in hook line and sinker and I still didn't know what the product was.

Snippets of conversation included environmental protection, global warming, deforestation, bio-diversity, overfishing, whaling, genetic engineering, anti-nuclear energy etc. etc. Remember this was the early seventies and as much as these expressions are common place nowadays it was Ancient Greek to me at the time.

I was told the business model was working in some European companies like Holland and Denmark and was built on creating environmental causes and seeking funding from all and sundry to finance the protestations. The deal was that as the South Pacific head I would be allowed to keep 20 per cent of all funds raised alongside a salary package including rent on a large home for entertainment purposes, cars and expense accounts.

There was only one major problem. I didn't have a clue what they were talking about. So out of the Dee briefcase came the folder with pictures and press clippings on a Dutch organisation called Don't Make a Wave who had sent a chartered ship, named Greenpeace for the protest, from Vancouver to oppose testing of hydrogen bombs in Alaska.

It only occurred to me years later that I had been offered the licensing, sometimes called franchising, of Greenpeace for the South Pacific for a fee of twenty thousand dollars a year. I expressed slight interest and hoped to receive more information before I could make a decision. However my mind was quickly made up as they excused themselves to go to the downstairs bathrooms and didn't return. Yes in Deeeeeeeed leaving me with the bill equal to half my week's wages. I now believe I turned down the charity version of Apple or Microsoft.

CHAPTER 18

When In Rome!

Spennymoor Grammar Technical School, as it was known in those days was very good to me and I did quite well in Mathematics and Physics with the arts subjects taking a back seat but I was able to pass exams in all subjects and I wasn't a bad footballer so I made the first team but never got to district level.

However we did have a boy one year ahead of me Bill Gates, no not that one, another one, who ended up captaining England Schoolboys and carved out a professional career with Middlesborough. He also had a younger brother Eric Gates who had a bigger career including a couple of games for England after a successful career with Ipswich.

Worth mentioning here that in 2012 while waiting for a table at the Bennelong restaurant, which is part of the Sydney Opera House precinct to celebrate my mother in law's 70th birthday we were seated next to the other Bill Gates, the American business magnate, philanthropist, investor, computer programmer, and inventor.

When I was fourteen years of age in 1960 the school arranged a weeks holiday for those interested to see the Olympics in Rome. I took on a Sunday paper round and told my parents this was to be money for me to go to Rome which cost eighteen pounds and included the train and channel ferry fares along with accommodation in what appeared to be an orphanage being run by Roman Catholic nuns.

We visited all the historic sites and took in a number of days in the athletic stadium for the games.

My first time of real travel and I was addicted.

Life took a bad turn for me when I was sixteen and my best friend from childhood, Billy Griffiths contracted leukeamia and after about three months in Sedgefield hospital he died in his sleep. This was a major reality check on life itself and made me more determined to live life to the full and fulfil my ambition to see the world. Things were better at home now. Dad had seen the writing on the wall for the coal industry and had taken a factory labouring job with Dorman Long in Newton Aycliffe and the change of job appeared to change his view of life and the mood swings stopped. In recent years I've come to the conclusion he was not a bad man but his life had been so full of frustration after losing his parents then a limb had caused the anger that had been exploding over the years into the violent behaviour.

Some years later I was back in Ferryhill and Lisa and I were having dinner with my sister Anne and her husband Stuart when I asked him what kind of man my father was. A strange question to come from a son but it should be remembered I had left home for college at eighteen then went to Australia at twenty three so I had had no time with him as a grown man but Stuart had known him for years as an adult.

It brought tears to my eyes when I asked him what he thought my father had wanted out of life and what

had he missed.The response had both myself and Lisa in tears when he said "He wanted to be you and live the life of travel and be the free spirit you are."

CHAPTER 19!

Turning Over a New Leif!

Then there was the time in nineteen seventy seven when I was totally immersed in television production and in particular pop and rock music programmes. Working for McCabe Collins, one of the more prolific television production houses I was producing, directing and writing five and a half hours of television each week for the Ten Network. This was made up of a daily thirty minute top forty run down using video clips supplied by the record companies and three hours live pop programming every Saturday morning. The afternoon shows were called Right On and the Saturday morning was called Rock n' Roll Milkbar. We were in demand from the record companies to play their videos and where possible to arrange television interviews with any local or visiting artists here to plug their recordings. This meant meeting a long roll call of pop stars including, Abba, even appear in Abba The Movie, Paul McCartney, Boz Scaggs, John Cougar Mellencamp, Billy Joel, Bonnie Tyler and too many others to list here. However one particular guest sticks out. This was the era of teen pop stars that came and went like confetti being thrown at a wedding and Leif Garrett was no exception to this much travelled path. With his shoulder length blonde curly hair and videos of him on skateboards, the fad of the time, he was the idol of every teenage girl in the country with hits like Runaround Sue and The Wanderer and as we were the number one teen television programme we had been airing his videos each and every day due to the demands of our audiences, so naturally we were first choice to do the interview and Phil Mortlock the promotions manager from Warner Brothers records put everything in place.

Under normal circumstances we would take the artist to the Channel

Ten Sydney studio and pre-record the interview to be edited in later but due to having Shaun Cassidy a few months earlier causing a near riot when word got out as to where and when the interview was taking place we had to find a new option as this had almost cost me my job. Ten's security company from then on had banned me from having any 'pop stars' on the premises unless we paid for the extra security which cost more than my weekly production budget. Our studio director, Eric Steen, had a friend with a cruiser that he volunteered to put at our disposal for a boat party on Sydney Harbour with food and some beer and wine supplied by Warner Brothers sounded a very good idea. All went well, beautifully shot scenes with the Opera House and the Harbour Bridge as backdrops how could it not. For a boy of sixteen years our star guest certainly knew how to drink, smoke and win the hearts of some models along for the ride and three or four years older than him. Proved a bit of drama when our host's girlfriend who he had invited along took a shine to Leif and on docking at Milson's Point she disembarked with him leaving our host to tie up and clean the boat. She was not seen for a week and as it turned out she had joined the promotional tour party for the rest of the Australian tour.

We carried on promoting Leif under demand from the fans and we were approached by a man called Michael Wilding, I know a famous name, but no Elizabeth Taylor on his arm, who had a small printing shop and had knocked up a few hundred posters of Leif Garrett and he was looking for a way to promote them and make some money from the sales. In those days we must remember marketing and merchandising was in its infancy so there seemed to be no obstacles to his plan. As a trial we offered some as prizes for our competitions and we were overwhelmed by the response and so we agreed with the printer to merchandise the product as best we could. He came back with more product including a pin badge about five cm diameter and iron on stickers for t-shirts with the same picture.

No experience in this at all we were pondering on how we could put this product to market when someone suggested we should get a stall at the Royal Easter Show coming up in a few weeks. Never having had the experience of visiting the Royal Easter Show I had no idea just how big an occasion this was. Ten days around the Easter holiday period where the country comes to the city and around two hundred thousand people a day turn up for all the festivities. In our naivety we called asking if we could book a stall for the ten days. The lady at the Royal Agricultural Society burst into laughter at my request and giggling non-stop advised me that people had been on waiting lists for ten years trying to get a presence at the Royal Easter Show. That appeared to be the end of that great idea or so we thought. Co-incidentally one of our sponsors, Allens confectionery called in that afternoon to drop off prizes and gifts for the crew and someone mentioned to him what had occurred re the show that morning. Not a problem, they have had a stall there for over thirty years and he'd ask back at the factory if there was any way they could spare one square metre for us to sell our merchandise. We received a positive response, which included a few free plugs and the hostess of the programme, Kobe Steele to make daily appearances at the stall. Little did we know what we were letting ourselves in for.Never having been to a Royal Easter Show I was totally unprepared for what occurred on the first day. The show bag pavilion opened at ten am and the rush was unbelievable. Thousands of people of all ages poured into the pavilion to get their show bags. I didn't even know what a show bag was until this moment. The explanation is that they are usually a plastic shopping bag stuffed with a company's product samples for sale at about half the retail price. But our stall was overrun by hundreds of pre-teen and teenage girls desperate to get their hands on any Leif Garrett memorabilia. We sold out of posters, badges and iron-one in a couple of hours and had to ring the printer for more with a promise to the kids that more product would be available in the afternoon. This went on every day for the ten days of the show with only myself and a friend manning the stall for ten hours a day. It was so exhausting when I arrived home I was too tired to reconcile the day's takings and merely stuffed every note under the mattress then collapsed and woke up the next day to start all over again. This was in the days of the one and two dollar notes so it's easy to picture the state of the money all crumpled up as we know youngsters don't carry wallets so there was no neatly folded wads of cash. The mattress had risen about ten centimetres as the money was stashed underneath it. Needless to say Allens, our hosts, were overjoyed at the attention and spin off they were getting. It was their best ever result from the show in decades.

When the show was over and it was time to reconcile the takings it took nearly a whole day to unfold the notes and count the dollars. Like something out of the Scarface movie without the cash counting machine.

All bills paid, McCabe Collins took the profits, very generously, not so, giving me a $250 bonus for putting in the ten days but an experience I'll never forget or so I thought.

It was some two years later when I was moving house after the divorce that as the bed was being moved I found another $1000+ in one and two dollar notes that I had missed being counted that day. So I got my bonus after all and I should say at a time when I needed it most.

Then there were other teen idols.............................

CHAPTER 20!

Old Father Hubbard!

Then there was the time in 1965 when I was going home from college in Newcastle to stay with my parents for the holidays in Ferryhill. A distance of about 40km, an hour on the forty six bus that stopped every two hundred metres or so including towns on the way, Gateshead, Chester Le Street and Durham City itself. But being the penniless student that we all were in those days to save four shillings, before decimal currency, was worth doing. So for sixpence the bus took me to south of Gateshead to a well known roundabout near Low Fell, the village that is now well known as the site of Antony Gormley's, The Angel Of The North, where at holiday times students would hold up a piece of cardboard stating their destination looking to hitch-hike home. A practice now frowned upon as dangerous and foolhardy. This was also before the motorway had been constructed which now takes the great majority of the North -South traffic.

I couldn't believe my good luck when a brand new Ford Zodiac, we knew production years of cars by their last letter on the number plate, this one had a letter C, hence 1965, pulled over and offered a lift. I opened the rear door to put in my rucksack, they became backpacks many years later, and had to position it alongside a number of cardboard boxes on the rear seat. The boxes were open and were packed with pamphlets and fliers of all shapes and sizes. But not looking a gift horse in the mouth I climbed in the front out of the biting wind which was always there in this part of County Durham.

The driver was average, probably could be described as non-descript, now there's an oxymoron, but he did have the kind of accent that I've always called soft American sometimes mistaken for Canadian. The ride began uneventfully with conversation mainly directed to what I was studying and my hopes and ambitions etc. As a 19 year old student I'd never considered my future, probably become a teacher or at least enter a profession that gave stability and a linear career path, so I presume I was a not too interesting subject for the driver who had now introduced himself as Lafayette, a very exotic name I thought at the time, never ever having been a student of American history.

As the ride progressed he asked me if I had done anything with computers, as a maths student that was easily answered as I had just completed a week's study at Rutherford College of Technology in their computer lab. Rutherford was attached to Newcastle University and was at the time in the forefront of computer technology. It was 1965 and a computer in those days occupied a whole building in the centre of Newcastle operating under the Fortran system which required thousands of punch cards to feed the machine utilising dozens of staff to punch the cards. Sounds archaic but we thought we were at the cutting edge of technology. Bill Gates and Steve Jobs were only ten years old at the time. They probably had it all worked out even then but were holding out for a better price. I remember my final thesis was on the future roles of calculators and computers in the future. Bearing in mind desk calculators were all mechanical at the time and electronic computers took up a whole building. Recently having a look at my thesis I picked up on my major error. I had not factored in the role of computers in the design of future computers thus not taking into account the exponential growth in technical knowledge. Never mind the internet.

The conversation in the car then moved to the human brain and how it was in fact similar to a computer with the more memory available than anything we know or are going to know and the only process we need to master was the retrieval of this information stored in the brain. He talked about all the things we had seen, heard, smelt, even touched and our emotional experiences were all there just waiting for the tap to be turned on. It was impossible to disagree with the his argument as it made a lot of common sense, and I must say even to this day I believe he was correct and now Google has taken over many of these functions and possibly made our brains lazy and working at a lower level than at any other time in history. His description compared our memory to a filing cabinet with tabs on the files and he made strong point that all we had to do was discover how as an individual we could go to the tabs quickly then open the file.

I was enjoying the conversation so much that as we approached the Ferryhill Cut on the old A1, locals will know where I mean, where I would normally get out and walk up Durham Rd. to the village, catch the local Martindale's bus home, this time I stayed for a further 10 minutes till we reached St. Aidan's church in Chilton from where I would walk down Chilton Lane, about 3kms to Surtees Terrace, where my family lived at the time. As I was getting out he reached over to the back seat and gave me a bunch of pamphlets which he suggested I read and if I was ever in Sussex to get in touch with him.

I thanked him and he said it was a pleasure and to make sure if I did get to Sussex use the phone number he had written on the Dianetics flyer and ask for Lafayette Ron Hubbard.

It's always been strange to me that whenever I've been stopped in the street by the Scientologists near Sydney Town Hall when I tell them I had personally met their founder they would cut the conversation immediately. Maybe he's been excommunicated or whatever it is Scientologists do to the de-converted.

CHAPTER 21!

Right Round Like A Record!

Then there was the time in 1974 when I made a foray into record production. The story has its genesis in 1972 when I was working as a researcher and television advertising executive for Leo Burnett Advertising one of the world's major advertising agencies. I was involved in determining the best ways to research viewing, listening and readership statistics as the media industry was embracing computers and the analysis that computerisation would bring. As the major TV buyer in the country I was feted quite a lot with lunches, dinners, theatre tickets and the like but I was true to the figures and statistics I was instrumental in producing.

One of the Sydney sales people for Channel 7 in Perth was an Englishman the same age as myself, John Hall, with whom I got on quite well and my wife and I socialised with him and his wife till she decided Australia wasn't for her and back to the UK she went. Soon after meeting him he left Channel 7 and took up the post of advertising and promotions manager for the major record label RCA. At the time RCA was one of the biggest record companies in the world which later was taken over by BMG records the German conglomerate. Their artist's roster included Elvis Presley the biggest rock star of all time till the Beatles came along.

Because of my relationship with John I was able to persuade them to move their advertising account to my agency and Burnetts found it wise to promote me to Account Director for RCA alongside my other duties. Initially RCA were never a major advertising account in terms of billings and expenditures but having RCA on the client list made good reading in the foyer of the North Sydney office. They became more important on the client list as television developed into the primary advertising medium for LP records and in particular for compilation albums which were the financial mainstay of record companies in the seventies.

The first campaign we did for RCA was for a John Laws album of trucking songs, Motivatin Man. John Laws was the number one radio personality in Australia at the time hosting a national talk back morning programme that usually once a week had him saving a caller from committing suicide and he portrayed himself as a friend of the battlers in society and regularly took calls from truck drivers plying their trade across Australia. We planned a launch and a television advertising campaign to support the obvious radio exposure we would get on his programmes.

Thinking outside the box we arranged for the launch reception to be held in the panel beater's yard belonging to Jumbo Jim set in one of Sydney's industrial areas in the unfashionable inner western suburbs, somewhere personalities, music reviewers and media personalities would never visit in normal circumstances. It was a great success. A typical Australian barbecue, steak and sausages just a little upmarket, plenty of wine and beer and about a hundred people in attendance. We even had Jack Daniels, one of his sponsors, package a bottle for each guest with John Laws - Motivatin Man on the labels. At the end of the reception when there was only John Laws, Bryan Nichols, John Hall and myself still hanging around complimenting ourselves on what a great success we had produced we realised we had forgotten to give the guests their bottles of Jack Daniels. So we did the obvious. We each brought our cars into the yard and took two dozen bottles each and left some for Jumbo Jim. I learnt to like bourbon in the coming weeks.

Having been introduced to Bryan Nichols, the youngest ever A & R manager ever appointed and at the age of 24 he was in charge of, as his title suggests artists and repertoire. Like myself he had started his working life as a schoolteacher. I had no ambitions as far as the music industry went, however one of our clients was Rothmans cigarettes and they were putting together a spectacular for the main arena in the Royal Easter Show, which is when the bush meets the city over ten days with just about everyone in Sydney attending for at least one day or evening. The Sydney Royal Easter Show, also known as the Royal Easter Show or simply The Show or (to exhibitors) The Royal, is an annual show held in Sydney, Australia over two weeks around Easter. It is run by the Royal

Agricultural Society of New South Wales and was first held in 1823. Queen Victoria, (1837–1901), awarded the society and its show the right to use the word "Royal" in its name. The Show is historically an event where "city meets country" and the rural industries of Australia can be shown and celebrated once a year. The Show comprises an agricultural show, an amusement park and a fair and combines the elements of each, showcasing the judging of livestock and produce. This comprehensive fair has many competitions including arts and crafts, photography and cookery, as well as tests of strength and skill such as wood chopping. The Show also has shopping, restaurants, commercial stands and exhibits, a horticultural display, a national accredited conformation dog show and cat show, and stage and arena shows. The Show currently attracts one million people per year.

It was assumed that because I was in charge of RCA I would know all that's necessary on music and in particular Australian traditional folk music. Could I put together a 15 minute tape of original recordings of Australian bush music to be the backing track for the spectacular. Didn't sound too difficult so I visited a couple of folk music clubs and put together a group of musicians including a well known Irish folk singer, John Currie, and into United Sound Studios we went. United Sound was recognised as Australia's version of Abbey Road as all major Australian artists recorded there with top engineers and producers. Feeling a little intimidated my merry band of musicians and myself went straight to work and four hours later I had the master tape which I took to the office the next day. I was now a record producer. Watch out Phil Spector here I come. The spectacular in the Easter Show involved replicas of Cobb and Co. stage coaches with eight horses, bushrangers galloping after them, staged robberies of gold transports and I do have to say it was a great success with the public.

The next thing to occur was that Bryan left RCA to join up with one of his U.S. colleagues to open Dyna House records in Australia. The business model was copied from the very successful budget label K-Tel in that it was inexpensive product with very expensive advertising campaigns. Their first few records were Polka Greats, Irish Lullabies, Hawaiian Hits etc. etc. and they were on a roll. It occurred to me that maybe Australian traditional songs could work if Polkas had sold. I put it to Bryan and was given the go ahead provided Bryan and I were 50/50 in the deal. So a letter of agreement was drawn up between myself and his company, Briandra Pty. Ltd.that gave us a 75c royalty on all sales.

I got back in touch with John Currie, he of the Rothmans spectacular, and we worked out a song list including all the best known Australian bush ballads and folk songs. Bryan had given us a six week deadline to have the master tapes ready and so we started to pull the required musicians together and arranged a few rehearsals.

But life is never that simple! A call from Bryan informed me that they have lost a licensing deal for their next promotion and with television time already booked it would cost them dearly to pull the ads so could we have the master tapes ready by 1pm next Monday to go to air the following Sunday. It was now Wednesday, not too much time to get things done but at that age we're all bullet proof. Let's go!

Bryan had taken the liberty of arranging with one of his friends, Col Joye, a once famous Australian pop singer, but famous now for producing Dirty Dancing the Stage Musical world-wide, for use of his ATA recording studio in Glebe beginning Friday at 8 am through till noon on the Monday. We had no choice of saying no.

Friday morning came. John Currie had assembled a motley crew of musicians and I'll try to credit all involved, apologies to those I've forgotten. Lee Williams guitar, George Cliff bush bass, Anne Cochrane vocals and flute, Sean Gilroy on fiddle, myself on lagerphone, Kate Delaney vocals, Don Hopkins mandolin, Maureen Cummeskey and Tony Suttor also adding vocals and others who made cameo appearances as word had gone around the folk music community in Sydney about what was going on.

We worked in four hour stretches with an hours break in-between, no-one went home the whole weekend. Exhaustion was rife, Anne, the flute player, her bottom lip was swelling, George Cliff on bush bass had to tape his fingers with major layers of Elastoplast so he could pluck through the pain. Voices were cracking but in the end come 10 am on the Monday all 34 songs were recorded and we left the engineer to mix them together and place them in the order I had suggested for a two record, two cassette set.

I suggested they all go to the Ancient Briton pub over the road for lunch and I'll be over soon to settle up. A courier arrived to pick up the master tapes along with a brown envelope containing two thousand five hundred dollars to pay the musicians.

We had kept good records on sessions played by each person along with information on how many instruments they had played in each four hour call so I now assembled all the time sheets and crossed the road to the pub. We were keeping good time sheets so that the musicians union could not come along later and bite us in the bum for underpaying. I distributed the time sheets to each person with the calculation of their payments, I then purposely pulled out the cash and spread it on the table for all to see. I then offered everyone involved a share of the royalties or their payment now in cash with them to waiver all rights for the future. I advised them all strongly to take the royalty offer even though it would take around three months for them to get paid if they went down the royalty path. I let them think about it and then on an individual basis they came and took the session fees. Not a bad sum for a weekends work probably equivalent to two weeks salary at the time. Only one, John Currie, the lead singer and guitarist decided to take the royalty option which I had advised everyone to take. Fair to say he was due for over $800 for his work so was he happy a few months later when I handed him a cheque for $8400. There was more joy for us as the records were released over and over again on different labels that Bryan launched in his career and that was probably the best decision John had made in his career as it provided a small income for a few years. I have only stayed in touch over the years with George Cliff the bass player and he still remonstrates with me 40 years later on why I didn't try harder to persuade him to wait for the royalty cheques.

But in those famous words 'Wait there's more............................"

Soon after the Australian success I was approached by a married couple who had called Dyna House to get my number and they wanted to meet me to discuss making records. I met up with them in Crows Nest and they told me that they had purchased some new technology which they had retro fitted on to a record pressing machine. The technology allowed pictures to be printed directly on to the vinyl. It was a breakthrough in those days. They wanted me to produce two albums, one was to be Christmas songs and the other was Bawdy Ballads. That meant find as many dirty songs as possible, record them uncensored and deliver the masters in a months time so they could get the Christmas market. They were paying handsomely so I rounded up the usual suspects, ie. musicians and singers, and using Copperfield studios in Sussex Street came out with the finished product. I was to deliver them to an address in Oxford St. Darlinghurst, where I would get paid on delivery of the masters. What a surprise I got when arriving at the address found out it was The Orgy Shop, quite a famous store as it was the first sex shop in Sydney and it had garnered massive publicity when it had opened. An even bigger surprise was on entering there was a young lady being served at the counter and as she heard me come in had turned around and she was holding a vibrator with frills and switched on it really was vibrating. Her face went red and she tried to explain it was for a girlfriend getting married later that week. A likely story!

I delivered the master tapes, took my money and asked when I could pick up some samples for the performers. Two weeks later I got the call that the samples were ready and I could pick them up from the warehouse in East Sydney. On arrival at the warehouse the next shock to my system. It was the warehouse not only for records but for all the imported sex toys and it was amazing to me how much of the product was there. Stacked up to the ceilings were boxes of sex aids including inflatable ladies and the like.

I later found out the couple were the publishers of the very famous Kings Cross newspaper, Ribald, a visitors sex guide to Sydney.

CHAPTER 22

The Wedding Singer!

Then there was Sydney Harbour opening up in front of me. September 1st 1969. An absolutely magnificent sight as the water was like glass, a beautiful southern hemisphere spring day about 6.30am. I defy anyone to say they have first set eyes on Sydney and seen it better than this. This was to be the start of a new life, but better than that it was the start of my life. Nothing I had seen or read about Australia could prepare one for this magnificent sight. Only 5 weeks before I had been a school teacher in the north eastern town of Jarrow, think hunger marchers and the television series 'When the Boat Comes In', I had taught my last class on the Friday, was married on the Saturday and on a ship from Southampton to Sydney on the Sunday. All this had been arranged in a few weeks after the NSW Department of Education offered me a mathematics teaching position if I could get things arranged to embark on this Italian emigration ship Flavia. The main thing to arrange was a wedding so as to enable my fiancee, Patricia, to accompany me. One thing life has taught me is that women can arrange a wedding in twenty four hours if necessary.

Emigration came as a shock to our families as we had only been discussing the potential of teaching in different countries probably in a year or two's time. Rhodesia was in consideration then Ian Smith announced Unilateral Declaration of Independence, Canada looked too cold, Bermuda offered me a posting but on checking salary levels we would have been living in comparative poverty. So when New South Wales offered the position and would pay all our expenses, including the ten pound emigrant processing fee our minds were made up. Emigration was a hot topic in Britain at the time as young professionals like myself saw it as a way out of this not so great Britain. It was referred to as the brain drain. The Australian model suited most young people with the promise of sunshine and great food and housing.

The wedding had gone without a hitch, including about a hundred kids from my school turning up. If I could have afforded to invite them all to the reception I would have. My wife insisted that the wedding was to be formal attire for men and a full white wedding for the ladies. That meant hiring morning suits and so I decided that if we were going so far that meant top hat and tails. Her father, Danny the postman, refused the tails but did wear the shorter version morning suit. I remember the proud look on my mother and fathers faces as they arrived at the church looking like they were on the way to the Royal Enclosure at Royal Ascot, light years away from theirs, and mine, coal mining background. I feel certain that they must have shown the photographs every Saturday night at the Chilton and Windlestone Working Mens Club which was the only place they ever went to for entertainment. For years we lived next door to a pub, the Surtees Arms, and I never saw either of them ever go into it. One other thing worth noting about the wedding, which only occurred to me later in life, was the band providing music both at the church in Jesmond, quite an up market suburb, and at the reception at the other end of the city in Scotswood, which in six months after our wedding was to become world-wide infamous for its resident Mary Bell, the eleven year old child killer.

Mary Bell a British woman who, as a child, strangled to death two little boys in Scotswood, an inner-city suburb of Newcastle upon Tyne. She was convicted in December 1968 of the manslaughter of the two boys, Martin Brown (aged four) and Brian Howe (aged three). Bell was 11 when she was convicted for killing Brown and Howe.

The band booked for the wedding reception was quite a well-known group of Newcastle musicians who went on to further fame and fortune in the years to come. However the star musician at the reception came as a complete surprise to everyone when my mother climbed on to the piano stool and joined in with the band. No rehearsal, no practise she was jamming along with people who could have been her grandchildren. Why was I surprised? In all my life we never ever had a piano at home, I had never seen my mother play the piano and obviously my brother, my sisters and I had no idea she was a musician. They couldn't get her off the piano and she then surprised us again with her beautiful singing voice and there wasn't a dry eye as she sang a solo version of Que Sera Sera, a Doris Day hit from the movie The Man Who Knew Too Much, followed by my father and her singing the Louis Armstrong classic, What A Wonderful World. A song my father had sung for years every morning as he woke up. Rather ironic I used to think at the time for someone who had lost half a leg when seventeen in an accident at the mine where he had worked for the past forty years. Later in the evening I was talking to my mother's sister Eva, our auntie, and after expressing my surprise at what had happened Eva was just as surprised that our mother had shared none of the family history with us. It turned out that their mother, our grandmother, had died very young and our mother being the eldest in the family had to leave school at thirteen to bring up her sister and two brothers. This was the practise in those pre-war days. The family had always been grateful for her to have given up her dreams of being a musician, singer and dancer. Our uncles and aunts could never do enough for her when things got tough when our father had his nervous breakdown and spent some months in psychiatric facilities.

I was reminded of this some forty years later when Lisa and I had returned to Ferryhill and on showing homes where we had once lived, a gentleman standing at his front gate appeared to recognise me and pointed out that I must be Freda's son that is Freda the dancer. Another irony in that she was married to a man with one leg for over forty years. The man was so kind and being only a couple of years older than me remarked how everyone had admired her during this tough period of her life.

The next morning, Sunday we caught the train from Newcastle Central Station to Southampton and that night we set sail. It had been a hectic few weeks.

A wonderful 5 week honeymoon cruising past The Azores, seeing Panama City, where I played football with the slum dwelling children, through The Shipping Canal, then Tahiti, a disappointment, as the beaches were all black volcanic soil, not what the tourist brochures promised,. However I do remember we rented a car with another couple to travel around the island and him being a mechanic he unplugged the odometer so we wouldn't get charged for the mileage. Auckland, where we saw the Haka for the first time and hundreds of voices singing the Maori Farewell as we pulled out of the harbour. Melbourne, not the best city to see as an introduction to Australia, and finally arriving in Sydney on this wonderful spring day with my young wife.

Were we brave? I don't think so, at that age we're all bullet proof. Nothing can stop anyone when you're so young and what a magnificent beginning. One of the most frequently asked questions over the years has been on what made us come to Australia. The short answer is that it wasn't the attraction of Australia it was more to do with getting out of Britain with its grey skies, grey roads and pavements, grey faced people wearing their grey clothes.

On the journey there were three main groups. Young Australians returning from their rites of passage working holiday in Europe, immigrants like ourselves and survivors/refugees from an earthquake in Sicily. I was asked to give English lessons to the Sicilian group, please remember I'm a Maths major but I suppose being a teacher qualified me. It came to me that this idyllic honeymoon cruise was also quite rewarding as I was being paid full salary for the summer holidays in the U.K. full salary from N.S.W. from the moment I embarked in Southampton and now a third pay packet from Australian Dept. Of Immigration.

We were in Paradise. Three meals a day parties and games day after day and exotic ports of call. The captain of the ship on hearing we were honeymooners took a shine towards Patricia and we dined every night at the Captain's Table, which is not to be sniffed at believe me, the food and service at top table was better and included the very scarce fresh fruit.

So here were at last. Patricia, I remember had dressed for the occasion with a blue two piece suit, dress and three quarter jacket with white trim and myself in jacket, tie and trousers. After all it was the thing to dress smart to meet people for the first time. Very un-Australian I learnt later.

Sailing past the unfinished Sydney Opera House, still surrounded with scaffolding, and not for one second realising the great part it was to play in my life. Under the Sydney Harbour Bridge and docking in a place called Pyrmont. I thought immediately that I'm going to like living here after growing up in the bleak North East of England in a pit village. Notice not a 'mining village' to the people who live and die there, they're not miners, they're pitmen, and forget any romantic notions of the proud working classes. Miners were fodder to the failing British industrial machine.

Where was the grey I was used to? The first thing anyone notices on arrival in Australia is the fact that people are smiling and laughing and in years to come I came to notice it at airport customs and immigration points. Even the uniformed customs and immigration officers on duty greeted you with a smile. This was confirmed some forty years later when our son brought his girlfriend to Australia from England and she said exactly the same things about Australians.

Never mind there was better to come. Worth noting here that Melbourne had been our first port in Australia. From a boring big town like Melbourne to a magnificent harbour city of Sydney lifted one's spirits and my thoughts were along the line of 'I think I'm going to like this place'. Melbourne and Sydney have always epitomised to me the difference between a big town and a city. A bit like London and Manchester. Those thoughts became a given not thirty minutes after the ship docked when we were paged to the purser's office and on reaching there found a flustered looking lady looking for Mr. and Mrs. Atkinson. On introducing ourselves we found she was from the NSW Dept. of Education and her job was to settle in new schoolteachers. She gathered our passports and then we noticed a man in a grey suit standing behind her who she told to go with me and to give me a hand getting our luggage from the cabin. He put on his peaked cap and followed me downstairs to our cabin.

The queues for customs and immigration snaked around the terminal, with friends we'd met on the trip lining up in queues like we are used to seeing in films of immigrants arriving at Ellis Island. So imagine their surprise when they saw us being waltzed to the head of the queue with our luggage being carried by a uniformed chauffeur. Out in 30 seconds into a black limousine parked directly outside the customs hall for everyone to see. Add that to our dinner being served at the Captain's Table for the past few weeks. The imagination can run riot in trying to work out what or who the other passengers thought we were.

What a wonderful beginning to a new life could it get any better?

Certainly can but nothing could have prepared us for what happened the next day ....

CHAPTER 23!

Pretty Baby!

Now that I'm a successful record producer or I certainly became one when the first royalty cheque for seventy five thousand dollars arrive. Had to divide it fifty-fifty with Bryan Nichols but let's go with the next one. At the time I had a desk in the offices of Bedford Pearce theatrical agency who were just starting up and would be actors and actors were filing in day after day looking for an agent. The agency became one of Australia's most successful representing people like Oscar winner Russell Crowe, Singrid Thornton from Sea Change, Liddy Clarke and countless other famous stars and I thank Martin and Shirley as they worked with me on Benny Hill in Australia and Kathryn Grayson a former Hollywood legend. I was secretly hoping this could lead us to a tour by Doris Day my own personal favourite.

Meeting Benny Hill was interesting in that on checking him in to the Sebel Town House his first request to me was where he could find working girls, that's a euphemism, as he always liked them two at a time. All those years I had thought of him being of another persuasion. It was a successful visit for Benny Hill as we were able to arrange a television special Benny Hill down Under with the Ten Network and through my old co-worker Leo Schofield a major advertising campaign using the line 'Nibblin Nobby's Nuts".

I was now a fully fledged impresario, or so I thought. Shows at the Opera House, record production, overseas artists seeking my promotional skills. What could go wrong?

We'll keep the answer to that for later.

For Bryan our next record was Treasury of Australian Poetry. An easy one to do. Use professional voice over people. Pay them union rates and here we are. No messing around with musicians. A moderate success.

The next television advertised record I produced was called Let There Be Drums, which was a collection of drum based hits such as Bombora, Let There be Drums, Apache etc. I had booked Atlantic Studios In the suburb of Earlwood and on meeting the engineer Peter Hood it turned out he was the drummer in The Atlantics, the band that had the world wide hit with Bombora. Gave me a feeling of great confidence until after about four hours I was asked if I'd give the rest of my day's booking to Gene Pierson a friend of mine from another record company who was wanting to lay down some demonstration tracks for a potential female singer. Not a problem, let me know when he arrives and we'll call it a day. Imagine my surprise when we walked out of the studio and in the lounge there was the 'potential star' none other than the stunningly beautiful Brooke Shields. To say I was tongue tied doesn't convey how startled I was. She was very well mannered and an easy conversationalist even at such a young age.

The next one was along the lines of a history of songs writing taking songs from Greensleeves through to the Beatles. We called it Four Hundred Years and that was about how many it sold. Never trust artists to pick the repertoire that's for A&R people meaning Artists and Repertoire. They don't get these titles for no reason. A postscript to this episode came in 2014 when Lisa's sister Sally and her family were moving house and as I was helping packing a copy of the record turned up in Sally's collection. Something I hadn't seen for close to forty years and she assured me she had been a big fan since the group had performed at her school decades ago.

Outside of the television marketing of records I was asked to produce a single for the riggers on the Harbour Bridge who were basking in the success of one of their own, Paul Hogan, who was by now a world-wide sensation with his movie Crocodile Dundee. The song they had written was 'Paul, Paul He's Our Mate' the next line being 'Paul Paul we think you're Great'. It was the worst song you could imagine and the guys themselves insisted they wanted to sing it. Their singing was worse than the song. But where there's a will there's a way. I hired a group of guys I knew who could sing and once we had the rhythm track down they put down the lyrics even with a few harmonies thrown in. The saying you can't make a silk purse out a sow's ear rings true. We sent the singers home, brought in a case of beer and the brass section were putting down their parts when the riggers / songwriters arrived. Free beer!! This is showbiz. The brass finished and in came the stars, pretty merry, very relaxed and ready to sing. Earphones on microphone stands erected, backing track playing, microphones switched off. That's right off! Here we go. We went through the motions of half a dozen takes. Singled out a few solo parts then called them into the booth. By mixing in the earlier singers the production was passable but these guys were overjoyed. They couldn't believe how all this modern technology could produce such great sounds.

The beer was drunk. The tape mastered. We gave them each a cassette to take home and I arranged for the master tape to be delivered to Seven Records in Brookvale.

Glenn A. Baker, Australia's rock historian voted it the worst record of the decade, which I have to say raised my profile in a not such a good way.

However some years later the Milli Vanilli miming scandal came as no surprise to me, maybe I was a trendsetter.

Not to be deterred I twisted Seven Record's arm that in return they would release the album recorded live by John Currie during his performance at the Sydney Opera House. Much to everyone's surprise radio stations picked up on an old Scottish folk song on the album, Four Maries. A ballad about Mary Queen of Scots and her ladies in waiting. Reached number four in the charts. So I was now back as a successful producer.

My next claim to fame in record producing was the discovery of the song, 'And The Band Played Waltzing Matilda' a song written by a Scotsman, Eric Bogle, and recorded numerous times over by artists such as The Pogues, Joan Baez, Dubliners, Doug Ashdown, John Williamson, Liam Clancy and many others.

It was an Easter Monday and a few of us were having a beer in the Glasgow Arms in Pyrmont, an inner Sydney suburb, and a girl we knew, Maureen Cummeskey, said she had just returned from the National Folk Festival in Canberra and had heard this song. She sang it unaccompanied and the whole pub hushed, and as she finished the people in the pub couldn't even applaud as all of us were so emotional. I remembered I had a cassette recorder in the car, as most record producers would have, so I asked if she would come to my car and I'd buy her a few drinks if she would sing it for me. Deal done. Cassette made and on the Tuesday I was in the office of Ron Hurst, head of Seven Records, and we were in the studio the next weekend. Chris Neal a synthesiser guru at the time laid down all the tracks, John Currie agreed to sing it and we had the finished single ready on the Monday. How opportune as it was Anzac Day, which the song's lyrics were about, in two weeks time so the song hit all the airwaves and was highlighted in all television montages produced by the networks.

CHAPTER 24!

The Wizardry Of Oz!

So there we were in the rear seat of the limousine with the chauffeur and the lady from the Department of Education in the front seats and giving us what appeared to be a guided tour of Sydney but in fact we were driven to a suburb called Dulwich Hill. In those days it would have been counted as a western suburb of Sydney nowadays it's classified as inner-west and has gone through a gentrification process. The car pulled up in the large driveway of an old Victorian mansion which was now, as we were told, being utilised by the Department of Immigration as a staging point for immigrants with professional qualifications. The facilities were five star, with an apartment to ourselves which was free of charge to us till we found a place to rent. What a great start to immigrant life, but it got better. The lady then handed us a book of cash value coupons that we could use for meals in all of the restaurants in the district and let us know that we would be contacted by a bank manager to offer us overdraft facilities, a real estate agent who would arrange accommodation with a months free rent and a furniture retailer who held a six hundred dollar credit for us. Sometimes too good to be true actually is true and this was one of those rare occasions.

We were now on our own in this land of milk and honey so we unpacked and went for a walk around Dulwich Hill and found a Greek restaurant and had our first meal on Australian soil. We then took a bus into the city, got off at Central and walked to Circular Quay. Sydney is getting better by the minute and on our return to our lodgings in Dulwich Hill imagine our surprise to find a bunch of newspaper journalists camped outside the building waiting to meet up with us.

What's going on we thought.

What had appeared of little insignificance on the voyage over was the fact that there had been six couples on the ship who were on their honeymoon and it so happened that we were the only couple with a double cabin to ourselves. The other couples had been separated as immigrant ships at the time had mainly four berth cabins that took four females or four males. It hadn't taken long for the other couples to find out about our good fortune and we used to allow couples to utilise our cabin at certain times of the day for their conjugal pastimes. Knowing what I know now we could have probably charged by the hour, thus creating a fourth income for the time we spent on the high seas.

Apparently the press had got wind of this and through the Department of immigration had discovered where we were living. So on our second day in Australia we were interviewed as celebrities with photos taken in the local pub/hotel with my first schooner in my hand and on the second day we were plastered all over the afternoon papers in humorous articles with pictures naming us as the lucky honeymooning couple who have just arrived in the lucky country.

What a start but it hadn't finished. The day after we appeared in the papers there was a phone message from Russel Mcphedran of the Sun newspaper saying he was a staff photographer and would Patricia be available for a glamour shoot. I returned the call puzzled as to what 'glamour' meant and was reassured that it was all above board and for us to check out page three of the Sun where we found the page three girl which was quite tame, mini skirt or bikini shots were orders of the day. The model in the paper of that day I remember very well as it was some years later that we actually met her with her husband who I ended up doing a lot of business with and strangely enough he had been a schoolteacher like myself early on in his professional life. Her name was Cassandra Styles and her husband of over forty years was Bryan Nichols whose funeral I attended in August 2013.

The result of the conversation was that Patricia was the page three girl within a week of our arrival and as a legal secretary she was very flattered to be offered a modelling contract which she took up part-time and even appeared in the Young Doctors an Australian soap opera for a time.

Things were moving very quickly and all the assistance we received made life almost perfect. As new chums we were unaware of where we should look for a flat or a house to rent so with a small town mentality we had at the time, the real estate agent assigned to help us find an apartment in Belmore. Why Belmore? I had received my posting and it was at Birrong Boys High School and Belmore was close and on the railway line. Made sense. The furniture retailer filled up the place with everything we needed. We opened a bank account with ANZ with a two thousand dollar overdraft. That helped as we had arrived with a hundred and twenty pounds and were eagerly awaiting the three pay cheques due. A few weeks after our arrival we were settling in very comfortably, with our neighbours Norm and Sheila, No I'm not joking, making us very welcome and inviting us to dinner and barbeques and it was now time to work.

Patricia had found a job with a legal firm in Margaret St. in the city and I headed off to my first day at Birrong Boys High School..............................

CHAPTER 25

A Little Knight In
With No Armour!

Then there was the time in 1970 when I was considering leaving school teaching as the holidays were approaching, and looking for other employment I found an ad in the Saturday's Sydney Morning Herald for a television advertising sales executive. Not having a clue what it was about I sent my application letter off along with a number of other positions I thought looked interesting and the next week I received a return in the post inviting me for an interview in the city with a Mr. Bruce Forsyth of Channel Seven Melbourne. An interesting name as Bruce Forsyth was a very famous English comedian at the time. Also a letter inviting me to an interview as paymaster for Ludowici Engineering, conveyer belt manufacturers in Lane Cove. Needless to say my curiousity was piqued by the television station job as I had no idea what it entailed, never realising for a second that commercials were sold to advertisers by the stations. In hindsight it made sense but television was a medium that arrived fully packaged into one's home and the business part of it never occurred to me.

On meeting Bruce, who it turned out was the Sydney sales director for HSV7 a Melbourne television station and having the position explained it seemed like a glamorous change for a maths teacher and my knowledge of figures would stand me in good stead and I was very pleased to be put on a short list from forty applicants down to three. I didn't get the job as it went to Tony Flanagan who had arrived in Australia with the background of working for London Weekend television however I got a call from Bruce the next week explaining his decision and pointing out that this advertising business was just the job for me and he would keep an eye out for any opportunities in the business.

Within two weeks he called me up and said there was a research job going at one of Australia's largest advertising agencies, Jackson Wain, what's an advertising agency I asked myself, and the media director would like to meet up with me.

From the mathematics teacher's staff room at Birrong Boys High School I called the number from the coin operated telephone and asked to speak to Mr. Neville Rydge and when I was put through and I asked if it was Mr. Neville Rydge. A very gruff response came that it was not Mister it was Neville. Not a bad start to the conversation and could I get to North Sydney this afternoon for an interview. Of course as long as he appreciated I was not suited up and I was coming direct from school. Created no problem meeting at 5pm 40 Miller St. North Sydney. The interview was short and not too sweet and I was hired within five minutes of my arrival subject to me starting the next week, fortunately school holidays coincided, taking a $30 weekly pay cut from my teaching salary which he would help make up if I would do some maths coaching twice a week with his kids.

Not a problem, nothing ventured nothing gained.

I was now in the media advertising business with a lot to learn.

First day at work in the commercial world was an eye opener. Directed to my office I couldn't believe it when I walked into the corner office with glass walls and the most magnificent views of Sydney Harbour stretched before me. Had the Harbour Bridge and the Opera House, still under construction, breathtakingly filling the windows and an uninterrupted view through to Circular Quay with ferries coming and going all day.

At the time not realising that corner offices with views are a sign of prestige in the commercial world I put it down to the fact that it was the largest space available which was needed to have all the research material and books filling up the other two walls.

My office became a very busy viewing stage a couple of months later when Pope Paul VI visited Australia and stayed in the Apostolic Delegation in the next street as the motorcade passed by every day of the pilgrimage.

But it was time to work and as a novice it was hard to believe my first task was to write two major reports for the company to send to the United

States for the Peter Stuyvesant people who were on their way to Australia to appoint a new advertising agency for the region and for them to have a background picture of what Australia was about as a country and also to give them a clear understanding of the media scene as it existed.

First report 'Australia'. Mainly statistical, economical and geographical all facts gleaned from the massive library of reports from the Commonwealth Bureau of Statistics office. All written reports, no Google or Wikipedia in those days. In one week had one hundred page report ticked off and now it was time to write Australian Media Scene.

This proved to be fascinating as I opened up this new world that I never knew existed. Newspapers, Radio, Magazines, Television, Outdoor Posters, Yellow pages etc. etc. and all intertwined within and without each other. Cross ownership, regulatory bodies and names such as Packer, Fairfax, ACP, Yaffa, Sungravure, Southdown and a small Adelaide company called News Limited led by a young Rupert Murdoch. To me it was like reading Harold Robbins novels with intrigue, back stabbing, takeover bids, political power struggles that recent television series have not done justice. My job was to paint a picture of ownership, readership, viewing and listening audience figures and make it an interesting read for the fifteen hour flight from the US west coast.

When it was finished after only three weeks on the job I took pride in that I probably had a better pragmatic view of the media industry that I never knew had existed three weeks earlier than any of the other twenty media staff in our office.

Given slight praise for what I thought was a very good effort in producing the reports I could now pull my head out of the reports and have a look around me and work out what the advertising industry was about and also take in a bit of the view of Sydney harbour.

For the first few weeks I acquainted myself with television ratings, print readership and radio listening figures and costs of advertising spots and spaces. People would come in and out of my office with predominantly statistical queries and I set up systems for people to make a written request and I'd have their reports ready in twenty four hours. This being my first venture into the commercial world from academia I had to learn about pecking orders and office politics and trying to discover what the people in the four floors above did which I learnt included account service, creative, they were the ones who wore jeans and t-shirts and were worshipped by the ordinary clerical staff.

Having never been above the first floor and never met any of senior management I had only heard names like Leo Schofield, Frank Grace, John McCormack, Dick Ash as the bosses of the Jackson Wain empire with Frank Grace's name only used in hushed whispers as the managing director.

So imagine my surprise when my internal phone rang and a female voice said that Frank Grace wanted to speak with me. My legs turned to jelly so I sat down and waited for God to speak. First questions were if there was any sign of Neville Rydge, media director and if not John Conway, the media manager. Couldn't see them about so the next barking question was if I was wearing a suit and tie, positive response, then ordered to get to the front door and greet Sir Frank Packer who was arriving in a few minutes and bring him up to the boardroom. Sir Frank Packer, a knight of the realm and someone I had spent a number of days analysing his media empire. No time to get nervous, first of all had to ask someone where's the board room? On the fourth floor in the same position as my office on the floor plan. So bravely I went to the front door and waited, wondering how do I address a knight, Sir? Mister? Your honour? Holiness etc. etc. As a young Englishman I was very worried about protocol. No need to worry.

Very soon a large American saloon car turned up at the front door out jumped the driver and held open the front passenger door and out stepped Sir Frank Packer. First impressions were of an ill-fitting suit and not highly polished shoes. Out went my hand to greet him. Ignored. Barked at me about fucking Grace not being there to meet him.

'Who the fuck are you?' To me.

I'm dying. Can't make any conversation. Push button for lifts.

'Should have been fucking fixed years ago' I'm told. Is this really a knight of the realm, an ugly, ill-mannered, foul mouthed pig of a man.

For the short ride to the fourth floor there was nothing but a tirade of abuse and four letter words about how Grace dragged him over the bridge every year so he could see Sir Frank Packer asking for the lion's share of the Jackson Wain advertising budget for his newspapers, Australian Women's Weekly and channels nine in Sydney and Melbourne.

Coming out of the lift on the fourth floor I thought I'll soon be out of this and hopefully have no more brushes with the gentry if this is how they behave. Didn't have to lead him to the boardroom he led me and there to meet him were four men who I soon found out were Frank Grace, Leo Schofield a gentleman who's name escapes me but he was advertising director of White Wings one of our larger clients and John McCormack. Thinking I was now off the hook I turned to leave but was told to stay grab a drink and 'get one for this bastard,' quoting Frank Grace, 'Packer'. I was addressed as Cliff by all that were there as if I had been friends for years and was part of senior management. It dawned on me that of course, this being a meeting about media expenditure someone from the media department should be present. Please remember I had only been in the company a few weeks and this was my first trip above the ground floor. I busied myself by serving drinks and speaking as little as possible but listening keenly to what was going on.

Next surprise, folding doors open and there's a dining table set for six, silver service and two waitresses seating us and then lunch being served from what I just found out was the White Wings kitchen which was on our fourth floor.

This was the world of big business. Two bulls in a paddock head butting each other, but not about cows, rather its allocation of millions of dollars of advertising revenue. As the wine flowed it became obvious that Grace and Packer enjoyed each other's company and this annual lunch was a highlight of the year for both of them. The lunch dragged on through the afternoon till about four o' clock and now we were all best friends. Apparently Sir Frank Packer had been told I was some mathematical genius that was going to ensure all the research figures were correct and I should be nurtured. What a load of bullshit I thought but went along with it.

I then escorted Sir Frank, or Frank my new best mate, as he was to me by now, to the lift and wobbly booting it to the ground floor and out to his waiting car he shook hands with me and said he hoped to meet up with me soon.

Never did but there's always Kerry, Clyde and James.

CHAPTER 26!

Settling in!

Here we are in Australia ready to begin our new life. Having rented an apartment in Belmore, a suburb chosen because it was close to a railway station and near Birrong where I was to begin teaching mathematics at the Birrong Boys High School. Patricia had found a job with an accounting firm in Margaret Street in the city and we first made friends with our neighbours Norm and Sheila who invited us to our first Australian barbecue. We then went looking for second jobs as we were determined to earn as much as possible in the shortest time. I took a job as an office cleaner at the ANZ bank in the city and Patricia took a job as a waitress in the newly opened Outrigger bistro in the Travelodge in York Street. I also approached the YWCA looking for youth work. I had already worked for them back in Newcastle so I was carrying a good reference and I now had a third job as a youth worker running their drop - in centre. I was teaching till three o clock in the afternoon then catching a train into the city to clean the toilets at the ANZ bank then off to the YWCA where I would work till around ten o clock. Never realised there was a hierarchal system in the office cleaning business where the lowest employee cleaned the toilets and the most senior drove the electric floor polishers. When I realised I was not going to be a polisher for a few years I gave up on the toilets and took up selling encyclopedia in the early evenings. It was some years later when I was in the boardroom at ANZ discussing some major financing project I let everyone in the room know that I had cleaned their toilets some years ago. To my surprise this admission resulted in everyone around the boardroom table telling stories of the worst jobs they had ever had. Could be another book in this.

Within a few weeks at the YWCA I was invited to a function at Admiralty House as Lady Cutler was their patron and the black tie event was a fund raiser for the organisation. Patricia was invited with me but she declined saying she couldn't get a night off from the restaurant as a friend of hers named Oscar was off sick, feeling stiff all over, and needed her attention so she invited one of her friends Pauline to accompany me. Very strange I thought as most women would jump at the chance of dressing up to dine at the best house in Australia. At the function there were not too many men as most of the YWCA ladies had come on their own and I was surprised to find myself chatting with the State Governor, Sir Roden Cutler. At the time I wasn't aware of his background apart from the fact he was the Governor but we got on so well he filled me in on his war years when he had been awarded the Victoria Cross and also had had a leg amputated. I could not empathise with him but having a father who had lost a limb we were able to make conversation about prosthetic legs. Pauline enjoyed herself immensely and couldn't get over the fact that here we were after me being in Australia only a few weeks and receiving such invitations.

The first few months in Australia can only be described as fast and furious having made friends with some people from Patricia's workplace inviting us into their social circle which involved sailing on Sydney Harbour, water skiing on the Hawkesbury river and something different every weekend.

CHAPTER 27!

Poker Face!

So having had my dealings with Sir Frank Packer I never thought or hoped our paths would cross again and history has shown we never did. However within a few months my research work in the media department led to me being promoted and installed as the first television buyer in Australian advertising. This put a few noses out of joint as television was considered the glamorous media taking up the majority of expenditure and media planners who had done the buying for their clients. It was also a well-known fact that the television sales people had more generous expense accounts for entertaining the media planners so it was understandable that a few of these old timers got to resent this young Pommy upstart whose experience was only as a schoolteacher.

It turned out that at the time I held the purse strings for more money than anyone else in the Australian advertising industry. Of course this led to some long lunches, best seats at the theatres, restaurants and nightclubs which incidentally led to a night out with Sammy Davis Junior whose Australian television special we sponsored for one of our clients British Paints. This was after we had convinced British Paints that if they spent the money for Rolf Harris to front the campaign 'Sure Can' which worked for decades but got lost somewhere in 2013 due to some small legal problems Rolf Harris failed to cope with. The Nine Network were market leaders and for years had taken the majority of the advertising dollars allocated to television so it was no surprise when the sales director of the network, Wilf Barker, called me and invited me to lunch in the city one Friday. I took up the offer and was surprised at the lunch at the Argyle Cellars, a restaurant in a very small tight lane, off Sydney's main thoroughfare

George street, next door to George Patersons, the biggest advertising agency in Australia at the time, now converted to one of Sydney's top night spots, The Establishment. The surprise waiting me there was to be introduced to my second Packer, Clyde, the son of Sir Frank who had been named as the boss of the Nine network. He was not a chip of the old block. In fact there could not have been any two people so far apart in their manners and outlook on life. Clyde was very affable and a man's man. He spent most of the lunch telling dirty jokes and never referred to business once. Over the lunch he invited me to a poker school in Artarmon that same night. Apparently this was a regular Friday night get together although still illegal by the New South Wales statutes, even though Sydney had a dozen or so illegal casinos operating at the time.

The game was held in the Artarmon Motor Inn on the Pacific Highway and in the room furthest away from the front desk and the main road. To my surprise the players included sales directors from both Seven and Ten networks and Clyde's younger brother Kerry, head of the Packer magazine empire. I am not and never have been a gambler or a poker player but everyone was insistent that I take a seat and play. Only having the basic knowledge of the rules of poker I was reluctant and as the stakes seemed not too high with two dollar ante and bets only up to five dollars I joined in. Call it beginner's luck but I soon found myself around a hundred dollars up which was close to a weeks wages at the time. As the bets started to get bigger it became obvious to everyone I wasn't comfortable and when Kerry suggested it was time for me to leave and take my pretty wife out to dinner I needed no more encouragement.

The game became a weekly ritual and so did Kerry's dismissal of me always when I was about a hundred dollars up. Talk about innocence and naivete. I really believed at the time I was getting the hang of poker. Could I have been given winnings as a soft bribe?

CHAPTER 28!

Moove Baby Moove!

So here I am making a name for myself in one of Australia's largest advertising agencies, Jackson Wain, mainly because of my knowledge of statistics and sampling methods for surveys of readership and time spent listening to radio or watching television. My recent short excursion into the inner circles had whetted my appetite for the 'glamorous creative' side of the business and after bringing the RCA Records account into the agency I had a few more people buying me beers in the Station Hotel, our after work meeting place. Just when I thought I was to be subject to the tyranny of statistics the internal office phone rang again. It was a feeling of Deja vu as once again I was asked where my boss Neville Rydge was and I didn't know so I was called into battle again. Upstairs to the fourth floor I was called, Frank Grace's secretary furnished me with a cab charge docket and instructions to catch a taxi to an address in Chippendale, near Central Station where Mr.Grace was waiting to meet me. Without any discussion, which would have been worthless anyway, I ran across the road to the taxi rank and was on my way. Not knowing what I was to do when I got there I just let it wash over me thinking the bosses would know what was required and I put all my faith into them.

On arrival I found we were at the offices of the Milk Marketing Board and we were pitching for their business. Please remember I had only walked into the commercial world a few weeks ago so the idea of presenting to a boardroom of executives was a totally alien concept to me. I had only just learnt that companies paid agencies to spend their advertising dollars so new business presentations was an unknown procedure for me. Whatever the senior executives of my company knew of my lack of business experience makes me shudder. In hindsight I believe no-one had told them that until a few weeks ago the only people I had presented to were boys at Birrong Boys High School and algebra had no place in advertising for milk all over Australia.

However the confidence they had in me fed into my psyche and I was ready to stand up to the challenge.

First up the big players from our agency did a selling job on how efficient our office procedures were, how talented were all our staff and then Frank Grace filled them in on the fact we were Australia's largest Australian owned agency and while that was not the only reason to hire us it should count for something. The next presenter was Leo Schofield our Creative Director who was so camp in dress, speech and presentation and this was before camp was a word that meant anything else but sleeping in tents but he charmed everyone with his history of Jackson Wain's successful campaigns for other clients with emphasis on our work in the food and beverage industry. Notice I'm now using first person plural. He then outlined, what I thought was a brilliant campaign, for flavoured milk. This was the days before power point and domestic videos so presentations were drawn in marker pen on flip charts

Fortunately advertising agencies had departments full of people who could illustrate quite effectively. The theory was that milk needed new markets and a new customer base to create new markets for the product. Hence the birth of one of Australia's most successful advertising campaigns for MOOVE FLAVOURED MILK.The presentation was summarised, a few questions asked and then given the good news we had been given the multi-million dollar contract and everyone was looking forward to working together for the next three years.

How easy was that I thought?

Next on the agenda was lunch. Again this was not finger buns and a pie from the school canteen but we jumped into taxis and transported to the Tai Yuen Chinese restaurant in Chinatown.

Another mind opening experience. I had never sat with eight others at one table and when the boss told the waiter to just feed us the food kept coming with beer, red and white wine for the next three hours I discovered the lazy Susan on the table and decided this was the life for me. I was now one of the team. How did I know that? The boss then started to discuss the next week's presentation in Melbourne for the Qantas account and I was invited to meetings over the next few days to discuss strategy. I had never flown in an aeroplane at this point in my life so could there be Something In The Way They Mooved Me?

CHAPTER 29!

The Original and the Best!

Then there was the time around nineteen eighty five when K-Tel our biggest client of the time went bust.

K-Tel were the TV gadget and record kings. We made hundreds of cheap and not so nasty commercials for them over a period of five years. One of the most lucrative production accounts in Australia how we got the account is amazing. At the time there was a pub in Cammeray a suburb on the lower North Shore of Sydney called the San Miguel and it featured live bands on Saturday afternoons which included names like Cold Chisel, Rose Tattoo, Angels and many others that went on to greater things. One Saturday I was enjoying the band and a few beers and needing to go to the toilet for a pee during an interval and it surprised me when the guy at the next trough started to talk to me. Trust me it's not good pub toilet etiquette to open conversation at such a delicate time so the surprise became pleasant when I realised I was not being propositioned for anything indecent, more so he introduced himself as Bob James A & R Director for K-Tel records. We didn't shake hands immediately for obvious reasons but he said he knew of me in that I knew something about television production and would I be interested in producing commercials for K-Tel.

Would I? This was the break every production company was looking for and here it was falling into my lap. The deal was finalised over a lot more beers before the evening finished and so began a long friendship and business relationship which I will come back to later.

Through the years of working with K-Tel I got to meet a lot of famous performers in my capacity as director. Most of them had re-packaged their hit songs into Twenty Greatest Hits and K-Tel agreed to promote them nationally and internationally on television. We produced the commercials in Australia for the rest of the world mainly because we were inexpensive, no let's be honest, we were dirt cheap and they had a promotional and tax scheme where each country where the product was to be marketed had to buy the use of the commercial for their market from the Australian arm of the company. This could result in Australia receiving around forty thousand dollars for use of a commercial they paid me four thousand. No complaints as we were producing so many we called ourselves The Production Factory.

Early on in the relationship we were assigned to make the ad for Burl Ives Greatest Hits. He was performing in a club in Tweed Heads near the Queensland border so Bob, the client arranged the air fares and hotels for my crew and I to have a couple of days in Surfers Paradise, the tourist centre a few kilometres north. On arrival we thought we'd pay Burl the courtesy of seeing his show and meet afterwards to plan the shoot for the next day. After working some years earlier with Chuck Berry I was aware of nuances associated with artists but was unprepared for Mr. Burl Ives who on being introduced to us sat us down in his dressing room, gave us a beer then told us politely that he wasn't going to do the commercial, he was too tired and he didn't need the money anyway. No room for discussion just finish the beer and thanks very much. Maybe not a little bitty tear but something let us down. Back in Sydney we solved the problem by using a friend of ours, the impresario, Frank Baden Powell, who had a very slight resemblance to Burl, and by shooting his back with a very strong spotlight on him we were able to convince the powers that be we had succeeded in getting Burl Ives to co-operate.

Following soon was K.C. without the Sunshine Band. We took him into a very small video studio in Crows Nest and arranged for him to mime to playback of his hits. He wasn't used to low budget productions and did nothing but complain because he had no stylist or wardrobe personnel and he had to make his own costume changes. After around four hours of moaning and groaning Bob from K-Tel took him aside, and in a voice just loud enough for all to hear, told him to stop acting like the queen he was and get on with it as he would cancel the deal and in his financial state that would have been catastrophic for him. He was well behaved after that and we finished in an hour.

Over time through working with K-Tel I met a number of stars, usually on their way down as obviously they were re-packaging their hits. I remember in particular being asked to arrange a barbecue at my home for an American visitor, Alan Carr, who was to deliver a large catalogue of music to K-Tel and as I was the only one living in a house with a garden, I agreed and to everyone's surprise when he arrived he had Davy Jones of the Monkees with him. I got a laugh out of him when I asked him if he was the kid from Coronation Street wasn't he?

The next one I cherish as it was with one of my own personal favourites, Dusty Springfield.

I had booked a studio in Crows Nest for a whole day and was like a nervous schoolboy waiting for her to arrive. I wasn't disappointed as she made the grand entrance one expects of a Diva, followed by the tiny Judy Stone, a famous Australian singer at the time, chasing after her carrying a mountain of costumes for the shoot. On being introduced as her director she easily picked up on my nervousness and she put her arm around me telling me not to be scared she only ate girls. At the time I didn't get the double entendre and I can't remember if that settled me or excited me more. She was a dream to work with. Totally professional and we were able to finish in half a day saving me studio fees that I used to take Dusty and others to lunch at La Grillade the restaurant across the street. This certainly helped our business reputation as all the television executives were regulars at La Grillade and all of them were looking for introductions and autographs, for their kids of course.

K-Tel at one point had an internal investigation after it was discovered that the warehouse manager had given courier business to his brother in law which it turned out to be found later at a much better price than they had been charged by the previous account holders and this had caused the managing director to initiate a police investigation into all the service providers to the company, including ourselves. This included early morning raids on offices and homes which resulted in finding absolutely nothing untoward at all. Caused me some consternation as they had arrived at my house early in the morning on the day I was directing the video clip for Cassandra Delaney soon to become Mrs. John Denver. Took them hours to find nothing which didn't surprise me as there was nothing to be found. However it did lead to one interesting incident some weeks later when Bob and myself were lunching at a restaurant, Buona Gusto in Chippendale, another inner city suburb of Sydney, and as the diners were thinning out we were invited to join a table of eight or nine guys who turned out to be detectives from the central police station a few blocks away. One of them turned out to be the infamous Roger Rogerson, the rogue detective notorious for shooting dead Warren Lanfranchi in a lane not a couple of blocks from this restaurant. The doors opened and in walked in the two detectives who had been assigned to investigate K-Tel and on seeing us with this motley crew of crime fighters they couldn't stop laughing and telling everyone they had known all along we were crooked but couldn't find anything on us. They actually believed we were friends with these soon to be disgraced group of detectives and our 'friendship' with them proved it. There's more to be told later.

After a long relationship with K-Tel and a turnover of approximately forty thousand dollars a month it came as shock when Bob came to our studio in Balmain to let me know early that K-Tel was heading for liquidation so not to let them get too much in debt for when the hammer would fall. Too late with the warning they went down owing us around thirty five thousand dollars which was a princely sum back then and created a lot of financial woe.

However in the dying days of K-Tel Bob repeatedly turned up at our place with boxes of master tapes of records they had issued and in particular a catalogue of classical music supposedly recorded by one of the world's top orchestras, the Berlin Philharmonic.

I was told to hoard them till a later date and maybe we could do something with them in the future. Up in the attic they went, safe but forgotten after a few months. Bob went to work for K-Tel's old rivals J & B records and we continued to make commercials for his new label but not to the same extent.

Next to go was J & B who on the Friday before their ASX IPO prospectus was issued on the coming Monday, which was to make everyone involved a lot of money, discrepancies were found in the audited accounts relating to royalties not being paid so everyone wiped their face and started to look for work.

Over a closing down drink Bob asked if I still had the K-Tel master tapes, which I did and so we retrieved them from the attic and went about cataloguing the titles and decided we had enough product to start our own record label and so began the gestation period for Mainline Music soon to become the bete-noir of the Australian music industry.

This was around the time CD's were being introduced and records and cassettes were on the wane. We realised that people were going to want to replace their records and cassettes with this new technology.

Bob pulled in a couple of favours to help us get CDs manufactured, with label printing and packaging with a line of credit for our first release package of ten titles of various classical composer's 'Greatest Hits'. We used classic paintings from all major art galleries of the world for cover design and here we were with five hundred Cd's of each title ready to go but not a customer to send them to.

As they said at the time ' let your fingers do the walking'. First stop O'Briens, the publishers of the Australian Yellow Pages in Milsons Point just over the harbour bridge, filled the car boot full of Yellow Pages covering all of Australia and back over the Sydney Harbour Bridge to the Glebe warehouse. So out with the yellow pages, open the book to record stores and let's go. We packaged small boxes of forty Cd's, four of each title, and then made out invoices to each of the stores advising that the product was sale or return in thirty days. That means if they don't sell them they don't owe us anything and all they have to do is return them. To this day it still surprises me that we got only one phone call from a store in Wagga Wagga telling us how cheeky we were to send out unsolicited goods but he admired our nerve and could we send another box. From over one hundred boxes we had two returned and all others were paid for within the thirty days. We now had a customer base and all we needed now was to get into the major chains and department stores.

Not a problem. We were on a roll. A telephone call from a Ross Farquhar of Grace Brothers, now known as Myers introducing himself as the buyer for the home entertainment department and he'd seen our classical series and he wanted them for his stores. Up to his office we went in the Broadway store and he handed us a purchase order for forty thousand Cd's and twenty thousand cassettes with packaging and delivery instructions and also claiming a discount of five per cent for payment within seven days from delivery. Wonderful one would think. Only sixty thousand problems and every one of them a dollar. How could we finance this?

We had a fairy godfather in Ross, as gay was not in the language as yet, if you understand, but now we needed another godfather and he turned up in the guise of the printer from Combined Creative Services, Kevin Wilson who backed us with the manufacturers and trucking companies. I was able to forgive him even for being a Chelsea supporter for this favour he was giving us free of charge, with one proviso that he would get all our printing and packaging work in the future.

Here we were a company not two months old and we had hit the big time but there was still more to come, and did we upset the status quo of the industry.

The next step.............................

CHAPTER 30

Shaking the Hand of God!

Then there was the time I got involved with World Cup football, not as a player I'm sad to say, and how I got to spend quality time with Diego Maradona. For those not familiar with the name, at the time he was rated the world's number one footballer akin to what Michael Jordan was to basketball or Don Bradman to cricket.

At the time with a friend Bob James, a South African frustrated rock star, we had formed a partnership to distribute re-cycled music tracks on CD and cassette. We had a warehouse and office in Lyndhurst Street Glebe, an inner suburb of Sydney. The business was ticking over very well, making good money, and we kept ourselves amused and having an interesting time fighting legal battles with the major record companies, and believe me there will be some very interesting stories to tell on the history of Mainline Records later in this tome.

It was late October in 1993 when the phone rang on this Wednesday morning and it was another friend of mine from my football playing days, I should explain I still play football at seventy three years old, my team mates in North Sydney over forty fives may disagree with the terminology 'play football' but Hector Martinez goes back to my better footballing days. He's an Australian citizen now and who came to Australia as a professional footballer from Argentina some years earlier, broke his leg and was now repairing shoes and coaching kids on Bondi Beach, very successfully I should say, including Tom Cruise and Nicole Kidman's son, Connor. He also taught our son Durham so we did have a brush with fame many Saturday mornings at Bondi Beach.

He had now been appointed as liaison officer for the Argentinian national football team in their World Cup qualifier to be played in Sydney on the coming Sunday evening.

The gist of the telephone call was that the Argentinian squad were on the team coach prepared to go to a training facility outside their hotel in Coogee and when they found out it was an hour drive to the outer western suburbs to Marconi Oval in Fairfield they were refusing to budge claiming two hours a day driving was a plot by Soccer Australia to create stiffness in the muscles and apparently there was a major slanging match going on in a number of colourful languages.

Hector was describing all the action from the public phone in the hotel foyer and there was a media scrum as people were trying to placate everyone and make arrangements to suit the Argentinians but Soccer Australia were refusing to change the venue. I learnt later, when in an executive capacity managing Australian Soccer through the company International Entertainment Corporation, this was typical of the intransigence of the people who ran Soccer Australia at the time. To this day I have tried to avoid doing business with people whose names end in a vowel.

Stalemate!

Can I help, was what Hector was asking. I asked if he could give me ten minutes and I'd get back to him. Told him to stay close to the reception desk, not too many mobile phones in those days, and I'll find somewhere. Why was he asking me? Don't know. The only sports administration I'd done at the time was as treasurer for the local North Sydney Soccer Club. These things just tend to fall into my lap. Looking up sports grounds in the yellow pages telephone directory, no internet as yet, intending to get the Marks Field, a good facility only 15 minutes from the hotel at Coogee Beach, and I made the call, booked the grounds for three days, charged it to Soccer Australia, with whom I had no status or business dealings, and they agreed to put up posts, mow the grass, mark the lines etc. within the hour. In fact they sounded overjoyed that their facility was to be used by the famous Argentinian squad.

Getting a little excited I rang the Coogee Hotel and told Hector I'd booked Wentworth Park. You've got it. Wentworth Park, the greyhound stadium in Glebe? What had happened to Marks Field? Yes in my excitement at being involved with something as important as the moon landing to me, I'd looked up the wrong stadium and booked the wrong facility not 100 metres from our warehouse by mistake. Had I stuffed up one of the world's leading football teams and could I face sanctions from FIFA? Fortunately for me I remembered they did have a football pitch in the centre of the park. However as far as football people knew they would have thought I was referring to the number of pitches surrounding the greyhound stadium which were used by the local footballers.

Too late to change things now. I convinced Hector things would be okay then tried to convince myself of the same so I walked down the hill, introduced myself to the head of the ground staff, and entered a hive of activity as all hands were at the pump. The Wentworth Park people were as excited as I was at the thought of entertaining Maradona, Batistuta and the like. Not twenty minutes later the media turned up in all their glory, TV, newspapers, radio, football groupies, this was shaping up as one of Australia's most memorable sporting occasions. I include myself in the last group.

The Argentinian coach, the bus that is, arrived, all the players and support staff aboard piled off the coach and into the ground then a full on training session started.

Posts were up, lines marked, training bibs issued, media placated with a few interviews and then all unnecessary people ejected. How good it felt to be one of the necessary who were invited to stay.

Later on in the day I was asked if I knew any people who could help with the training the next day.

Is the Pope a Catholic? What does a bear do in the woods?

Of course. So the next day I turned up with football kit and half a dozen players from my club North Sydney promising them a training run with Maradona and others. Not quite. All they required us for was to form walls to help them practise their free kicks. A dangerous position even at our own level never mind defending against the world's best. The equivalent is following the circus elephant with a shovel and bucket in the parade but loving being in show business. This went on for three days.

I was now part of the Argentinian entourage. Must point out here I am and was a total supporter of Australia but didn't feel like a traitor as I was now hob-nobbing with Maradona. Not a very sociable relationship as his knowledge of the English language matched my Spanish so our grunts had to cover as conversation.

It was also galling to an Englishman like myself to be making friends with the man that had 'The Hand Of God' that had destroyed a previous England's World Cup efforts, but I got over it. The Hand of God refers to Argentina v England, played on 22 June 1986, in the quarter-finals of the World Cup in the Aztec Stadium in Mexico. The game was held four years after the Falklands War and was a key part in the already intense football rivalry between Argentina and England. It was also a match which included two of the most famous goals in football history, both scored by Diego Maradona.

The first goal, after 51 minutes, was to become known as the "Hand of God", which Maradona scored by using his hand. Seen by everyone in the stadium and those watching television all over the world apart from the referee and linesmen on the day. When questioned after the game he never admitted it but said afterwards, it was perhaps the Hand of God. The second goal he scored was brilliant. No arguments there.

From there Argentina went on to win the World Cup. What was strange about Maradona was his total detachment from the rest of the players and team management. Maybe he actually believed he carried the hand of God. He would sit in a corner of the lobby with a glass of juice where we would meet regularly. Success was getting a photograph of our seven year old son Durham with the man himself. I also got him to speak to Bob, my business partner on the phone to convince him I wasn't bull shitting him as to why I was away from the office and warehouse. Bob wouldn't have known anyway who it was as Maradona spoke in Spanish, not one of Bob's most fluent languages.

Wentworth Park had worked out very well for the Argentinians, however Soccer Australia were not too happy and advised the Wentworth Park Trust to invoice me for the four days bookings.

Seriously guys, can you imagine this is the FIFA World Cup we are talking about. Suffice to say I didn't pay it and to this day have wondered just who did.

It was then the Thursday before the game and I was invited to the hotel for dinner with the squad and over the red wine came the surprise request.........................

CHAPTER 31!

Rocky Mountain High!

Then there was the time in 1994 when Bob, my business partner at the time talked me into playing golf. I had a short history with golf in that during my college days my flatmate was Harry Ashby a top amateur golfer and in 1968 I caddied for him to win the Durham County Amateur Championship and a few years later he won the English amateur title twice. Unfortunately for me I was already living in Australia at the time. Deciding to do things properly I booked myself in at Woollahra golf club in Sydney's eastern suburbs for six lessons with the club professional and he taught me how to hit a ball without standing like a giraffe drinking water from the river with legs spread so wide my forehead could almost touch the ball.

Bob and some golfing friends had a permanent booking at Castle Hill Country Club, one of the better courses in the Sydney basin, following the ladies who had the course to themselves every Thursday morning and we were allowed to tee off when they were at least four holes ahead or suffer the wrath of the lady members.

It was an eclectic bunch of guys with handicaps ranging from scratch to the thirty six they allowed me as a beginner bending the rules to fit me in.

In 1982 I had produced and directed a pop video clip for Cassandra Delaney using a lot of friends and favours to get in on budget and I stayed in contact with her for some time as she struggled with a country music career with her mother as the Delaney Sisters and it came as a surprise that in 1986 she had left her long suffering boyfriend, Andrew, and had run away with a real country singer, John Denver, who she married in 1988.

Andrew tells the story involved in the genesis of the romance with a great sense of self-deprecation. The Sebel Town House in Kings Cross was the favoured hotel for visiting pop musicians and the cocktail bar at the front of the hotel always had the girls hanging round in the bar hoping to meet up with someone famous. On the Wednesday night I had been having a drink with Cassandra and she was moaning about how tough her life was and she felt like she was getting nowhere with her career and also asking if I had any commercials work for her. As the story goes when I had left for home John Denver and his party had come into the bar for a night cap and the inevitable happened. As Andrew the ditched boyfriend told us later he was out of town at the time and he had had a phone call from Cassandra saying her and her mother, The Delaney Sisters, had landed a week's work touring New South Wales clubs and she would be back in Sydney in a week's time.

The Denver Delaney romance blossomed in that week and John had proposed. Talk about whirlwind romances! Andrew and Cassandra lived in one of the apartments at the south end of Bondi Beach overlooking the beach recognisable by the red and white exterior décor. They lived on the top level. As Andrew told the story he said that on her return Cassandra had owned up to what was happening and she was leaving. Andrew wanted her to stay and as he had an important meeting in the city that morning he wanted her to stay at home till he returned and they would discuss what to do. Cassandra's mind was made up so Andrew thought the best thing to do was to lock her in the apartment. Off he went to work and when he got back she had gone. Turned out she had climbed over the balconies, throwing her suitcase ahead of her, until she had reached the ground and off in a taxi to the airport. Andrew headed off to the airport and on arrival talked his way into the airport lounge where he confronted John and Cassandra. John took him aside and explained how this was not just a fling but it really was love and he would look after her and sorry that someone had been hurt. Andrew then said they remained civilised had a couple of drinks and as he was leaving the lounge he used John Denver's own lyrics to say goodbye. Well I guess 'You're Leaving on A Jet Plane' He often told the story over the years laughing at his own joke.

About a year later Cassandra was back in Sydney and she wanted me to compile a show reel for her and on asking how life was going for her she said the best thing was that she knew she would never have to clean a toilet ever again.

However it turned out that John was a keen golfer and had played a few times with our Thursday group when he was in Australia and when he did his 1994 Australian tour he took up residence in the Quay West apartments in Sydney's Rocks district where he would travel everywhere on his high powered motor bike. It came as a surprise to me but apparently not to everyone else when he showed up on the Thursdays at the country club and joined the group for a few weeks as he was taking an extended break after the tour finished.

I have to say he was an all-round gentleman with no pretensions and always stayed for a beer or two after the golf had finished then he would sling his golf bag onto his back and climb onto his motorbike and head back into the city. Now this motorbike was something special a Suzuki GSX1100, a real monster. I couldn't even hold it up it was so big. He then asked if I could take care of the motor bike while he was away. Keep it in the garage and turn the engine over every couple of weeks till he made his next trip to Australia. Sounded OK to me and he arranged for me to pick up the keys from the concierge at Quay West with his helmet and gloves. I had forgotten to mention that I didn't have a motor bike licence so when the time came to pick it up I had to get a friend of mine to do the honours. The irony in this is that the friend was Brendon Redmond a footballing friend who was a motor bike aficionado and also was the actor I used as the antagonist in Cassandra Delaney's video clip some years earlier. This was all happening long after the marriage had broken up with a lot of bitter recriminations which John had talked about easily as he was aware of our connections with Cassandra, and as by now a long time had passed he could talk about it with humour which hadn't happened while the divorce was happening. One of his thoughts was that in future when he slept with a lady he'd just give her a million dollars and a house. It would save a lot of time and legal fees.

The bike was garaged, gloves in the helmet and having a talking point for dinner parties that John Denver's motor bike and accessories were in my garage nothing to worry about. Brendon kindly offered to take the bike for a spin every few weeks to keep it in trim. Every few weeks soon became every Saturday and Evil, as Brendon was now known, enjoyed taking it around the Northern beaches where he lived.

Things were going too smoothly until Bob's son mentioned to one of his friends, Nick, who rode motor bikes, that this powerful beast laid idle ninety per cent of the time and he volunteered himself to take it for a run up and down to the Blue Mountains, a round trip of a hundred kilometres.

Not a problem! But yes the inevitable happened, he came off. Not too much damage to stop him riding it back to our garage with bent front forks. He offered to pay for repairs and got quotes to fix it up. As this was a special bike, only a few that size in Australia, the quotes were all around the three thousand dollar mark which was a lot of money to a young guy getting married in a few weeks. It was agreed that as we had heard no word from John on any dates for a return trip we would leave the bike as is till he could get the cash together or when John announced another tour, which we thought wouldn't happen for at least two years.

Guess what! Four weeks later the phone rings, yes it was John who had just arrived in Sydney for a promotional tour and could he pick up the bike tomorrow. I explained what had happened and the phone went dead. Early the next morning there was a knock on the door and there was a motor bike repair van with trailer outside sent by Kevin Jacobson, John's Australian promoter, to pick up the bike. Off it went.

Later that morning I'm listening to the radio when John Laws, Australia's number one radio personality at the time, announces he's got John Denver coming on the show in a few minutes.

I had to listen and after the usual platitudes and stories, a few tracks from the new album and in conversation John Laws asked him about his motor bike and was he looking forward to getting out on the open road. I quote John Denver's response, "I would love to John but a _former_ friend of mine had an accident and didn't get it fixed for me."

Another irony in the story was that the helmet and gloves are still in my possession all these years later and led to a few jokes in bad taste inferring that if he'd been wearing the helmet in the micro plane crash it may have made a difference.

CHAPTER 32!

A Party With The Lot!

So here I am living the dream, maybe only one of my dreams, and assisting the Argentinian football team including one of the greats, Diego Maradona. I'm considering myself a bit of a traitor as the memories of the Hand Of God in Mexico 1986 World Cup still felt sore but never mind I was having my brush with fame and learning a little Spanish at the same time. What I do remember is that he was a lone wolf and could be seen in the foyer of the hotel sitting by himself with a brooding look on his face. Training was going OK, facilities were up to scratch and things were going very smoothly. I was then asked to meet up with one of the management team in the bar at the hotel which I dutifully did so hoping to be told I was on the payroll for all the work I'd done. No such luck. But what I was asked to do shocked me, maybe not to the core, but certainly a big surprise. The game was to be played on the coming Sunday and the Argentinian squad were due to fly out on the Monday afternoon so I was informed the whole squad were looking forward to a night out in Sydney after the match. I took this to mean a meal in a decent restaurant and admission to one of Sydney's better nightclubs. Shouldn't pose any problems I was a bit of a man about the town at the time and knew all the nightclub people and taking a crew of forty or fifty very rich footballers to their venues would stand me in good stead for the future. Plenty of time for the club owners to let the girls of Sydney know that these guys would be there from about ten o' clock on Sunday.

Not so fast I was told. What they were looking for was 'a party'. 'A party' to me can mean a lot of things and I asked for him to be more specific.

Yes there would be somewhere between forty and fifty men, have to invite visiting journalists of course, food was needed, obviously, drinks, yes full bar, drugs, Oh Oh! the smoking type and the white powder known affectionately as coke, and of course girls and music. I am now getting out of my depth here I thought and was convinced when it was pointed out that the girls had to be 'willing'. I must stress at this point that this conversation was not with any of the players or in their presence. I nodded and made my departure and having no idea where I could find forty or fifty 'willing' ladies thought my days of being a football groupie were coming to an end.

Next day went to work wondering if I should call the hotel and let them know they would have to find another party organiser until I mentioned the request to my business partner, Bob, and he said it wouldn't be a problem he knew exactly where there was a place that catered for such functions. He made a quick phone call and we jumped into his car, left Glebe and headed towards the city. We stopped and parked in Pyrmont, a small suburb, ungentrified at this stage, just half a kilometre from the CBD across the Pyrmont Bridge. He then led me to what looked like an old public house on the main corner, three or four stories, very tasteful exterior and a double door with security cameras pointing at everyone who chose to enter or leave the premises. It was on the corner of Pyrmont Bridge road and Harwood Lane and the house had a sign telling us the house was called Harwood Lane. Bob rang the doorbell, identified himself, and in a few seconds the door opened by itself and we entered into a front foyer that could have been any office of any profession such as doctor, dentist, accountant solicitor or the like. A well dressed lady, about forty five years old shook our hands and led us into another room which, must to my surprise, had a fully stocked cocktail bar. She gave us a drink then we sat at the bar and I gave her my brief without mentioning who it was for. She said that shouldn't be a problem and then took us on a guided tour of the building. Excuse me, she took me, Bob seemed to know his way around. It was similar to being given a guided tour by a real estate agent trying to sell me a house. Here's the seven bedrooms, each with a spa bath and shower, mini fridge in each room, full room service, the kitchen that can cater for up to sixty people, but if anything else was needed the Sheraton Hotel was just around the corner and they had a special delivery deal with them. All very professional and somewhat detached regarding all the exotic requests that I had mentioned in my brief. No problems. My innocence in these matters was taking a battering and I wanted to get the deal done and out of there as quickly as possible. Yes I had just realised this was a brothel, knocking shop, whorehouse or any other synonyms that describe what could be going on in there very soon, after lunch she said was their busiest periods. They would close the place on Sunday night for our 'private party' and the fixed fee was minimum of forty bookings for a night with the lot $170/head. Not meant to be a pun!

Couldn't get out of there quick enough and as soon Bob had negotiated a couple of freebies as commission on the deal we were back on the pavement.

Being new to these kind of activities I rang the Argentinian contact, told him the deal and discretion guaranteed. Not a problem I thought, rang the lady confirming the arrangements with a rider that I would 100% confirm once I had the $6800 in my hands and at the latest Friday lunchtime.

This is the kind of story one would normally keep to themselves if things went smoothly. However things didn't so maybe I'm taking a little revenge by disclosing. You see the party never happened. Why?? Come the Friday, no cash to pay had arrived so a number of calls eventually resulted in a call back from my contact saying the party was off. Why?? Because they couldn't find any local Argentinian individual, company, government body or anyone else to pay for it. A truism it is that the more wealthy people become the more they expect things for free. Okay no hard feelings. Do I have any other ideas? Fortunately one of our favourite restaurants in Sydney was the Rancho Amigo in Petersham. Close to the city and specialising in Argentinian barbecues. The proprietor jumped at the opportunity and when I asked how much he said it was free provided Maradona turned up. Of course it happened. We didn't get an invite. The match was a draw and the coach went direct from the Football Stadium to the restaurant.

My first venture into sports promotion but not my last and Argentina was on the horizon..........................

CHAPTER 33!

What's Up Doc?

So here we are, Mainline Music, a customer list including Myers one of Australia's largest department store chains, David Jones the other department store chain quickly came on board so it was now time for us to obtain licences for material other than classical as the public appeared insatiable for this CD alternative to records and cassettes. In trying to licence from the Australian record companies we were knocked back by everyone as they were completely against budget priced product as they were intent on keeping compact discs at the world's most expensive level, over thirty dollars, not a bad mark up as we could manufacture a compact disc, with a high quality printed insert into the plastic case, all up one dollar. Take into account artists and composer's royalties and distribution costs still didn't get near five dollars. Bob James, my partner, had been artists and repertoire manager for K-Tel for years so he had other sources for product and they all met at Midem, the music industry's annual trade fare in Cannes in the South of France. Bob being experienced in these festivals stressed the importance of looking wealthy no matter how young to the business I was and that meant staying at either the Carlton or Martinez hotels across the road from the Palais des Festivals the main venue for the festival. As the festival is held every year in late January early February we only had a few weeks to register and make arrangements. How relieved I was to find out all hotels in Cannes were booked out for the conference once I knew what price they were looking for people to pay for a room. The only hotel I could find available was in Grasse, a small town about twenty kilometres out of town in the hinterland. This would require rental of a car duly arranged, and we drove to Grasse from Nice airport. A pleasant town and not a bad hotel.

The first morning at breakfast in the hotel had its own memorable moment when, as we looked out of the window from the restaurant, up pulled a massive limousine with blackened windows, a car in front and another behind. It looked like something out of the movies as the driver, and what appeared to be body guards, formed a protective pattern, just like you see the American Secret Service do guarding the President, to let in a very important looking coloured man. I said that to maintain any political correctness people care about, as he was a very black man as was the rest of his party. He was dressed immaculately with a silk suit and shoes that shone so much you had to cover your eyes.

The maitre-de came over to our table and politely asked us to move, when I say ask I mean told us to move, and as we were the only people in the restaurant it struck me as strange that they moved us to the furthest table from the one we had which was now being hurriedly set for this obviously honoured guest.

Bob and I tried to guess who it was, which ranged from Lionel Ritchie to Chubby Checker and a lot of names in- between. However it became obvious this was no music personality as the body guards placed themselves between the door and the table and us and the table.

Then when we stood up to leave, the bodyguards kept a respectable distance from us but maintained the human barrier.

Strange as it may seem we were not perturbed too much by what had transpired over breakfast and off we went down the hills into Cannes and our first day at the festival. At the festival we met up early with a group of Australian delegates and on telling them the story we were shocked, to say the least, to find out it was the deposed dictator, former Haitian leader Jean-Claude, Baby Doc, Duvalier. He was President of Haiti from 1971 till he was deposed in 1986. He was supposedly in hiding from Haitian justice, which says something about the people who were looking for him.

Bob and I made quite a meal of the story and with a little elaboration on our side it became a story where the Duvalier party could have thought we were professional assassins set to murder him.

It was now down to business and in the main hall we explored the stands and made notes and appointments with people that Bob thought would be useful in signing licensing agreements for a number of catalogues. It was decided we needed music from certain decades which included forties, fifties, sixties and anything else that emerged. The next day we kept our appointments and signed up a number of titles to be paid on a royalty basis, very encouraging as there were no up-fronts but I couldn't understand why Bob was doubling up on a number of singers and their back catalogues. It was then explained to me that there was no way we could check the bona-fides of the companies offering the product as most of the artists involved had changed record labels a number of times in their career and each new label made it a term of their contract that they would re-record all their previous hits. For instance there were eight different versions of Chuck Berry singing Maybelline and only scientific research could pick the difference. It was a given around the international music community that the best way to cover one's self against piracy charges was to have a number of royalty contracts for the same artist and their recordings which could be produced if the major labels asked the source of our product.

By the end of the Midem Convention we had licensed hundreds of tracks covering all decades of recorded music and we were ready to enter the mainstream.

On our return to Australia we launched our new product with great success. Hits of the Forties, Greatest Hits of The Fifties, Sensational Sixties, Disco Divas the list went on and on then they were recycled and put out with other titles. We were meticulous in keeping accounts up to date and at one point we pinched the Financial Controller of Warner Music to work for us. It was of paramount concern that we paid publishing royalties which ensure the song writers get their due rewards and every quarter we remitted funds to the companies we had licensed the product from. It was just as well we did as the majors began to see us as a threat to the status quo and began to apply pressure.

First up Sony Music took out a writ against us quoting a series of serial numbers of some of our products accusing us of piracy. This was to be heard in the Federal Court in Sydney and on checking the writ I discovered that the serial numbers belonged to another budget record label, Hughes Music. I took this to mean we didn't need legal advice or representation as I would tell the judge the case was nothing to do with us.

How wrong could I be? On being called into court I stood to explain that the case had absolutely nothing to do with us. The federal court doesn't quite work like that. The judge asked me to sit down as I started to speak. When I asked why I was informed that I didn't have the right to ask the question. I protested and the judge made me resume my seat. Barristers, solicitors, journalists and others began filtering into the court to see what was going on. It was beginning to look like something from an Abbott and Costello film, then finally an officer of the court took a hold of me and took me outside. Once in the foyer I was approached by a number of laughing legal eagles saying they hadn't had so much fun in all their time in the legal profession and one barrister said he'd enjoyed it so much he would represent us free of charge. Yes I know that's hard to believe, a lawyer doing something for nothing. I've always believed they would defend my rights to my last dollar. He explained that in Federal Court only barristers are allowed to address the judge, not even solicitors. The legal profession have it all tied up. We went back into the court, the barrister pleaded not guilty on our behalf, we were absolved of guilt and the legal people of Sony Music were given a dressing down for not having their facts straight.

Outside we were nearly mobbed with handshakes all round and even the Sony legal team had a laugh with us. So maybe we thought that was going to be the end of legal problems or how wrong could we be?

CHAPTER 34!

Here We Go, Here We Go, Here We Go!

Then there was 1999 when I was in the process of arranging the Maximusic dot com company as described in other parts of this book when I got a call from a friend of mine Dominic Galati. We went back a long time as when he was seventeen and an apprentice plumber he had an accident which injured his back and plumbing was now out of the question. He was also a potential football star with a junior contract with Marconi, Australia's number one Italian supported club. After my divorce I had bought a house in Hunters Hill and had seen a note in the local laundromat window inviting soccer players to sign up for Gladesville Ravens and that's how we met sometime in the late seventies.

We had the Production Factory up and running making commercials and video clips and Dominic asked if there were any jobs going. We took him on a casual basis paying him by the day and as proven in the future he had an appetite for work that eventually made him indispensable to the company. At the time we had picked up some contracts to cover football for Australia's new multicultural television network SBS TV and Dominic took charge of this part of the business. One day the SBS Director of Sport, Peter Skelton, who I had known from his days at the Ten Network asked if I knew anyone that had television experience and was looking for a job as he needed an assistant. I recommended Dominic with the added information that his name ended in a vowel so he would fit in immediately and he also spoke Italian.

The job was his.

Within twelve months he was the staff representative on the management board and after another six months he was Director of Sport and the sky seemed to be the limit.

Fast forward to 1999 when I got the phone call from Dominic and he asked me if I could give him a hand with the upcoming tour of Australia by Manchester United, the current holders of the European cup, the F.A. Cup and English champions and arguably the number one football club in the world at the time.

Would I?

Definitely a rhetorical question. I was at his office in the city before he could have hung up his phone. There were two matches arranged, one in Melbourne and another one in Sydney. The only disappointments at the time were that Alex Ferguson their manager couldn't make it as he had an appointment at Buckingham Palace to receive his knighthood and David Beckham couldn't make it as he was getting married to Victoria. So when we were in Melbourne this created a joke that Beckham wasn't in Victoria, Oh yes he is came all the retorts.

Both games were sold out with the Sydney game filling the newly finished Olympic Stadium for the first time. Sponsors were lining up and the promotion was a resounding success both financially and football wise. Dominic was being backed by the flamboyant Sydney stockbroker Rene Rivkin, who put up the two million dollars needed to get the show on the road. It was the same Rene Rivkin who was the victim of a witch hunt in 2003 which saw him sentenced to weekend detention for insider trading which gave him a massive profit of $2600. Always a gentleman and fun to be around.

It's interesting to note that during the wash up and the profits distributed Rene pointed out he had hedged his investment, as he had no idea who Manchester United were and didn't have any faith in the project. He had sold hundred percent to his friends and clients and kept nothing for himself. Apart from the house tickets that I had arranged to be sold for cash to Glasgow Johnny No Names, an 'admission facilitator'. An easy thirty thousand dollars.

Dominic gave me the role of host at the pre-match lunch with all the V.I.P.s which caused some red faces at the Sydney match.

Lisa and I took our positions at the number one table and greeted Mrs.

Edwards the Manchester United's chairman's wife and their sons who had flown in from Hong Kong. Martin Edwards arrived. The air was electric, conversation was perfunctory. Even Ian Thorpe the Olympic swimming champion at our table found the going heavy. After a few red wines the atmosphere relaxed a little but never reached the usual convivial state.

It was only the next day when I picked up the International Express newspaper and there on the front page was a headline article on Martin Edwards being caught in a compromising position with a young lady in Brazil just before he had flown out to Australia.

That explained a lot.

After the success of this promotion Dominic set up IEC and took over financing the Australian national soccer teams which included the Socceroos, Matildas, Olyroos and the National Soccer League. It was a simple arrangement along the lines of IEC would guarantee Soccer Australia the two million dollars a year they needed to operate and IEC would finance the national teams and the league, arrange sponsorships and once the two million dollars had been raised a percentage split between IEC and Soccer Australia came into play.

I went back to my Maximusic dot com business with some good memories.

However come 2001 Dominic called again and I was employed full time by IEC the first full time job I had had in twenty five years and as it was a qualifying year for the 2002 World Cup to be held in Japan and South Korea the world was smiling on me. We often make the joke that I gave Dominic his first job and he gave me my last.

We were so confident of Australia reaching the finals I had been sent to Korea and Japan to tie up marketing rights for Oceania. During that trip I learnt how popular karaoke is in Asia and my impersonations of Tom Jones singing Delilah made me a must guest for dinner most nights out. In Seoul on the last night I fell for the old trick over dinner. Korean cuisine is usually a number of very small dishes, probably around ten, with a mixture of meats and sea foods washed down with wine and custard tarts for dessert. On the last dish of the main course I noticed my Korean hosts were looking quite amused and having small giggling fits behind their hands. Only after dessert was finished did one of my hosts ask how I'd enjoyed the dinner and in particular the last plate of the main course.

It all seemed fine to me and I said so. Then all four of my hosts started to bark like a dog. Woof woof! Yes I'd eaten dog meat. Turns out it's a custom in Korea to trick us wide eyes in this way and yes, it tasted like chicken.

As part of the preparation for the Socceroos play-offs against Uruguay we had arranged a friendly fixture against France, the current FIFA World Cup Holders at the MCG. This was a coup in itself even though it was costing an arm and a leg with a touring party of 75 including a large press contingent. They were contracted to bring out the full squad including Zidane and the Arsenal team which was everyone's favourite French team at the time. Tickets went well, Australia were able to bring all their first choice players from around the world and it looked like a bumper crowd was expected. Pity it poured down the whole day of the game and we had to be happy with a gate of 59,000. Not bad as it was the first time in two years since we took up marketing rights that a profit was made.

As the date approached we had what could be called a financial hitch. One of our sponsors for the Socceroos was Qantas, the Australian national airline, and as well as a cash component in the sponsorship the deal involved all Socceroos to fly business class while we paid only the full economy fare. This applied to everyone apart from one Harry Kewell, who had a separate deal that ensured he flew first class. Always strange as he went on the plane before everyone else and turned immediately left into first and everyone turned right into business or economy. Great for team spirit. We were able to negotiate with Qantas the same deal for the French touring party of seventy five and duly issued tickets for all carrying the dollar price of business class ie. $7,600 but actually costing us $2200. This was in the times of tickets being paper booklets with a page for each stage of the journey, no e-tickets like today.

What could be the hitch? You may remember someone called Osama Bin Laden and his friends that on the ninth day in September of 2001 they flew planes into the twin towers, the Pentagon and a field in Shanksville, Pennsylvania. 9-11 caused major upheavals in most parts of the world and in particular the business of security. Living in Australia we're usually immune from the woes of the northern hemisphere but not in this case. The French government decided that the national football team is a national treasure including all the individual parts thereof and it would be too much of a risk for them to travel on commercial flights so they would fit out an Air France 747 into all business class seats and fly the team at their cost, less the expense of our already purchased tickets and would include a fighter plane escort accompanying them over what they would call hostile territory.

Early October we received this news along with a DHL package of seventy five Qantas business class tickets and an invoice from the French government for $570,000. Did that hit the bottom line considering they would only have cost us $165,000.

As mentioned earlier it rained all day on the Sunday of the game but the MCG held up well and an entertaining match ended in a one all draw. The only drama was in the dining area when Ian Knop, the chairman of Soccer Australia, had his nose out of joint when he realised the French ambassador was not on his table but had been allocated seats on the promoter's table ie. Mine! As is usual in visits by high profile rich sportsmen there were always young and not so young ladies making themselves available by hanging around the hotel bars and the French team was no exception. There were three ladies in particular that appeared to have taken up residence in the hotel and it came as a surprise to me when they approached me after the game back in the hotel asking who was to be paying for their rooms. Unbeknown to them the French team that they had been accompanying had left for France in their chartered 747 immediately after the game because of security concerns. I had never met the ladies before but I believe I heard one of them remarking that she was very big in Bollywood.

But never mind Uruguay were next and could that be any more exciting..........................

CHAPTER 35!

Just Local Customs!

How the major record companies must have hated us. We had beaten them twice in legal proceedings costing them a great deal and we wondered why they didn't have the sense to make us an offer to buy us out and close us down. Our next challenge was to break the parallel import ruling which the record companies had used for years to keep the prices of records, CD's and cassettes at the highest retail price in the world. The main stumbling block was an agreement the majors had amongst themselves to ban the importation of any recorded material from anywhere resulting in a cartel running a monopoly. That may sound as incorrect grammar but it was the case that had existed for years. Comparisons in prices had a popular CD selling for $32 in Australia while in America the identical product was below $20 and in Asian countries and developing markets the same product was retailing at less than $10. The majors tried to make it sound as though it was to protect local artists and composers from piracy which would result in lower or even no royalties. This was a real furphy as we were to prove.

Having the reputation we had earned as buccaneers of the industry it was no surprise to be invited to meet with Professor Allan Fells who was running the Federal Government watchdog on price fixing. It was establishing a good name with the public and its political masters as an effective body protecting the public from cartels and price fixing. In an informal off the record meeting Professor Fels asked us how the major record companies were able to maintain this price fixing when some budget labels such as K-Tel were able to deliver the same local product at a massive discount. After pointing out to him that the cost of manufacturing a CD then putting it into a jewel box with a printed cover cost only one dollar, mental arithmetic told him there was something not too kosher going on.

Did we have any ideas on how to break the cartel?

Not yet but give us a couple of weeks and we'll come back to you.

Having recently been in Jakarta on business, ironically selling CD's and cassettes to music distributors and retailers in Indonesia, we discovered that all major product identically packaged was retailing at under $10 throughout Indonesia. With a wholesale price of under $6 the plan started to take fruition. On my return we met again with Professor Fels to discuss a plan going forward. He was not able to offer us any guarantees as that would be doing exactly what ACCC was there to prevent, but he did promise that if the record companies approached any retailers in Australia threatening retaliation if they took our imported product he would make them show reasons why they would adopt such a stance as he believed it would be illegal under any circumstance for someone who had a monopoly on a product to take that position.

Feeling, if nothing else we had some support, we switched into subterfuge mode as per the live recordings and arranged our first shipment. Not a great deal but a pallet load, ie. four thousand units CD's and cassettes, of current hits and on arrival we let the retailers know they could have the exact same product for fifteen dollars, with a recommended retail price of nineteen dollars which was less than what they were currently paying wholesale. Not a bite! Word was out and the majors had made veiled threats along the lines of the product was pirated and while they would not stop servicing the stores they could arrange for our product to be confiscated by the anti-piracy unit. Nothing for ACCC to get involved with but a guardian angel turned up in the guise of Big W, a chain of stores owned by the retail giant Woolworths who said they would take all our product and would help us in the future if we could guarantee ongoing supply. We even had a teleconference with Roger Corbett, CEO of Woolworths, who gave us his promise he would support us by ordering more product to assist us to cover any legal expenses incurred. That was good enough for us so we delivered the first batch to Big W and on using the Big W reception the discount two dollar shops came on board and our next shipment was ordered, packed, shipped by air freight to Sydney. The majors didn't give up so easily and as we were waiting for the product to be checked by customs and released from the bond store the phone rang and it was Her Majesty's Customs asking us to send a representative to the bond store to help customs inspect the product that they believed could be illegitimate and subject to refusal of entry. I went out to Mascot but not till after I had called my father in law who was quite senior in the customs and he gave me a tip to make it as difficult as possible which could include inspection, not only of every box but every single CD and cassette. What should have taken an hour was now fraying nerves and adding major overtime expenses as hours after hours passed until they finally gave up and were ready to let us have our product when a summons arrived which was from Sony Music accusing us of importing pirated product and it was not to leave the bond store until at the earliest after a court hearing scheduled for the next day. Federal court again. We didn't make the same mistake of going unrepresented this time and when the judge wanted to set another date for the full hearing our case was that we needed the product out of bondage as it was part of our marketing plan with Father's Day only ten days away. The judge agreed with us it would be unfair to penalise us financially without anything being proven and ordered the release of the goods and if we were found guilty of piracy the record companies would have the right to claim any compensation for any product we were to sell or import in the future. Good Lord we had just been given the go ahead to carry on importing.

With the full hearing set down for months in the future we carried on with our arrangement with Big W and the two dollar shops but we couldn't get the record retailers to stock our product so we decided on another approach. We would retail the product ourselves. How? If we had no retailer in a town we booked the local town hall, scout hall or any vacant high street retail store and shipped the product to the venue thus inventing the pop up shop concept. We booked television advertising time on the local TV station. We would then arrive on the Thursday meet the people who would be providing the trestle tables needed for display, visit the dole office and hire on a cash basis anyone who looked likely to help us for four days setting up, selling then cleaning up afterwards. Over the next few months we must have visited half the towns in Australia flying/driving in, taking the cash and making a hasty retreat being chased by the local record retailers.

There's always greener pastures so let's tackle New Zealand.

We booked the television advertising, booked the old disused customs wharves jutting out into Auckland harbour and this time gave ourselves one more day to arrange things as we were in a foreign country after all. Not that it ever feels that way and that's where we nearly came unstuck. We had flown in around ten pallets of product and as a precaution we had found a local father and son who had a little knowledge of the business as we had met up with them on our Tasmanian sojourns where they had been on holiday and we were relying on them for local knowledge. Never again. On arrival on the Wednesday I found New Zealand Customs had impounded our stock until import duty was paid which was to be no great problem as I was carrying enough cash I thought to pay any duty incurred. On arrival at customs house it turned out duty alone was not the problem rather they were questioning the veracity of the import forms with special attention devoted to the price of goods we were declaring. They were so used to the exorbitant prices Australian record companies were charging their New Zealand retailers they didn't believe our prices and thought we were trying to minimise the duty. Fortunately for us we had had the product shipped direct from Jakarta and a couple of the palettes had the original rupiah invoices. After a nervous afternoon customs and excise agreed to free the product on payment of the agreed fee. Not out of the woods yet. I was about two thousand dollars short but shouldn't be a problem I'll just go to a branch of the ANZ bank, our Australian bankers and get some more cash. That's when I got the reminder I was in a foreign country and ANZ Australia is a different entity to ANZ New Zealand. The manager was very friendly and wanted to help but he couldn't just give cash to a foreigner who didn't even have a bank account in the country. I now was facing a disaster and a major financial hit so I had to use all my powers of persuasion to get him to call our bank manager in Balmain who promised him the funds would be telegraphically transferred immediately but wouldn't be seen in my newly opened ANZ New Zealand bank account till the next morning. The New Zealand bank manager and handed me the necessary funds. A quick taxi ride back to Customs House only to find the people who handled accounts had already left for the day so there was no-one to accept the payment thus freeing the goods. The customs guy was feeling a little sorry for us having put us through the ringer all day and the trucks were waiting at the bond store he called his superior and on my promise that I would be back there the next day on the step as they opened we could take the goods now. What a relief.

The stock was delivered later that evening and I kept my word and paid the duty first thing in the morning.

It was now Thursday setting up day. Everything went to plan for the first time on this venture.

The next morning, opening day Friday, I woke up in my hotel room which was across the road from the venue around seven am, ate breakfast in the restaurant then went back up to my room to collect all that I needed to get me through the day. As I looked out of my window at the venue there were hundreds of people queuing up obviously waiting for opening time. Wherever we had been this had never happened before so what a pleasant surprise. Over the road we went made sure everything was in place then opened the doors. It was like Boxing Day sales in Australia or Black Friday sales in America. People grabbing CD's and cassettes by the basket load. Nothing had prepared us for crowds this size and as the tills started to overflow I had to make some very quick decisions the most important one being what to do with the cash. Not wishing to draw attention to myself I decided the best way was not to make a big security deal but be in full sight taking out the garbage. I filled a plastic garbage bag with the paper money, not yet bundled, and headed off to my new bank manager about a kilometre along the harbour frontage. On arrival at the bank I made a deal with them for them to loan me a clerk to count and deposit the money. I made this trip three times on the Friday and my biggest worry was what I was to do on the coming Saturday and Sunday. We had taken about thirty thousand dollars and Bob, my partner had called from Sydney asking how things were going and I gave him the good news.

After a very tiring day I limped back to the hotel and flopped on the bed. The phone rang and it was Bob. He asked me if I felt like a drink, which I thought was a little strange him being back in Sydney. Not the case he'd been so excited at our success he'd jumped on a plane and was downstairs in the bar. That solved my money counting problem. I was able to take the bags of money back to the hotel on the next two days for Bob to count.

Suffice to say it was the biggest event in Auckland up until the time they won the America's Cup. How did it happen? I'd forgotten I'd done a fifteen percent of takings commission deal with the television network and they had gone overboard with the number of spots they had broadcast giving us every unsold commercial spot for the week.

The next few months were taken up with us going to New Zealand every fortnight taking in Wellington, Christchurch, Dunedin and Invercargill with the same success.

One amusing episode was the weekend I took Lisa and our son Durham with me. We were in the hotel on the first morning having arrived the previous evening. I was in the shower and there was a knock on the door. Our eight year old son answered it and I could hear him talking to Lisa saying, 'One security guard, one policewoman, and a policeman'. I got out of the shower and asked what was going on and I was accused of using a stolen Visa card. Easily explained as our travel agent had used the stolen card number of mine when making the booking as it was what they had in their records and they hadn't updated with the new card. But I had used my new card on checking in! Apologies all round and they had the grace to give us free dinner with wine that evening. A satisfactory result.

CHAPTER 36!

It's Only A Game!

Having seen the French football squad back on their own chartered Boeing 747 which left Melbourne Tullamarine airport within an hour of the game finishing it was now time to prepare for the upcoming World Cup Qualifier against Uruguay.

The Uruguay first leg was set for the Melbourne Cricket Ground so we stayed in Melbourne for the two weeks leading up to it. The promotion went without a hitch, unless one remembers the tax man insisting GST was on the total turnover not just booking and ticket fees.

The hotel in Crown Casino was a hive of activity with some minor hitches including heated discussions on payment for players for signing shirts for memorabilia. But come the day of the game with a full house of ninety five thousand Australia won the first leg one nil thanks to a penalty from Kevin Muscat. So it's off to Montevideo. The plane was arranged to fly out to Buenos Aries immediately after the game and a major disagreement ensued on the tarmac. The Australian squad were seated in the business class area and the Uruguayans had reserved the seats at the rear of the plane but over one hour after the scheduled departure time there was no sign of them. Ian Knop, Chairman of Soccer Australia, incidentally with his full knowledge of football gained by watching his son play under eights at Northbridge, insisting that the plane hold take off till the Uruguayans arrived. Some of the hardened football people, including myself, were pushing to get the plane moving without them. World Cup Qualification is something that needs every advantage you can gain and sportsmanship does not fall into that category. With only five days to go for the second leg in Montevideo it seemed like a great opportunity to gain a great advantage if they had to re-schedule flights within that time. Sad to say Ian Knop won the day and we waited another couple of hours.

On arrival in Buenos Aries it was a quick transit onto a local airline for the short hop to Montevideo.

Then in Montevideo airport stuff really hit the fan. As the Uruguayans were met by cheering crowds outside of customs the crowd waited for the Australian squad. After being held up for an hour by Uruguayan customs, the Socceroos emerged to be greeted by a surging crowd of punching, spitting Uruguayan fans.

'Security was barely adequate to keep the mob at bay. It had become a diplomatic incident, with the Uruguayan ambassador being called in today to see Foreign Minister Alexander Downer and Australia's ambassador to Argentina crossing the River Plate to insist on better security for the Socceroos in Uruguay.' (source: ABC TV)

There you are Mr. Knop. Told you so.

To say it was frightening doesn't explain it adequately and what would happen if we knocked them out? Didn't bear thinking about.

As it came to pass we were beaten easily three nil at the Centenario stadium in front of fifty thousand baying fans. An amazing stadium that resembles something from the days of ancient Rome and the crowd creates an atmosphere that is awe inspiring. The play-off system spelt the end of Australia's World Cup dreams that night for the second time in succession. After losing out to Iran for a place in France 98, the Socceroos went into the second leg of their qualifier against in Uruguay full of hope, hanging onto a 1-0 advantage from the first leg. However, they failed to make their advantage, a late penalty from Kevin Muscat at the Melbourne Cricket Ground, pay as a confident home side triumphed 3-0.

After the match was over all of the Australian party, including a dozen or so supporters who had flown in from Argentina, were ushered downstairs into the dressing room area where we were assembled under the watchful eyes of heavily armed soldiers from the Uruguayan army. We were then escorted onto the coach, players, supporters, officials, standing room only once we were loaded. The coach had been driven tight up to the dressing room doors so we did not have to walk any distance at all and we soon found out why.

As the coach pulled away with a fully armed escort, out riders, front, back and sides, the journey to the airport was horrendous. For the whole thirty minutes it took to get to the airport bottles, cans, vegetables fruit and just about anything that could be used as missiles were deployed against us. I believe we all realised then just what it would have been like for the Christians on their way to the Coliseum, or the aristocrats on their way to the guillotine.

I turned to the lady sitting beside me and wondered out loud what would have happened if we had won and knocked Uruguay out of the cup. Turned out she was from the Australian embassy in Argentina and she nonchalantly pointed out to me that there had been military helicopters on standby ready to land inside the stadium and fly us direct to Buenos Aries.

This incident brings back to mind the quote of Bill Shankly former manager of Liverpool.

'Some people believe football is a matter of life and death, I am very disappointed with that attitude. I can assure you it is much, much more important than that.'

Four years later, not under our management I must point out, we had our revenge in the Olympic Stadium in Sydney where we saw them off after a penalty shoot - out.

But our days as management of Australian football were numbered.

CHAPTER 37!

Too Hot For Handlin!

So here we were Mainline Music the arch enemies of the Australian record industry. Every major had the knives out for us because of our attitude to imported product and the 'Unauthorised' catalogue we had issued and were having great success with both branches. Our retailers were supporting us with our legal expenses by ordering more product as the civil cases proceeded in the Federal Court. It would be easy to believe that I was always an enemy to the record industry but there was a time in the seventies when I was one of their great supporters having landed a position with a major television production house, McCabe Collins, and I was producing five and a half hours of pop music television every week for the Ten network. Right On was broadcast at four thirty for a half hour Monday to Friday and Rock N' Roll Milkbar went to air live for three hours every Saturday morning. This meant along with Countdown on the ABC and Sounds Unlimited on the Seven network we were a very effective promotional medium for the record industry to use to break artists through programming of their video clips.

There was a pecking order amongst the television shows with Countdown having first choice of clips followed by ourselves and Sounds then offered to local stations as fillers.

Our production schedule for Rock N Roll Milkbar involved us flying to Brisbane on Thursdays, pre- production on the Friday then live to air nine am Saturday morning. This presented a great opportunity for the Queensland promotional people to get some clips aired nationally so Fridays were usually taken up with visits from all the record companies asking us to play the clips. Worth remembering they would have been given the clips weeks after they had been offered to the Sydney and Melbourne producers.

The promotional junior in Brisbane for CBS was a fresh faced young man called Dennis Handlin, a real hard worker and would hardly ever take no for an answer.

One Friday he turned up with a reel of 16mm film which had five songs from a newly signed artist to CBS, Boz Scaggs. The tracks were from his album Silk Degrees which had just been released four or five weeks earlier. The first single was 'What Can I Say' and Dennis explained to me that Sony had been unable to gain any traction from television and radio in the major markets so the film had landed on his desk and could I play the single and he would buy me lunch, not a bribe, called payola in the music business, and would give me six albums to give away on the show. An offer too good to refuse so I promised to play it this coming Saturday.

He also came up with the line 'Boz Is the Buzz' and I sent the film to facilities to be transferred to videotape and I programmed in four minutes for 'What Can I Say' thought no more of it and finished my production duties. Come Saturday and it's time to go to air. There's nothing as exhilarating as live television with the chances of Murphy's Law being enacted at any point and three hours is a big call for live television. We had had a lot of practise so the well-oiled machine was swung into action. The Boz Scaggs single was scheduled for about two hours into the programme with the Boz Is The Buzz promotion to come immediately after the single had been aired. Listening through the headphones to the director and production crew as the clip started I got the bad news that one of our playback video machines had broken down and we couldn't play the following clip until it was back up and running. Trying to keep things rolling I remembered that the film Dennis had given me had five songs on it with Boz performing in concert. I asked if we'd transferred every track and receiving a positive response chanced my luck and asked if they were all on the same tape now playing. The gods were smiling on me, we had all five tracks on the tape on the working machine, giving us twenty minutes in which to fix the other video machine. My instructions were to keep the tape running till we were fully operative and so on national television Boz Scaggs was seen for the first time in Australia performing, What Can I Say, Lido Shuffle, Lowdown, We're All Alone, and Georgia. Our switchboard lit up. Everyone wanted Boz Scaggs and Silk Degrees. By accident we had made a hit in Australia of an artist no-one else would touch. As we came off air there was Dennis waiting to greet me and thanking me for playing all the tracks, something that would never have occurred under normal circumstances. Taking a little license I told him that on seeing the whole tape the night before I had decided it was so good I would play the whole five songs. Never mentioned the broken video machine. I was now a hero to Dennis and the follow up was that Silk Degrees became the biggest selling album in Australia in 1976. This led to Dennis being promoted into the national promotions office in Sydney followed by a meteoric rise to the number one position of Chairman and CEO of Sony Music. He has been a great supporter of charitable causes and recently was deservedly awarded the Order of Australia for his service to the music industry.

Fast forward about ten years and our paths had crossed a few times at functions over the period and the greeting was always Boz Is The Buzz, and I must confess I lapped up all the credit that was given to me and only now I am confessing it was by accident and not my intuition about what makes a great album.

It was late one night and Lisa and I had stopped at the cocktail bar in the Sebel Town House for a nightcap and Dennis was there holding court with some of his staff and when he saw me he dragged me into his circle and started telling the story about our great success with Silk Degrees and after buying drinks all night got me to tell the story and was using it as motivation to his sycophantic minions on how to get to the top in the industry through hard work and persistence.

As we sat down later in the evening like old chums and reminiscing about the good old days he then asked me what I was doing as a job now. When I told him I was a director of Mainline Music the mood change was instant. He stood up never spoke a word to me and stormed out of the bar with his juniors in tow. He had just realised that I was involved with the Unauthorised and importation of product. I guessed that was the end of that friendship and the only time I have seen him since then was when playing soccer a few years later against a team that he sponsored and again I was given the cold shoulder.

Justice was achieved in both of the legal actions when charges of piracy featuring the live albums were found to be unfounded as we had operated strictly within the law and the record companies were admonished for not checking out their own rules and regulations and the fact that we had made it obvious we were acting honestly with our warnings on the covers. We were awarded costs and only the importation legal battle to finish. Again the majors tried to convince everyone the CD's were pirated and were being pressed in backyard plants in Indonesia. They ended up with egg on their face when we pointed out in court that in fact all the product we had imported had been manufactured in their own factories here in Australia. How did I know this? Surprisingly the record companies did not know their own processes. In the clear part in the centre of CD's there is a number stamped and this number denotes which CD pressing machine pressed the CD. We were able to prove these machines were owned by the Australian record companies and they had in fact made the CD's and had their export records intact proving they themselves had sold the product into Indonesia at less than half the price they were receiving from Australian retailers.

We got this news in good time with damages awarded as a few months later my partner in Mainline, Bob James, died of a heart attack while holidaying in Bali. RIP.

CHAPTER 38!

Bend It!

So I was now doing something I love and getting paid for it. I was a sports administrator for International Entertainment Corporation the company that held marketing and promotional rights to all the Australian national football, soccer that is, teams and the National Soccer League. We had failed to reach the 2002 World Cup Finals and we were copping a lot of criticism, unfairly I must say, as the factions within Soccer Australia and the National Soccer League were impossible to control and were continually striving to position themselves better rather than for the good of the game. There were nationalistic egos at stake with each of the ethnic groups involved steadfastly refusing to enter any discussions where the status quo could be altered. The vultures were circling due to the lack of success but we played a trump card. We arranged to play England, in England, for a friendly match. In meetings with the English FA in Soho Square we were adamant with them that any game against Australia would be a sell out and they should play the match at Stamford Bridge, the home of Chelsea or Old Trafford the theatre of dreams. The final decisions were to be made by the England manager Sven Eriksson who didn't appreciate Commonwealth rivalries and downplayed the match as unimportant and opted for the small West Ham ground Upton Park. As we predicted the game was a sell out within minutes of tickets going on sale and we knew we were going to have a large number of ex-pats now living in Britain. Who couldn't wait to see Australia put the boot in to England on their own turf at their own game.

On arriving in London I found out I had a lot of very good friends that I hadn't heard from in years but they would like to meet up with me and if possible could I find tickets for the game. Don't know to this day how they found me but I was unable to help anyone apart from one gentleman who was introduced to me as the CEO of the One North East Development agency which was a government body with an annual budget of two hundred and fifty million pounds for development and job creation in the North East of England my old stomping ground.

It turned out he was the best friend of Tony Blair the British Prime Minister of the time from school and university days. This was too good an introduction to miss. Knowing he was looking for a ticket to the game I headed to Soho Square and asked the FA for an access all areas ticket for the game that evening. The mean people of the FA charged me for the pass.

I couldn't believe that even Tony Blair's name didn't hold any sway where tickets were concerned. Armed with the ticket I had been sold and the address of 104 Pall Mall to meet there for pre-match drinks onto the tube I went down town. It was only when I got there I realised it was The Reform Club, a very salubrious and genteel private club. Fortunately I was suited up but as it dawned on me that this was the equivalent of a working man's social club for the rich, powerful and famous of Britain whose history had been that every Prime Minister of Britain became a member automatically. They had to change their by-laws allowing female members to accommodate Margaret Thatcher as it had always been a gentleman's exclusive club. After joining the small party my guest discovered I was from the North East originally and said we should meet up the next day to exchange stories and ideas. As we were leaving for Upton Park I also remembered that the Reform Club was the starting line for Around the World in Eighty Days, the book by Jules Verne and the movie starring David Niven and Cantinflas.

Yes it really is A Long Way From Ferryhill I thought to myself.

As Upton Park has its own tube station it was more convenient to catch the train rather than get traffic trouble by driving or going by taxi but the inevitable happened as it was February in London. The underground system was failing all over London and we were stuck in tunnels for quite a long time. Thankfully it was announced that the kick off time had been delayed because of traffic problems and we eventually took our seats as the game kicked off.

Much to the disappointment of the English at half time Australia were leading two nil and the crowd were getting restless. At this time I thought I'd use my access pass and visit the dressing room areas to use the bathroom and as I passed the English dressing room which was tightly closed and the door flanked by security guards I couldn't help but hear the shouting and screaming going on in the room. There were some very angry voices being raised and where as I couldn't understand what the arguments were about it soon became very clear. Sven Eriksson made nine substitutions for the second half including a number of debutants and famously amongst them Wayne Rooney. Later it came out that the English players were arguing with Eriksson that he shouldn't make the wholesale changes as this was Australia that was beating them and tried unsuccessfully to make him change his mind. Years later in his book he pointed out that he hadn't realised the importance of sporting events between Australia and England until he saw the ticker tape welcome given to the English cricket team when they won the Ashes.

We went on to win three one and afterwards at the post match reception under the main stand I was in football paradise, we had won, and I was surrounded by most of my sporting heroes. Without realising who was next to me I was celebrating the Australian victory with all who would listen before I was thumped on my right shoulder, forcing me to spill some beer and drop my sausage roll, I turned to face the perpetrator ready to give him a mouthful and was stunned to see it was Alan Shearer, former England striker and captain, and my hero. We got into a friendly conversation and he was surprised that with my accent I was supporting anyone else against England. It was when I reminded him that between him and me we had scored thirty goals for England the conversation was more relaxed and I have never washed that suit jacket that has Alan Shearer's knuckle prints on the right shoulder.

The conversation ended as did everyone else's in the room as the main attraction arrived. Turning around I saw coming through the door four of the biggest men I have ever seen in black suits forming a guard around, who else, David Beckham and Victoria. How good was this and they were heading towards me, or maybe it was Alan Shearer they were heading for, but let's not split hairs. Beckham shook hands with Shearer then turned to me, shook my hand, saying nice to meet me and then wandered off. It would have been easy to think of the Beckhams as tossers but it should be remembered that only a few days earlier there had been kidnap threats against their children by Croatian criminals so security had been beefed up. For those who have been in a coma for the last 30 years David Robert Joseph Beckham OBE, is a retired English footballer. He has played for Manchester United, Preston North End, Real Madrid, Milan, Los Angeles Galaxy, Paris Saint-Germain, and the England national team for which he holds the appearance record for an outfield player.

The Australian party made our exit after a polite hour or so and we returned on the coach to our hotel in North London which had been our base using Tottenham Hotspur's training facilities. Then the real celebrations started. The bar was kept open and media interviews were being conducted all over the bar area. Television and radio were steaming as it was first thing in the morning in Australia and Australia had woken up to this great news. Finding a quiet corner after all the excitement I found myself talking to a young guy who introduced himself as Tim Cahill who I had heard of as he was playing professionally for Milwall in England at the time. While enjoying the moment he was a little disappointed as he wanted to play for Australia but due to him having played in the1995 FIFA under 20's World Cup for Samoa, Cahill made his debut for the under-20 team at the age of 14, thus he was disqualified playing for Australia. This problem was resolved within months and he went on to become one of Australia's leading players. This was our last major promotion in the football world as the Australian Sports Commission took an interest in soccer for the first time and we entered into a long and acrimonious legal battle against one of Australia's wealthiest men, Frank Lowy of Westfield fame and fortune and a lover of football.

The English press gave it to the English team the next day with headlines along the lines of 'Can we beat Australia at anything?'

The day after the match I was scheduled to fly to Glasgow for a meeting with the Scottish Football Association to arrange games for Australia against Scotland either in Australia or Scotland but on arrival at Stansted airport found the planes grounded so it was back to the hotel.

Before I returned to Australia I met up with my friend from One North East and this opened a few doors and included my dealings with the third generation of the Packer family.

CHAPTER 39!

Wombat of Wall Street!

Then there was the late nineties dot-com bubble. We had been running Mainline Records and Much More Music quite successfully having fought off the major record companies in legal battles over copyright and import regulation when the phenomenon of the internet engulfed everyone on the planet. Amazon had started selling books on-line with massive success and a share price going through the stratosphere. People were looking for the next product to market on-line and CD's seemed the perfect fit. We knew absolutely nothing about the stock market on how it worked or any potential for us. We had seen Brian Nichols float his J&B records on the ASX making him a multi-millionaire but it still meant nothing to us.

I was approached by a friend I played football with at North Sydney, Rene Kerstens, a Dutch Australian that I had had very few dealings with up till that time, and he let me know that he was a stockbroker with BNP Paribas in the Sydney CBD and would I be interested in talking with someone who was looking for a product to back-door into a listed company. This was all gobbledegook to me but ever the adventurer my curiosity was roused and I agreed to a lunch with whoever the interested party was.

On a Tuesday we met with the gentleman who introduced himself as Ian Murray, chairman of a number of listed companies, and they wanted to climb onto the dot-com express train that was picking up speed and accelerating. Ian was a white haired gentleman, very urbane and sophisticated, dressed in only the best attire and the smoothest conversationalist I'd ever met at that stage. He drove a convertible Porsche 911, you know the car we love driven by the guys we hate, but I must say at his age his difficulty getting in and out of it took away all the glamour that may have been associated with it.

Over this one lunch at The Mixing Pot our favourite Italian restaurant in Saint Johns Road, Glebe it was agreed that I would receive $95,000 and millions of shares, be appointed Deputy Chairman of a company listed on the London U.K. stock exchange. The company was Barker Securities Plc. But was to be renamed as Maximusic dot com Plc. My head was swimming with all this talk but I managed to maintain my knowledgeable expression as details were written on the paper napkin, hands were shaken and I was moving into a new world.

Did this new world spin fast! The next day the cheque was in my hand, reams of documents were signed so quickly I could have been Faust making a deal with the devil, which in hindsight is what I almost did.

I was advised to buy new clothes, including a suit. Remember I was in the 'music industry' where we thought we were too cool to wear anything but blue jeans and leather bomber jackets, and prepare Lisa and myself for a flying visit to London to make things official and sell the newest dot-com company to the market. First presentation 11 am the coming Monday. Two first class tickets were supplied for the Friday, which I altered to the Saturday evening as I had an over 35's football match at Cammeray Oval on the Saturday.

Must get our priorities right.

Lisa picked me up immediately after the final whistle had blown and fortunately I was neither man of the match or mug of the day which could have held me up for another hour to scull a schooner of VB in the Oaks Hotel which has been a long tradition with North Sydney football club and hopefully will remain so. It irks me to this day that in my first game ever for North Sydney I scored four goals out of our five scored and didn't get Man of The Match. It went to the goalkeeper.

We arrived exhausted at Heathrow late on the Sunday, saw the driver with my name on his piece of card, and we were whisked to the Park Lane Hotel where Ian and his wife were waiting to take us to dinner in a Chinese restaurant in Mayfair. Having been a critic of English cooking whenever I had been in Britain this was a pleasant surprise.

Actual Chinese cuisine in England, unheard of.

How long has this been going on I kept asking myself.

Private jets and motor launches next?

Over dinner I was briefed as to what was required of me over the next ten days which included presenting our dot - com, having had the company change its name to Maximusic dot com Plc. to the major broking houses in London. Thank heavens my distant past as a high school teacher meant I had no fear of public speaking and I assured myself I knew more about the music business than any stockbroker.

Tired and pleasantly wined and dined we retired with the instructions to be ready at 9.30 the next morning, bright eyed and with shiny shoes.

The Monday came and Ian picked me up at the hotel in a taxi and drove me, much to my surprise, to a Lloyds bank where I was given the very pleasant surprise of eight thousand pounds in cash as my expenses for the ten days I was to spend in the U.K. Costed at eight hundred pounds a day I thought this was going to be a very profitable trip until I was told I had to pay the hotel bills out of this. On checking out I discovered how expensive London can be especially in Wimbledon fortnight. Enough said when I realised the VAT on the bill was more than I had ever paid for a suite even in five star hotels in Australia, U.S. and Asia.

Now came the period in my life when I was a paper multi-millionaire.................

CHAPTER 40

Roll The Dice!

Having had dealings with two generations of the Packer family it comes as no surprise that I eventually caught up with James the son of Kerry now heading up the Packer Empire

It came about from a quite unexpected source emanating from the England Australia football match at Upton Park in the February of 2003. I had been introduced to a gentleman who needed a ticket which I procured for him and as previously mentioned we met at the Reform Club before catching the tube to the football stadium. It turned out he was the best friend of British Prime Minister Tony Blair harking back to their university days. He was not a politician but a career public servant who had risen high up in the service to now have a billion pound budget to create industry and jobs for the North East of England. Apparently there were a number of depressed areas around the country that had been allocated budgets to revive industry in the same areas. Being from the North East myself I took an interest in what he was planning and we agreed to meet for lunch the next day. On picking up the newspapers in the morning the headlines were about reforms to the gambling industry and in particular the casinos which were very strictly regulated including members only policies etc. Over the lunch I suggested that this was a great opportunity for creating jobs and services in depressed areas and they should probably start lobbying for the larger casino complexes which include restaurants, cinemas, theatres, food courts, shopping malls and anything else that would fit into the resort type complex. I was basing my reasoning on the success of Crown Casino in Melbourne which on opening had become the heart of the city and all roads led to Crown. The idea hit a nerve with the people around the table and I was hired to prepare a paper stating facts and figures relating to Crown then extrapolating them into what it could offer areas in the United Kingdom. On returning to Australia I talked with Dominic the head of our company as to how could we get information on Crown. How fortunate it was that Dominic had been working for Rene Rivkin, one of Australia's leading stockbrokers, who had been a mentor to James with the blessing of Kerry. So Dominic knew James quite well and an appointment was made for the next day and off to the Park St. office in the city we went. On arriving there another surprise was James's personal assistant a Scottish lady Jacqui, I knew through one of my football team without knowing anything about where she worked. So it was smiles all round and then after a few minutes we were led into the inner sanctum.

On entering his office the first surprise was the fact that he was in his stocking feet which after introductions he planted on his desk. We told our story and we obviously sparked his interest as it was well known that James was intending to get out of the media business and create a world-wide gambling empire. He was already in partnership with Aspinalls, one of Britain's oldest casino operators whose founder had died only a few years earlier. After about an hour's discussion it was agreed that Crown would co-operate with us in putting together a paper with meaningful statistics to help the lobbying firm in Britain. It should be noted that at this point the lawmakers were still thinking along the lines of relaxing the licence procedure but still maintaining the boutique style premises that were already in place and adding more of the same.

With the assistance of the Crown staff we were able to quote figures like ten thousand jobs created during building stages of three to four years, then thirty thousand full time jobs once the complex was open and operating. Also take into account another ten thousand jobs in the community which would be servicing the complex that's the butchers, the bakers, candlestick makers etc. I was then invited back to England to present the project to the interested parties.

On arrival I was met with the good news that a site had been earmarked as available for the development in the seaside town of Redcar a town well known to me as it was where we spent our annual holidays as a family. It's only other claim to fame being the birthplace of the singer Chris Rea whose father owned the ice cream factory in Redcar and owned the ice cream vans that roamed the county before Mr. Whippy.

The site was the old Dorman Long steelworks on the river Tees opposite the ICI plant at Billingham, probably the ugliest river estuary in the country if not the world. Dorman Long had a connection with Australia in that they had built the Sydney Harbour Bridge. The company had been nationalised and became British Steel and eventually was taken over by the Dutch company Corus. The company was down on its knees unable to compete with cheaper steel coming out of Eastern Europe so the possibility of selling the land had great appeal to them. It was estimated that a billion pounds would be needed to clean up the land to a usable site for commercial interests. This didn't pose a major problem as the government already had legislation in place for such clean-up projects.

As I still have a sister living with her husband in Peterlee a town only twenty kilometres from Redcar I invited myself to stay with them and on telling them what I was doing there it was like the return of the prodigal son including thoughts of a knighthood in the family if the project ever got to completion.

There was another site mentioned and that was Redcar racecourse owned by Lady Zetland who would agree to a land swap if it became the chosen site.

First meetings were held at the North East England Regional Development Agency where the staff were enthusiastic and could see it made more sense to have one major job creation project rather than a piece meal approach to development.

The second day involved a meeting in the VIP lounge at Teeside airport with local MPs, lobbyists and a representative from Ryan Air. This idea had grown wings with all these big hitters involved with discussions on a major revamp of the road systems from the airport and the major motorways. Ryan Air promised daily flights in and out from all European cities with special emphasis on the Eastern European bloc. Telephone calls were made to ministers in London and it appeared that discussions had taken place using my model on construction of six or seven resort casinos in the depressed areas identified some years earlier making the assumption that even though it was easier to consider the major cities the mantra "Build it and they will come." had become the catch call. There was obviously some wheeling and dealing to be done and I could see some of it happening already in the lounge. The next day was a field trip around the district visiting current gambling venues which turned out to be massive bingo halls that had sprouted like mushrooms in the seventies and eighties. I remember one venue in particular as when five of us all wearing dark suits and ties left the car and on entering the lady who was obviously the day manager approached us saying she had rung the police so could we leave now. She had thought at first we were policemen but in second thoughts had decided we were stand over men and so had rung the police.

I returned to Sydney feeling quite satisfied with what I had put forward and no doubt full of my own self- importance as to potentially making historic social changes in my old locality and looking forward to the parliamentary debates that were to take place on casino regulations in the near future.

Some months later the legislation went through parliament, watered down and nothing like our proposal and all I could think was what a missed opportunity due to pressure groups with vested interests.

CHAPTER 41!

Dot Bombed!

So here we were staying in the very expensive Park Lane Hotel with eight thousand pounds cash in the wallet, ninety thousand dollars back in the bank in Sydney and a rosy future ahead of us. Lisa was off to Harrods as quickly as she could while I was picked up by a chauffeur driven limousine and escorted to the Barker Securities Plc. offices in Chelsea where I had to sign a number of documents, that I must admit, I didn't read, but was being assured everything was to my benefit. As I left the office I discovered I was Deputy Chairman of a FTSE company Maximusic.dotcom Plc. the owner of millions of shares and stock options worth at the time around a million pounds sterling, WE WERE RICH!!

The next five days were spent presenting to stockbrokers in their boardrooms all over London gaining support for the company and letting them know their clients were all looking to invest in dot com companies that were going to take over the financial world. Fortunately I am not a shy person and I felt comfortable making these presentations and we were assured of support for the stock. We only hit one snag and it was while presenting to about twenty brokers at Cannacord, a large city broker, when one of their brokers stopped all proceedings saying the dot com industry was a bubble and a confidence trick and there was no way that any sales figures could justify the valuation we had on the company. He stormed out slamming the door behind him. Everyone else in the room apologised for his boorish behaviour and promised to get as many of their clients involved that they could.

How prescient of that broker when we see what occurred in the future. However Lisa and I were not complaining as we were now living the high life we always thought we deserved and after a hectic ten days in London, a quick visit to the north east to see the family and we were on our way back to Sydney. The next few weeks were hectic with meetings in Australia with brokers and merchant bankers, all promising their support. Then we had to find someone to build the website and in those days there were a lot of carpetbaggers thinking as it was a new business they could con anyone out of massive sums and on hearing we were a listed company the prices seemed to reach unbelievable heights. After starting with a couple of groups that we found out were charlatans we settled on a young guy who said it was a very simple process and could be constructed for around five thousand dollars. After the others quoting between thirty and a hundred thousand dollars he was hired and in a couple of weeks we were on-line and ready to go. One thing I learnt very quickly in this short period of time was that there is absolutely no correlation between actual sales revenue and share price which determines the value of the company. Our marketing strategy was directed solely at raising the profile of the company which in turn had the desired effect on the share price. From being what is described as a penny dreadful the share price soared and it was now determined we would be going to the market to raise more capital. Note we had no sales at this point. I signed everything that was put in front of me and I trusted the chairman Ian Murray implicitly. There were no shenanigans or insider trading going on as we were not allowed to sell our stock as we had received it at no charge we had to wait twelve months before we could cash in. Things were going beautifully, the share price had increased nine fold and on one Thursday I worked it out I was worth nine million pounds in paper and a capital raising to be put to the market the following Thursday that could have raised the value to a potential 90 million.

Alas it was not to be.

Between the Thursday and the following Tuesday, Tuesday being the closing date for our capital raising, the dot-com bubble burst and my nine million pounds was worth nine hundred pounds, if I could have found a buyer. Being philosophical it was something I'd never had so I never missed it and I look back now and realise we did have a few months living the life of multi - millionaires. Also it was good to find out that my partners in the original company had made quite a killing. As part of taking over the music company I had given them free trading shares which they had sold at the top of the market.

From now on I was hooked on the stock market having seen what could be won and lost and I was determined not to waste any of the knowledge I had gained so I went back to college to learn how it worked properly and gained certification as a responsible executive and compliance officer. I was now ready for the big time.

One post script to this period came a few years later when a television channel ran an expose/documentary on a very infamous horse racing scandal known as the Fine Cotton Affair where one horse had been swapped for another to win a race in Brisbane. Some very colourful racing identities were involved in the scam. Some of the players were warned off racecourses in Australia for years, and to my surprise, large as life on the screen was the urbane Ian Murray who had been placing the bets for the major players in the rort while in Tasmania on holiday. He was referred to as 'The Silver Fox' and I couldn't think of a better name for him.

CHAPTER 42!

Long Kick To Freedom!

Then there was the time in 1987 when I was working for a television production company HM Productions in Chatswood a northern suburb of Sydney. The company had its own outside broadcasting facilities and a medium sized studio where Harry Michaels, the HM of the company title, is a Greek Australian television producer and director who pioneered Greek television in Australia. He is also a former actor and television host. He has been involved in the companies Harry Michaels Productions and zer0-1-zer0 (now known as Silk Studios) and at the time produced a comfortable money spinner programme Aerobics Oz Style. It consisted of 30 minute episodes of an aerobics instructress, June Jones, calling the shots in front of another six physically fit girls/women following her with the exercises. Interestingly enough one day in 2014 I saw one of the shows being repeated on a community channel. The schedule involved a fortnightly recording of ten episodes in one day which left everyone exhausted but it did keep production costs down.

It ended up helping to make Harry a very wealthy man as we sold it on to Sky in the U.K. and through Europe as pay television was gobbling up content, and the beast that was pay television had an insatiable appetite for any type of programmimg. What began as ten pounds per episode per broadcast per country grew into each episode being telecast four or five times a day in about 20 countries. When more episodes were needed than we were able to produce I came up with the idea that we recycle all the episodes but give them a new episode number and alter the date of recording on the identification frames at the head of each episode. Over three or four years no one noticed that we were re cycling the programmes and each one could have had four or five different identification numbers. It illustrated to me one of two things. Either no one ever watched the shows or alternatively the fashion styles of aerobics clothing never changed in that period.

However this story does not concern scantily clad ladies performing physical exercise on channel 10 at 6.30 every morning but is about one day in Melbourne when we were to produce a live telecast of Australia playing the English football champions of that year Everton. Don't think they've won anything since.

In the days leading up to the match there was a flurry of activity around the studio with solicitors turning up at all hours, threatening phone calls, shouting matches on who owned the rights to the television rights for Australia's games. Was it SBS, Soccer Australia or HM Productions. Reams of purported contracts and correspondence were being waved around and slammed on desks with no resolution in sight. Threats of night sittings in the Supreme Court were being bandied about but no-one even knew which state court held jurisdiction over these either legal or bogus contracts. Because all this had been done before I had been hired I had no idea where the truth lay but Jack Reilly, a former Australian goalkeeper and now a commissioner of Soccer Australia, and a very successful businessman at the time, was adamant that as they had contracted Everton it was their match to televise and on-sell the broadcast. Harry was undaunted and on the Tuesday put the OB van on the road to Melbourne and to the Olympic Park where the match was to be staged. We flew down that afternoon expecting fireworks on arrival and we weren't disappointed. Meetings in smoke filled hotel rooms came and went. I was then given instructions to ignore all that was going on and meet the OB van and crew at 7am the next morning at the Olympic Sports Ground, called that because it had been used for training and warm ups for the nineteen fifty six Melbourne Olympics which were held next door at the Melbourne Cricket Ground, and get everything and everyone set up while Harry would continue the heated negotiations.

The next morning I caught a taxi to the ground and as bold as brass got the chief groundsman to open up and off the trucks came the cameras, microphones, all cabled up to the outside broadcast van etc. The groundsman was aware that discussions were under way on rights but he couldn't make contact with anyone from Soccer Australia to get up to speed. He took my word for it that whoever won the contractual argument our facilities would be used to facilitate the broadcast. Only a small white lie, but I could convince myself that that's what would happen as we were settling in all the commentating facilities for the SBS sports journalists.

As is usual it takes about 5 hours to set up the equipment and we then locked in the transmission equipment for live-to-air on SBS-TV.

We were now ready to go which served us well as no-one else could be ready in the short time left.

The rest of the day was spent in checking and re-checking then when I was satisfied everything was in order my job was done and I made my way to the VIP lounge which I always knew had the free food and beer.

There were a number of' 'dignitaries' already in the lounge enjoying the hospitality and as it was in Melbourne most, if not all, were strangers to me, but I noticed one gentleman alone at the bar in a very expensive looking suit and his face was very familiar. I approached him and introduced myself and asked him if he had ever played football in England and in particular for the very successful amateur club Bishop Auckland. The response was positive and I knew it was the guy who played left-half for a number of years. He was a very memorable character for us growing up in the North East of England as he was a dark skinned Australian aborigine, a very exotic person. The North East of England had the least appeal for any immigrants and I can remember only two coloured students attending schools I attended over 15 years. Obviously we lived in the least attractive part of Britain.

Some information about Bishop Auckland Amateur Football Club will not go amiss as background. In those days professional footballers were on a maximum wage of 20 pounds per week so it was well known that you could earn more playing 'amateur' football for boot money, usually more than 20 pounds and tax free as it couldn't be disclosed. Bishop Auckland lured large crowds and won the Amateur Cup at Wembley Stadium more than any other club. Ten wins and eight losses at Wembley in the finals. They had the largest number of players in the England amateur team and were crowd pleasers in their two blues chequered strip. One little known fact about them is that in the two weeks following the Manchester United Munich disaster of 1958 which saw the majority of the 'Busby

Babes' as they were then known, killed returning from a European Cup game in Belgrade, most of the Bishop's team were offered contracts with Manchester United and a number took up the offer. As a sequel to this in the late nineties the club was going broke and about to be turfed out of Kingsway and a Bishop Auckland fan wrote a letter to Sir Alex Ferguson explaining their plight. No-one at Manchester United had memories of the gesture but when advised they sent a Manchester United team to play a testimonial and this testimonial match bailed the club out. When Old Trafford was being upgraded they gave their old floodlights to Bishop Auckland as another gesture of thanks. I explained to him my memories of these times and let him know how exotic he appeared to us kids in the North East and we talked a long time about those days. In fact we missed most of the match walking down memory lane as he explained he was living in Manchester at the time and he and Harry Sharrat the goalkeeper used to drive to the North East every week and that was the extra money they needed to get through life in the North West of England.

He was also a real Anglophile. He loved Britain. It had been so good to him and he told me it was the first time in his life he had been treated as an equal and even confessed to being treated as more than an equal by English girls.

Then we swapped tales of our playing careers in Australia. His was a bit more spectacular than mine, but we discovered we had some mutual playing partners despite the age difference.

To me I was talking to a childhood football hero of mine, little did I know how important a personality was Charlie Perkins in Australia but I soon learnt!

CHAPTER 43!

Shiver Me Timbers!

So having scored a slight victory over the major record companies we thought we should probably take some legal advice to ensure there would be no more charges of piracy levelled against us. Fortunately we found Robert Scard a solicitor who had just opened his new practice after working as in house legal counsel for Sony Music and the first thing he gave me was a twelve page booklet called Guide To Music Copyright in Australia. This wasn't going to gain me a law degree but it did outline all procedures necessary to stay on the right side of the law including royalty payments and record keeping. It was while browsing through this tiny, Copyright for Idiots, booklet, one paragraph jumped off the page, and to say I was surprised doesn't afford any description of my real shock. The paragraph referred to the Treaty of Rome 1960 Copyright Act. The reason it jumped off the page to me was due to the fact as a schoolboy I was in Rome in 1960 for the Olympic Games. I read it over and over again. It was the actual quotation from the act that stated that no artist/performer royalties existed on recordings of live performances. That is not to say composers rights were cancelled, only the artists performances. I checked this out with Robert our counsel and he agreed with me. There was no ambiguity in what it said. Artists are not due to any royalties on recordings of live performances and it also applied to any performances that had been broadcast live through television or radio. He was more surprised than I was as to how this loophole in the law still existed. How could we utilise this?

We were aware that in Italy there were departments in their record stores with the title Bootlegs and they were live performances so we sent our junior, Frank, off to Italy to buy as many CD's as he could in these stores and bring them back to Australia. Frank was back within a week with a suitcase full of CD's from the world's top artists all performing live. These were not recordings made by a member of the public with a small recorder, they were all professional quality recordings from artists such as Michael Jackson, ABBA, U2, Beatles, Madonna, all in all over a hundred titles. It was decided we would put on the CD cover that the recordings were UNAUTHORISED by the artists and we printed UNAUTHORISED twice the size of any other information on the slick so there could be no doubt about what we were doing and were not misleading consumers.

We did have one major problem in that we knew the normal music outlets would not stock them for fear of retribution from the major record companies so we looked for alternatives. Before we began pressing the CD's we approached the two dollar shop owners and asked if they would be interested. They jumped at the opportunity and unbeknown to most people these chains of bargain shops all worked together when it came to purchasing product. We decided to launch with fifty titles and expected to manufacture about five hundred of each and two hundred cassettes. Imagine our surprise when the order arrived for two hundred and eighty thousand CD's and a hundred thousand cassettes.

On receiving the order we went into action. First up we set aside funds for composer's royalties and maintained meticulous records for APRA. We arranged for our CD supplier to begin manufacturing as soon as possible and let us know when delivery was. We swore him to secrecy as he had contracts with the majors and to keep heavy security on our product as the last thing we wanted was to be discovered before the product went out. Our reasoning being that if the majors cottoned on to what we were doing before the product was distributed and paid for, they could slap injunctions on us that would send us broke. When the goods were ready the subterfuge continued as we rented out a number of storage sheds from Millers Storage a few suburbs away from our warehouse and when it came time for packaging the goods into boxes of a hundred we hired a dozen backpackers at ten dollars cash per hour to do the picking and packing. They obviously didn't know what we were doing was something a little borderline and they were happy to get a weeks work in for cash payment. Come the day for despatch the McPhees trucks arrived and out went over a hundred pallets packed with CD's and cassettes. At the time there was price fixing in the Australian music industry which kept prices at a very inflated level around thirty dollars a CD. Our costings were similar to theirs at one dollar for pressing, printing and packaging plus the composer's royalties we were able to wholesale at five dollars for a ten dollar retail price point. The product went flying out of the stores and within a week we had orders, again from the two dollar shops, for the same again. They paid us up front so we paid APRA for the composers. We repeated the operation including adding another twenty titles to the mix and so it came as no little surprise when the proverbial hit the fan. Fortunately it took the majors a few months to swing into action and by then we were comfortable financially and prepared for any legal action.

During this time we were contacted by a Los Angeles based music distributor who had followed our story and having made contact with us placed orders for a Japanese music distributor. Their story was that they had taken the advice that we were acting legally on an international basis but they couldn't convince local manufacturers to produce the product. So on a weekly basis they would send us a list of titles with orders for one thousand of each and they would pay on order for everything including freight. That means money up front. They even created compilations of different artists each singing one track each, along The Greatest Hits type of album. This was a good way to make money. We never saw or handled the product. On receipt of payment we supplied our manufacturer with a master disc and as soon as they were pressed the transport company picked them up at the factory gate and off they went to America or Japan.

After a few deliveries, which were working for all parties involved, they decided they'd like to call on us in Australia and thank us. So it was arranged that they would fly in from Los Angeles and Tokyo the next week and we would give them the guided tour of all our facilities and treat them to all the pleasures Sydney had to offer.

They were staying at the Park Hyatt and I agreed to meet them at their hotel on the Friday morning and then grab some lunch at our favourite restaurant, The Mixing Pot in Glebe.

My normal work clothing was fit for warehouse work, which usually amounted to shorts, t-shirts and sturdy boots and I would usually drive a diesel fuelled, two tone grey, Nissan Patrol workhorse but because of our overseas visitors this day I dressed up in my best linen pants and casual shirt topped off with my three hundred dollar Ray Bans and I drove my white Jaguar convertible XJ sports car meaning to impress our clients.

After meeting up with them for coffee I then headed to the warehouse in Balmain and as I pulled up outside the loading bay I stepped out into a pack of pressmen with TV cameras rolling and journalists firing questions at me. I must have looked like a Colombian drug lord or at the least a music pirate. After forcing my way past the horde, in the warehouse were over a dozen people compiling lists of everything in the offices and warehouse. Bob, my partner was in his office like a stunned mullet and letting these people, who by now I had found out were federal police officers, have free reign throughout the premises. Had he rang our solicitor? No. I told him to do that now then I asked who was in charge then demanded that all action stop until I had read the warrant for the search. Turned out Sony and Polygram had issued writs against us for piracy and with it being a federal criminal offence they had called the federal police, followed soon after by a few calls to the press, and all hell had broken loose. One would have thought it was the criminal bust of the decade. Incidentally I then remembered there was about thirty thousand dollars in cash in my desk drawer being takings from some market operators who preferred to pay that way. I made a few noises and did a bit of nit picking on the warrant noticing offices were not mentioned only warehouse and storage along with our manufacturer's premises which were being raided simultaneously, then went into my office, stuck the cash down my trouser fronts and made my way to the coffee shop next door and asked him to look after these envelopes for a couple of hours. Sounds risky but in those times you'd probably have trusted a stranger more than a policeman when cash is around. Our solicitor had arrived by now and he took charge. Then a magic moment. The officer in charge had picked up a ledger and was thumbing through it and he asked me what it was. When I told him it was our schedule of payments to APRA he realised they had over reacted and slowed down all the action while he discussed it with the Anti-Piracy representative who had come along with them as advisor. Because they were now committed he ordered stickers to be put on all the 'suspect' pirate copies which meant they had been impounded and we couldn't sell them or even give them away.

All this time I had forgotten about our overseas visitors so I asked Bob to pick them up and not bring them to the warehouse as previously arranged, imagine the scene that could have greeted them, and take them direct to the Mixing Pot. Things quietened down, the press and television had lost interest when they had been told what was really going on, everyone left and I arrived late for lunch without missing a beat and carried on as if it was a normal Friday. I'd told Antonio in the warehouse to move the stock around to hide the stickers so when we arrived back after lunch no-one would have suspected the goings on of the morning.

CHAPTER 44

Burn Baby Burn!

So here we are two people who loved football drinking beer in the VIP section of Melbourne Olympic Park waiting for the Australia versus Everton game to kick off. Reminiscing a lot about the North East of England which Charlie had loved all the time he was there then the conversation drifted around to our own football careers. It just so happened I'd missed playing with him for Bankstown in the NSW State League as he had retired in 1965 three years before I signed with them. At the time it didn't mean much to me that we were left on our own with cursory acknowledgements from other VIPs but it made sense some months later when I got to understand just who Charlie Perkins was. When I asked him if he was still playing he said he wasn't as he thought he was far too old and it was then I told him about a pick-up game that went on every Sunday morning ten am kick off, don't dare to be late, and all were invited. The game was played every Sunday morning at Lyne Park in Rose Bay one of Sydney's most affluent suburbs and has been there for over fifty years without missing a beat. When I mentioned that there were guys well into their sixties taking part alongside comparative youngsters like myself he sounded interested. I then mentioned a couple of names, Frank Hearn, former Crystal Palace and Australia, Roy Blitz, Portsmouth and Australia, Johnny Roosenthal, Matt Guildea a former New Zealand international, along with a number of retired professionals. The games had been going on for about forty years at the time and even if Christmas was on a Sunday the game went on, that's how keen these Golden Oldies were. Well it turned out Charlie knew all these guys and had played with and against a number of them. His surprise at the fact that they were still running around, I corrected him on that, no-one could ever say they were 'running', was enough to ignite the flame and he would be at Lyne Park on New South Head Rd. Rose Bay this coming Sunday.

True to his word the following Sunday he turned up with his young grandson Tyson.

There was back slapping all round as this bunch of old warriors of the football field reminisced. It was the custom that after the match we all met at the Golden Sheaf hotel in Double Bay for beers and Charlie joined us there where he had his favourite ale, Guinness.

The week after he turned up for the game with a newly purchased pair of football boots and from then on he was a regular whenever he was in Sydney. It was during the sessions in the Sheaf that I was able to find out about his political career as the first aborigine to graduate from a university and the first to head up a Commonwealth Government department. A lot of people think that Charlie was a politician which is false in that he was a public servant. There was also his history as a leader in the aboriginal civil rights movement where he was said to be Australia's equivalent of Nelson Mandela without the prison term. As time went on he would tell us about his fight with the Prime Minister of the time, Bob Hawke, about some dealings with a licensed club in the Australian Capital Territory which were affecting his position in the public service. It is history now that soon after he resigned under pressure and began a new career as a consultant to business on aboriginal matters such as land title etc.

It was during one of these afternoons in the Sheaf that he told us he was to appear on a midday television show the next day and how he was going to give it to the hostess Kerri Anne Kennerley who had made some unfavourable comments about him. We tried to talk him out of being aggressive and after three or four Guinness he agreed.

What happened the next day is folklore as he went on a verbal rampage describing the viewers of the programme as a bunch of the blue rinse set who had no opinions worth listening to and finished off with his never to be forgotten line that if nothing was done to assist the aborigines it would be 'Burn Baby Burn'. So much for our talk in the pub. He made headlines around the nation and was remembered for all time.

Anyhow he continued to play with us on the Sundays and the game was starting to attract some celebrities including David Hill the managing director of the ABC, Graeme Souness former Liverpool and Scottish international hard man, Massaro from an Italian world cup final team and a number of visiting English rock stars. One German guy known as Ziggy had us all convinced that he was the East German soldier famously photographed jumping to freedom to West Berlin. We never verified that it was him but it was a good story anyway. There is always a game, rain, hail or shine. Christmas Day or Mother's Day no exceptions.

We also found out that he was the longest post-kidney transplant survivor anywhere in the world and for that reason his wife Eileen would only allow him ten dollars if he was going to the pub with us. For that reason he copped a whole lot of teasing about the fact that he never bought drinks for anyone else but he made up for it about four times a year when we were all invited to his home in Newtown for barbecue lunches. We remained friends for years and Eileen and Charlie were guests at our wedding which certainly impressed the in-laws. At the wedding he took me aside and told me how grateful he was that he had met me in Melbourne that night and convinced him to take up playing football again as he described it he was going through a major crisis in his life at the time and had considered suicide on a number of occasions and his counsellor had asked him if there was anything in life he really looked forward to. He told him it was playing football on a Sunday and the counsellor quickly told him that that should be enough to keep on living. I must say there was a tear or two shed between us and it was one of those moments when I felt very proud of myself.

It was in 2000 when the kidney disease reared its ugly head and Charlie was admitted to Prince Henry Hospital at Randwick he knew the end was coming and when I visited him I took him a couple of books one of which was Nelson Mandela's Long Walk To Freedom. Imagine my surprise when he told me he had never read a book in his life, a surprise considering he was a university graduate.

When he died he was afforded a State funeral which was held in Sydney Town Hall with hundreds of dignitaries and us footballing friends. Afterwards there was to be a freedom march to the Sydney Opera House for the wake in which a few thousand took part walking through Hyde Park and the Domain. As we left the town hall my mobile phone alerted me to an SMS message I'd received and when I opened it it was from my son Durham who had been watching the service on television and knowing Charlie was to be cremated he sent me the message 'Burn Baby Burn' as a tribute to the man he had grown to know very well. I saw the humour in it and turned to the man walking beside me and I showed him the message he laughed with me and then I recognised him it was Sir William Deane the Australian Governor General.

Thank you Charlie.

CHAPTER 45

She Was Only Sixteen!

Then there was the time in 1981 when I had my own television production company, The Production Factory, named because of the sheer number of television commercials we produced weekly. Our clients included K-tel, Telmak, and Concept records for whom we produced their retail commercials usually about six a week, not major productions as they usually required editing together parts of the artist's video clips with a voice over spitting out the titles of the songs and artists in these compilations. Not very creative but quite lucrative. We also produced corporate videos and the odd pop video clip.

We had quite a reputation amongst the record companies for bringing in product quickly and on budget and as such we were usually invited to the promotional functions for visiting rock acts or record launches. So it was no surprise when I received a phone call from Sam Hamilton, promotional director for Polygram music, asking for a favour. It turned out that they were hosting a function for Dr. Hook and the Medicine Show to launch their Australian tour at a country music venue in Chinatown that evening and they had only realised that only men had been invited and they needed ladies to soften the function.

Free dinner and drinks, no strings attached and as I was involved in producing television commercials I should know a few attractive models to make up the numbers. Not a problem as only the day before our director of photography, Fitz, and myself had been at a party with a bunch of models in North Sydney so did Fitz have a contact number and if so get in touch with them and make the offer. He jumped at the opportunity and came back thirty minutes later with a list of names from Viviens model agency who had agreed to turn up. No problem so far until my phone rang and it was Viviens wanting to discuss fees for the ladies which had never been in anyone's thoughts till then.

I was able to reassure the agent that the event was all above board but there was no budget available but I promised all my work for the next twelve months for models.

The agent agreed and put me under a threat worse than the inquisition if anything was to go wrong and I was to be responsible for the girls' well-being. They were to ask for Cliff on arrival and I had to promise they would get dinner and drinks, but not too much.

Deal done could now get back to work, assured Sam there would be ladies attending and he owed me the next two compilation commercials for my efforts. Little did I know I was to receive a much bigger, if not my life's biggest reward that same evening.

Come 6pm off I went to the function. Arrived a little early and at the bar was a former friend of mine, John Brommel, head of Warner Chappel music publishing. I say former friend as some two years ago I arranged for my girlfriend of the time to be hired by John and would you believe it, of course, he stole her away, in hindsight I should have thanked him but at the time it seemed like a betrayal. However this night John was at the bar looking miserable as sin with a beer in his hand and he invited me for a drink, he even offered to pay for it before he realised it was a fully catered event.

Apologies all round, shaking of hands and let's be friends, yes, she had left him that very same day for another man hence the forlorn look as he spoke of his regrets for leaving his wife and family. I had met his wife and son some years earlier at a barbecue in their backyard and it turned out to be an interesting afternoon as a friend of his, quite a famous performer, Digger Revell and John came to blows. Rolling around in the grass we had to separate them. Without any of us knowing what it was about things calmed down eventually. Maybe it could have been related to the same Digger being a guest of Her Majesty for dealing in the marketing and sales of marijuana.

I was able to half cheer him up by telling him how good single life had been since his betrayal and he'd get over it. The function was now filling up and we were now the best of buddies again when the maitre-de approached me and asked if I was Cliff. My response obviously being yes, well can I come to the front door as some people were using my name to get admission. At the door was a vision to behold. Eight of the most beautiful creatures you could ever imagine, all asking for Cliff.

In they came, I couldn't resist it, straight to the bar to introduce my renewed friend John to these beautiful young women and by now he was looking so gob-smacked I thought his jaw would hit the ground.

The girls were well behaved but had decided they were going to stretch the joke on Cliff for the rest of the evening. Every time they wanted a drink they would ask for Cliff as instructed by their agent. If anyone asked them to dance they told the guys they had to ask Cliff. This even applied to the stars themselves so I was soon the best friend of Ray Sawyer, he's the one with the eye patch, and Dennis Locorriere, he's the one with the beard, as everyone had to ask permission from Cliff. Sounds like I was acting a bit like a New York pimp but I didn't have the bling or attitude but the joke was certainly going down well but I certainly had an inflated ego and swagger as the evening wore on. By now John Brommel was looking forward to his new single status.

As the event was drawing to a close the suggestion went around for a late night visit to The Cauldron, Sydney's number one nightspot of the time, and of course' Cliff's girls were high on the invitation list.

The limousines arrived and we all piled in and headed for Kings Cross with the girls still hanging on to the joke and not doing anything without asking Cliff.

Into the VIP lounge we were led, more free drinks courtesy of Polygram, lots of flirting going on, yes, I was guilty of it too. Amongst the girls was one in particular stood out but she was either too shy or too beautiful and haughty for me to approach but circumstances had us sitting next to each other.

When she whispered to me that as it was getting late she needed to go home or she would be in trouble with her father. Being the older, wiser, I have since learnt these two qualities do not necessarily go together, person I suggested that fathers only worry about their daughters and she should give him a call to tell him where she was and in safe company.

I provided the forty cents for the pay phone, remember mobile phones not yet in every person on the globe's hands, but she returned crestfallen as her father had demanded she get home immediately.

I had never even asked her name. I arranged for a taxi, never even got to know her name

and that was the end of that.

Or so I thought..................

CHAPTER 46!

Hubble Bubble Mama Mimi!

Then there was the time at Mimi's an Italian restaurant in Darlinghurst the suburb adjoining Sydney's centre of sin, Kings Cross. It was summer of 1984 and we used to frequent a night club, The Cauldron, usually on Tuesdays and Sundays. We were an arrogant lot being television producers and directors and making certain everyone in the bar knew so, especially budding television models. We avoided Fridays and Saturdays as they were the nights out for 'The Westies' now referred to as Bogans. The Cauldron was owned and managed by a dapper gentleman, Charles, who was very particular about his clientele, particular in the fact that you had to look as if you were able to pay his exorbitant prices, which encouraged not quite your young crowd that worked the stock exchange, more the car dealers and drug dealers with their flash cars parked ostentatiously in the no standing zones but in sight of the girls queuing up in the lane for entry. This was also the early days of bling even though it wasn't called that then. Probably should point out that Fitz, my best friend at the time, drove a convertible Porsche and I drove a Mercedes four fifty SL sports car but we will deny to our dying days we were flashy, just cool. Even wore Gucci sneakers.

The Cauldron, along with Rogues, were the two most exclusive nightspots in Sydney at the time and I can remember literally bumping in to many famous personalities including after the cricket one Tuesday evening there was Mick Jagger, Elton John and David Bowie chatting with Michael Parkinson at the bar. No-one bothered them and unbelievably they were paying for their own drinks. Another time I was in the crowded bar not realising who was standing beside me when the guy on my right asked me if I would introduce him to my friend George who was standing on my left. I looked to the left to check out who 'my friend' was when I recognised him as Doctor George Peponis, Australia's rugby league captain. Unfazed I tapped him on the shoulder and introduced him to the guy on my right who shook his hand introducing himself as Alan. Would you believe it I had just introduced Australia's rugby league skipper to Alan Border, Australia's cricket captain. For the next hour or so I was in the middle of the conversation, enjoying their hospitality, that is free beer, when Alan Border went to the bathroom and George asked me how I knew Alan. When I explained the story they both had a good laugh as they had both thought I was a friend of the other. Then there was the night I was making my way past the queue of wannabes when a voice with an American accent was heard asking how one got in this joint. I told them they were my guests so come to the front. How surprised can one be when I find myself with Sylvester Stallone and two young ladies hanging off his arm. First impression was how short he is. However Charles cleared the doorway and created a VIP area and the beer and wine flowed. Worrying what my wife would say when I got home so late 'Rocky' told his sidekick to get his limousine driver to take me home. Thinking I wouldn't be believed I made the driver wait outside in the driveway so I could wake Lisa up so she could see the limousine. There are many other stories associated with the Cauldron but this is a story of a night we didn't go there.

It was late on a Sunday evening and I was with Fitz, our cinematographer and two beautiful girls, Lisa and Vicki all of 17 years old and TV and fashion models. Would not call this dating as we believed we were far too old at 38 for these girls to be interested in us, even if we were producing TV commercials for a living. We were two very modest characters at the time. We decided to go to Mimi's the Italian restaurant next to the Cauldron on Victoria street even though it was around 11pm. The place was closing but seeing we were regulars they let us in provided we'd eat and drink and be out in 30 minutes. Downstairs we went, doors closed behind us and a table for four with no choice of the menu but to eat the pasta they gave us. That wasn't a worry as their pasta was probably the best in Sydney.

It was noticeable that besides ourselves there was only one other group of three still drinking away at their table and much to our surprise they invited us to join them for drinks. At the time I would have believed that they were interested in talking with Fitz and myself but nowadays with some hindsight I'm certain it was Vicky and Lisa that attracted their attention, not Fitz and myself.

Imagine my surprise when on joining them I realised it was Justice Lionel Murphy, High Court judge, former Attorney-General in the Whitlam Government, instigator of the Family Law Court, leader of raids on ASIO along with Senator John Button and another lady who faded into the background alongside such bright stars. Not including ourselves in such company, bright stars that is.

The red wine was flowing and it became very obvious as to why Justice Murphy had the bulbous nose usually associated with drinkers like W.C. Fields. As we were at their table we made the assumption that they were paying so even though we were not red wine drinkers we forced ourselves to enjoy their hospitality.

Changed my life. I've been drinking red wine ever since. Justice Murphy turned out to be very charming, did not try to hog the conversation and at times even acknowledged us two guys as well as the two beautiful ladies. He also seemed genuinely interested in what younger people were looking for in Australia and kept reassuring us that they would value our opinions on what we hoped our politicians could do for the country

It was now getting very late and the wine and conversation were flowing but we had to remember we had two very young ladies to return home to their families and having had Lisa some weeks before being told off by her father for staying out late. She had told me her father was a Labor voter so I convinced her he would be impressed by the fact that she had been eating dinner with Senator Button and Justice Murphy.

The other lady at the table had been looking very disinterested in the conversation until the Justice remarked on his current position sitting on the Lindy Chamberlain appeal to the High Court of Australia for a hearing in the High Court. She was trying to close the conversation, pay the bill and obviously was uncomfortable with the direction the conversation was heading. To no avail, Justice Murphy had something he wished to say along with another bottle of red to drink.

Senator Button, who had been enjoying the evening began to make a move but Lionel, that's what we were able to call him by now as his new best friends, ordered another bottle of red and in our slightly inebriated state we couldn't refuse no matter how hard Lisa and Vicki tried to get us moving. Our 30 minutes was now over two hours.

It was becoming obvious to me that the lady and Senator Button were becoming very worried about how they could finish the dinner and get the Justice out of the restaurant before too much more was said.

Within a few minutes it became clear why they were concerned.

What Justice Murphy then told us was a real shock.

CHAPTER 47!

Evie Part 4!

So having arranged for the taxi home for Lisa from the Doctor Hook reception I thought no more of it and got on with life which at the time was producing and directing television commercials and rock videos. However Fitzy our cinematographer had kept in touch with her best friend Vicky another young television and fashion model and a few weeks later Lisa and Vicky turned up at a party we were at and I was taken by surprise that they remembered my name and the telephone call between Lisa and her father.

At this party I spent some time with Lisa but never for a moment thought there could be anything between us because of the age difference however in the next few weeks there were a lot of coincidences when Vicky and Lisa turned up at places which we frequented and some places we didn't.

I took the plunge and asked her out to the movies and was surprised that she wouldn't let me pick her up at her home but chose to meet me in the city where we saw a double feature of Poltergeist and Raiders of the Lost Ark. Over the next few couple of weeks we met a few times, nothing passionate or romantic, or so I thought, and the longer she wouldn't allow me to pick her up from her home my thoughts were that she was either ashamed of me or worried what her parents would think about this much older man. I would pick her up beside the Eastern Suburbs cemetery.

Then one Friday we arranged to go for dinner at Martin's Bar, a well-known night spot on Oxford street. Martin's was a bar/restaurant with a speakeasy decor and atmosphere including the black front door with a peephole that only Martin himself was allowed to use. He was famous for his photographic memory and I can recall him recognising me by name on my second visit some eighteen months after my first. During the day I had been directing some filming for Alberts Music, the home of AC/DC, John Paul Young, The Easybeats, Ted Mulry Gang and a full stable of other artists being produced by George Young and Harry Vanda.

As an aside, that very same day a Dutch music magazine were in Alberts for interviews and photographs with Flash and The Pan, a recording name for George and Harry that were number one in Europe at the time with their hit 'Hey Saint Peter' and AC/DC who were recording in the studio that day. The Dutch wanted a picture of the band, but there was no band! Flash and The Pan was only George and Harry. So Ted Mulry and I were drafted into the band picture. Somewhere in the world there's a photograph of Flash and The Pan featuring yours truly.

This Friday afternoon after finishing the shoot Stevie Wright, who was working at the time at Alberts as a promotions manager, and myself went to the pub next door and had a few beers discussing next week's work which was to include a video clip for John Paul Young, well known at the time for his global number one, Love Is In The Air. Turned out he had written a song about Kingston Town, a very famous racehorse of the time, called Get A Beer For The Horse which we shot in the Grand National Hotel in Paddington where they actually brought Kingston Town to the pub for the shoot. Some background on Stevie Wright for non-followers of rock n roll history was formerly billed as Little Stevie, an Australian musician and songwriter who has been called Australia's first international pop star. During 1964–1969 he was lead singer for Sydney-based rock and roll band The Easybeats, widely regarded as the greatest Australian pop band of the 1960s. His solo career included the 1974 single, "Evie (Parts 1, 2 & 3)", which peaked at No. 1 on the Australian Music Singles Chart. Stevie has had problems with alcohol and drug addictions, by 1976 he was hospitalised and undertook methadone treatment, and in the late 1970s he was treated at Chelmsford Private Hospital by Dr Harry Bailey who administered Deep Sleep Therapy with a combination of drug-induced coma and electro shock. Stevie himself told us the story of him waking up in the middle of the therapy and 'escaping' only to be caught naked hiding in the bushes somewhere in the middle class suburb of Beecroft.

Stevie had been a massively successful teenage rock star but had hit the hard drugs and life took a really bad turn for the worse which ended up with him in re-hab and working with the Salvation Army. George and Harry took him under their wing and launched Stevie Wright as a solo artist with one of Australia's biggest ever hits Evie. After another relapse and more re-hab, Alberts, taking care of their own, gave him a job as Promotions Director and as a result we had become very good friends.

So as I explained I was going out to dinner that night with a 'potential new girlfriend' he invited himself along and said he'd bring a date with him.

He made his telephone call and then I realised I was running late so we jumped into my car and off we went to meet Lisa at the cemetery gates. On arriving at the cemetery nature called on both of us and we were desperate for a toilet so throwing caution to the wind I knocked on the door. Lisa's mother opened the door. I introduced myself then Stevie and asked to use the bathroom. Over her shoulder I could see Lisa holding back hysterics and her two sisters looking to see who this mystery boyfriend was and what he looked like. As I used the bathroom Stevie started to play the piano in the front hallway, remember we had had a few drinks, and to this day Lisa's mum still brags that Stevie Wright serenaded her on her piano with a rendition of Evie. Lisa hurried us out of the house as quickly as she could and off we went to dinner. Stevie still had one surprise up his sleeve. On arriving at the restaurant much to our surprise, but not his, his dinner date was waiting, and the joker had invited my previous girlfriend, the one who had left me for her boss mentioned in a previous chapter, the night I first met Lisa. Stevie had done it on purpose without telling her it was me they were dining with. A tense situation for a little while and as I found out later that evening the former girlfriend had whispered to Lisa to get away from me as any other man would treat her like a princess. From that day on I have always referred to Lisa as 'Princess'.

CHAPTER 48

Who Took The Baby?

So there we were after midnight in Mimi's restaurant and a more diverse group you could never find sitting at the same table anywhere in the world. A High Court Judge, a member of the Australian Senate, a failed rock singer now working as a cameraman, a schoolteacher now a nearly famous TV producer, two fashion and television models aged sixteen or seventeen, not old enough to drink, and another lady who said very little but we assumed she was a solicitor as she was obviously close to Justice Murphy. All five of drinking age were in different stages of inebriation due to the free flowing red wine. The restaurant was now closed and as usual the manager and the barman are looking very impatient as Lionel kept ordering the red wine. The conversation was being led by the Justice and contrary to his image as a professional politician, he was asking questions, not pontificating as most politicians do in their misplaced and exaggerated view of their own importance. His main concern appeared to be what did the next generation seek from their leaders. To his surprise Lisa and Vicki, the young models, told him they expected nothing, they would do things for themselves. What followed was a discussion on the lack of leadership being shown anywhere in the world with the justice and the senator nodding sagely at the views of the next generation. Thank heavens we were all inclined to the left side of politics, either by our own volition or what parents had said in front of us. So no major arguments erupted. The conversation, again led by Justice Murphy turned to our legal system and what part it played in our lives. I was able to flatter him by telling him I was one of the very first divorce cases held under the Family Law Court which had been a major change in the law sponsored by Lionel Murphy.

I hadn't been too happy at the time but hindsight gave me a much better perspective on the result. Now we could see Senator Button and the other lady getting slightly agitated as he started to talk about how privileged he was to serve his country in his position as a High Court Judge. The conversation moved along at a pace till he came to his current trial. He took some time explaining how judges had to make decisions according to the law that was in front of them and only parliament could alter laws. The girls were now yawning if not asleep already. Take for instance his work at the time was one of a High Court appeal with three members of the High Court, including himself, by Lindy Chamberlain, who was seeking permission to lodge an appeal in the High Court as all her legal trials and appeals were under Northern Territory law, territories under the constitution came under federal government law. The Lindy Chamberlain saga is now Australian folk lore and was even turned into a movie, Evil Angels, starring Meryl Streep with probably her only failure at accents in her career. Lindy Chamberlain a New Zealand-born Australian woman who was at the centre of one of Australia's most publicised murder trials.

Originally accused and convicted of killing her nine-week old daughter, Azaria, while camping at Uluru (then known as Ayers Rock) in 1980, she maintained that she saw a dingo leave the tent where Azaria slept on the night she disappeared. Eight years later, her conviction was overturned after the discovery of new evidence, and both she and her then husband Michael Chamberlain were acquitted of all charges. She was adjudged wrongly convicted after having spent three years in prison for murdering her baby, and having given birth to her fourth child while a prisoner. In 1992, she received $1.3 million compensation from the Australian government for wrongful imprisonment. As the result of a fourth inquest in 2012, an Australian coroner made a ruling that a dingo had indeed taken baby Azaria from the campsite in 1980 and had caused her death.

Unasked for, or should I say he blurted out, how sad he was that he had to adhere to law as it is written as in his words. "She killed the baby, of course she did, we all know she did, but that's not what we are there for. We have to make a decision in law and I just hope we don't help in setting her free."

At the time it was not an earth shattering moment but what it did do was close down the conversation as the senator and friend decided that was enough and we made our thanks and goodbyes and to the relief of the restaurant staff out we went.

The first good thing that came out of this is that once Lisa had told her father she had been socialising with Lionel Murphy and John Button I became a bit more acceptable to him as he was, and still is, a staunch Labor Party supporter. Thought nothing more about it till some months later when the High Court tabled its judgement on the appeal and the other two judges voted to dismiss the action with Justice Murphy dissenting on a point of law, and she should be allowed to appeal. I thought at the time that at least he was honourable in sticking to principles of law rather than what he actually believed to be true.

CHAPTER 49

Just P.M. Tension!

While working for HM productions, as written about earlier, I received a call from a Stefan Kamasz, who headed up Soccer Australia, the body that governed and managed, or mismanaged, depending on who you spoke to, about their annual presentation of awards for the season just finished. They had a problem in that as this was Monday the awards were planned for the coming Friday at a black tie event to be held in the Grand Freemasons Lodge in Goulburn St. in the city. The problem was that they only had a hall booked and nothing else. SBS television were to televise the event live and both parties believed the other had taken care of all the preparations. As was usual in soccer circles at this time no-one had done anything, so in comes the Lone Ranger, me, to the rescue and I accepted the brief for the princely sum of $1000 for the weeks work. This didn't suit Harry Michaels of HM productions and he fired me again. Worth noting here that Harry said "You're Fired" to me more times in two years than you would hear it watching Donald Trump featuring in The Apprentice on television. A very volatile relationship you've gathered. No worries, he always called to get me back, so back into live production I went.

Working out of Soccer Australia's Sydney city office it became impossible to get a decision on anything as administration was in Sydney but the board all were based in Melbourne including the Chairman Sam Papasavas. No money could be spent without his approval even for taxi cabs. It was a case of taking the bull by the horns and making up my own budget and making all decisions myself, which were never questioned or remarked upon. It appeared to me that the feeling was the event was going to be a disaster and people were distancing themselves so I, as the outsider, would cop any flak afterwards.

But not to be perturbed I ploughed on, booked Vince Sorrenti a comedian of Italian heritage, notice name finishing with a vowel, as host for the evening. Televised part of the evening was to be hosted by Les Murray the SBS soccer guru, at which point I realised there were no trophies organised. Got a list of awards, drove to trophy shop in Willoughby and arranged for trophies to be delivered to Grand Hall on the Friday. Had to pay extra, sorry, Soccer Australia had to pay extra for ordering with such short notice. Sent my wife Lisa, one of Australia's top models of the time, to the most expensive dress shop in Double Bay to borrow an evening dress so she could hand the trophies to the presenters. Should say she looked a million dollars as usual, she didn't need haute couture. Everything appeared to be coming together with nothing more than about four panic situations a day including the one I vowed to stay away from. The seating plan. In the short week I was employed what I found out was that in the world of the beautiful game the politics, friendship, hatreds, old grudges, and new grudges took over everything when decisions had to be made. Then an article appeared in a scandal sheet suggesting that the Prime Minister was having an affair with Mrs. Papasavas. What else could happen before Friday?

Back to the seating plan. When I was told the guest of honour was the Prime Minister that's when I put my foot down on seating arrangements. Someone from Soccer Australia had to make the decisions on who sat where. I arranged name place cards for all the guests that were on the acceptance list then left them in the Soccer Australia office with the table plan and instructions that I needed someone to arrange seating placements. This was going to be more difficult than a wedding when both sets of parents are divorced but I had a little faith in that they could do this one thing.

Friday arrived. Early morning start around 7am with the television bump in and set up, tables to be set with cutlery napkins etc. staging to be arranged and things appeared to be going smoothly. Fortunately for me the head of sports at SBS was a very good friend of mine Dominic Galati. So that meant for all of the Friday things went smoothly and we were all set up and ready around 5pm for a 7.30 kick off. Time for having a quiet beer. Yes you guessed it. Where were the place cards and the seating plan to be posted outside the hall? Nowhere to be found. Calls to Soccer Australia shed no light. All staff had gone home to dress up for the occasion and obviously no-one had bothered to look at the plan.

Guests were now starting to arrive, cocktails were flowing in the reception area, I was panicking. Then Stefan Kamasz arrived and off he raced back to the office, picked up the plan and the place cards and at 6.30pm we scrambled to arrange as best we could and at about 7pm we were able to open the doors and let the guests find their places. Bear in mind the television part of the show was to be live to air at 8pm.

I was still in my t-shirt, jeans and work boots relieved that my part was now finished, everything was looking good and I could relax and take my time to have a cold drink, then get changed into my tuxedo and sit back and enjoy what I had created. Not quite!

I feel a tap on the shoulder and I'm greeted with the query am I Cliff Atkinson? I gave a positive response then noticed a small wire coming out of his ear and a tiny microphone around his collar. He introduced himself as from the Prime Minister's security detail and who was to greet the Prime Minister when he arrived? My assumption had been that the President of Soccer Australia, Sam Papasavas would have that dubious honour. Yes but where was he? You've got it, not here yet. The guy then mumbled to someone at the other end of his communication device to slow the car down as there was no-one to formally greet Mr. Hawke who I gathered was being driven through Rushcutters Bay as we were talking with about 15 minutes to his arrival if they cleared all traffic lights on the way.

Ok. Did I have a dinner suit?

Yes!

Let's get it on you!

Without a shower I asked.

Bear in mind I'd been working non-stop for 12 hours.

OK we can manage a few minutes.

While in the shower I was quizzed as to my background with all my responses being relayed to the PM's car that was quickly approaching. So many questions about me were asked nowadays one would think I was going on E-Harmony or RSVP looking for partners.

The security guy never let me out of his sight and kept hurrying me along as he was able to monitor where the motorcade was at any time and as we entered the lift I heard him tell the driver to slow down as Cliff Atkinson would be outside on the steps in two minutes.

Just as I left the lift, walked the 15 metres to the front doorway up pulls the government car, with motorcycle outriders, and it's now Showtime!

The Prime Minister bounds out of the back seat and comes directly up to me tells me how good it is to catch up with me again, oh yes again??? He then grabs me by my right elbow and with a far reaching grin on his face keeps nodding in a friendly manner at every other person in the foyer and whispering to me out of the side of his mouth as to what was planned for him.

Dialogue, as far as I can remember, went something like this:-

PM-"What time am I speaking?'

CA- "About 8.15"

PM-"Not fucking about! What time?"

CA- "8.15"

PM-"How long do I speak for?"

CA-'About three minutes"

PM-"Not fucking about! How fucking long?"

CA- Warming to conversation with a very sore elbow. "Three minutes 15 seconds"

PM- "Where the fuck is Papasavas?"

CA- "Don't fucking know."

PM- "Where the fuck are we heading?"

CA -"The fucking VIP lounge."

At this point I saw Sir Arthur George having a drink in the VIP lounge. I had never met the man but I had seen him in the media and he cut a distinguished figure with his long white hair and as a former chairman of Soccer Australia I took it upon myself to introduce them and make what I thought was a dignified farewell to my hosting duties. Not so. Ten minutes later the security detail find me again, frog march me back to the VIP lounge with instructions to take the PM to his seat.

My elbow was taken captive again and back up the stairs we went heading towards the dining room.

PM-"Why did you leave me with that old fart?"

CA-"Sorry about that, thought you knew him."

PM-"Don't move more than ten metres from my table in case I need you to get me out of boring situations."

CA-"OK. If that's what you really want"

The rest of the evening went like clockwork with only one faux-pas as Les Murray made some inappropriate joke about rumours that the PM had a strong friendship with the Victorian Soccer Chairman and his wife that went down like a lead balloon and I had started moving towards the exit and safety.

As the telecast finished and the evening took on a less formal atmosphere I got the invitation to join the PM at his table and to bring along Lisa my wife for a couple of drinks. Strange how a beautiful partner ensures lots of invitations especially from men.

Remember the Murphy evening?

In the end I can't say I was sorry to see the event come to a conclusion but it had taught me a lesson on how many things senior politicians have on their minds. So have everything worked out for them. Never use the word "about" ever, as we cannot ask them to think on the run. Or even to get them to think about anyone but themselves.

However it was a relief to see my new best friend climb into the back of the government car and I've never washed my right elbow since. It's still too sore.

But never mind there's always more Prime Ministers.

CHAPTER 50!

Dead Man Walking!

Then there were the times that I am certain I was dead or at least at death's door. Of all the people I've come across in my life I wasn't ready to meet my maker. The first time occurred when I was working in Melbourne over Xmas 1998. We were in the middle o f a massive legal battle with the major record companies, and in particular Sony Music because of our efforts to bring down the parallel import rules that had been in effect keeping the price of a CD at $30+ in Australia while other countries were selling the exact same legal product from $10 - $20. The reason we were in Melbourne was due to the fact that the record companies had threatened music retailers that if they dealt in our imported product they would have their accounts with them closed. Actually, an illegal threat on their behalf as it came to pass, but we had decided to take our product direct to the public. We had imported from Indonesia about 30,000 CD's and cassettes of the world's leading artists, including the yet to be released Bee Gees 'One Night Only'. We booked the Convention Centre by the River Yarra for the seven shopping days leading to Christmas. We mounted an advertising schedule on Channel Nine and waited for the customers. The customers came in their thousands and our stock only just lasted till Christmas Eve. A very successful but exhausting week. Working about fifteen hours a day for the whole week took its toll and Christmas Day saw my wife Lisa, son Durham and myself having lunch in the Windsor Hotel, one of Melbourne's old dignified hotels. Boxing Day saw us at the Melbourne Cricket ground to watch the opening day of the test match between Australia and the West Indies. Channel Nine had invited my son and I to join them in the VIP lounge. This invitation was a dream for Durham as the importance of the

Boxing Day Cricket test is iconic in Australian sport. The most amusing incident was when a famous AFL player, Dermot Brereton, asked Durham if he wanted his autograph but Durham being a Sydney boy responded as to why and who are you. Sydney people are not so enamoured of Australian Rules football which is a religion in Melbourne.

We were due to fly back to Sydney the next day so we packed the bags and decided to go to Chapel Street, a famous street in Melbourne for good restaurants. After lunch on a hot day I felt a little queasy so we climbed into a taxi to head back to the hotel and as we approached the city centre I became nauseous and asked the driver to pull over to avoid messing up his cab. On getting out I felt really ill and sat down in a bus shelter. Trying to stand up is the last thing I remember as my body gave up and down I went. I remember nothing else till waking up in intensive care in Royal Melbourne Hospital. I was told I'd had a major heart attack and fortunately for me we had pulled the taxi up across the street from the hospital. Someone sitting at the bus stop had called for an ambulance and I was on the operating table in a few minutes. Lisa and Durham had been told to expect the worst but somehow I came back. As I've been heard to say many times it was because there wasn't anything there, very boring, so back I came. That put paid to returning to Sydney that afternoon.

For the next few days I was stuck in bed with tubes going in and out all over me and by New Year's Eve I was going stir crazy. Durham had returned to Sydney to stay with his grandparents and Lisa had hung around getting completely bored. On New Year's Eve the chief heart surgeon was doing his rounds with the interns moving from room to room, picking up those charts they hang on to the end of the bed. On reaching me he spent about fifteen minutes going through what I had went through talking as though I wasn't even in the room. As they were about to leave he asked me if I had anything to ask and when I asked if I'd be able to play football after this he said yes, which I was grateful for and replied that that's good because I couldn't before, and I heard his response as he was walking out saying to the interns that patients usually ask if they'll be able to play piano afterwards. Can't beat their sense of humour.

Having survived this medical emergency I altered my lifestyle as the doctors instructed, changed my diet, stopped smoking, exercised vigorously on a daily basis and in the words of the therapist avoided becoming a coronary cripple. However I was not prepared for my second appointment with my maker either timing or location.

One of the results of this heart attack was the birth of my new nickname which I carry to this day. Having had the heart attack in Melbourne, on December 30th I learnt how never to let the truth get in the way of a true story. The rumours of my death, crippling injuries, wheel chair purchase etc. had taken on a life of their own back in Sydney and to quote Mark Twain, 'The Report of my death was an exaggeration' so it was a major surprise when I turned up in March for the first training session of the football season at Cammeray oval for North Sydney. I was immediately named Dead Man Walking, and since then the club have provided me with a new shirt every year with my age as my squad number and my name Dead Man Walking across the back.

To this day when Lisa and I are at club functions the younger players are always quick to introduce me as the guy that had two heart attacks on Cammeray Oval and died twice in the ambulance afterwards. Lisa has now given up on telling them the real story as the legend now has a life of its own that keeps on growing.

CHAPTER 51

No Cuckoo Clocks.

So here I am recovering from my friendly episode with the Prime Minister Bob Hawke which ended up quite convivial at the end of the night as he invited my wife Lisa and myself to his table for a few drinks, that is we drank, he didn't, having made a pledge that if he ever made Prime Minister he would give up the demon drink. Now he was super friendly, which I put down to the fact that he had realised I was married to the model on the stage handing the awards to the presenters.

My next brush with a Prime Minister came about a few years later when we had purchased a property in Neutral Bay, an upmarket suburb on the lower north shore of Sydney. It was in fact a duplex with two three bedroom apartments. We lived on the ground floor and we advertised the upstairs for rent. It went very quickly due to its location and the tenant turned out to be Patrick Keating, the son of the Prime Minister Paul Keating, and his girlfriend Amber.

The names did not ring any bells at the time as we were too engrossed in our own home making and it was only on the day they moved in that the significance of the name hit home. There in his shorts and polo shirt was the Prime Minister helping his son to move in. Carrying boxes and other small items of furniture it painted a very different picture of a man usually dressed in three thousand dollar Emernegildo Zegna suits.

I said hello, shook hands then for some inexplicable reason I excused myself to go to The Oaks Hotel to talk English football and check our Fantasy Football scores with Bill and Scrogie, never ever did know his real name, the painters. House painters I should say. After about half an hour I realised what I'd done, I mean not done. I had been in a position to probably invite Paul Keating into my home for a beer or a cup of tea and I'd blown it.

I drank my VB quickly and jumped back in the car, rushed home, but yes, you've guessed it, the move in was complete and no sign of Paul Keating, who could have been my next best friend.

I was hoping he didn't count it as a snub but about ten years later I met him at an antiques fair in The Rocks and when I said hello I got the impression he recognised me from that fateful few seconds some ten years ago and he snubbed me. Just to get his own back. I'll remember that moment and I can't wait till I'm a best- selling author and I may have the chance to cut him again.

My other experience with Australian Prime Ministers came in Melbourne at the Cricket Ground before the Australia Uruguay World Cup Qualifier when, as the co-ordinator of all pre game festivities I had to escort John Howard, the Prime Minister of the time, onto the ground for presentation to the teams. I had no idea how many people could dislike me as I walked out of the tunnel to be met by eighty thousand people booing me. What a surprise it was to think they recognised me.

We had arranged for a singer from Sydney of Uruguayan descent to sing the Uruguayan national anthem, and as we all know these South American anthems can seem to go on forever, so it was no surprise to anyone that the singer stood there without singing a word for what seemed an eternity then started singing and the music stopped a few seconds after he started singing.

Making our way back down the tunnel with the Prime Minister we were joined in the lift by a very angry Uruguayan singer complaining about not being able to hear the backing tape. He was using every four letter word I'd ever heard with a few more I'd never heard. The security detail were apoplectic but good on John Howard he took it all in his stride and calmed the guy.

The only time I ever came close to an Australian Prime Minister after this episode was at a Mick Young charity function at the Four Seasons in Sydney but to my disappointment my wife was invited over to Julia Gillard's table and I was left to my own devices.

But never mind still a few Presidents left to meet in the World.

CHAPTER 52!

Is There Any Wonder?

Then there was the time in 1975 when I had to make a trip to London and New York for negotiations on future tours. The tickets were issued by Pan Am an American airline that was one of the world's biggest and most successful at the time but since has gone broke and out of existence. Because I had an arrangement with Pan Am for flying our touring artists I had an arrangement for issue of free tickets for my personal or business use in return for mentioning Pan Am in all our advertising. The route to London was what we would have called a milk run as it stopped so many times on the way. First up was the 707 to Hong Kong via Denpasar in Bali. My first wife and I had done this trip a year earlier and had spent time in Bali on the way. A beautiful island hideaway that now has been taken over by indulgent westerners and is not the island paradise it once was. An overnight in Hong Kong and then to pick up the 747 PA 002 which was the flight number when travelling in a westerly direction around the world and PA 001 was the flight number when flying in an easterly direction around the world. First stop after Hong Kong was Bangkok in Thailand, and then New Delhi.

As I was travelling on contra tickets, which means that they were issued to me in return for advertising time which I had arranged, the price part of the ticket read F.O.C. which in one way is translated as Free of Charge or otherwise Friend Of Company. Either way it almost always meant being upgraded to either business, or in this case first class so I was travelling in the best way possible and I thought it was getting better when a very attractive hostess came around distributing the disembarkation cards as we approached New Delhi. As I had no intention of visiting India I politely declined and she remarked how disappointing that was as she was hoping someone would be able to visit the Taj Mahal with her as all the other flight staff had done the trip many times before. Being the kind hearted man I was, and still am, and maybe because she was so attractive, I said I would put myself out and accompany her if she could arrange to get me and my luggage off the plane. Ten minutes later it was all arranged. She had arranged for me to be part of the flight crew for ground transfer and hotel bookings at Pan Am's expense. After all I was a Friend Of Company. It was never explained to me how far from New Delhi is the Taj Mahal. But with the assistance of the hotel and the financial clout of Pan Am a car with driver was hired and off we went. Nowadays they will tell you it's a three hour drive but back then a nightmare drive of around four and a half hours each way was the norm. This didn't include the impromptu game of cricket at Mathura that I was dragged into when they found out I was from Australia, and they kept calling me Chappelli, not too pleased at that as I was a strong English supporter back then, however I did have the fashionable moustache of the time. I was dragged into the game as we had stopped for refreshments and the Indian kids gathered round and demanding our attention with calls of hashish, hashish. Obviously they had dealings with white tourists before. The barefooted kids of about seven or eight years old had set up a cardboard box as a wicket, a bat that had no rubber left on the handle and a cricket ball that was missing most of the leather covering. The wicket itself was not as one sees at the Melbourne Cricket Ground or Lords, with dust flying as the ball pitched and spinners being assisted by ruts and rocks. The biggest debates were about who was Lillee, Thomson or Marsh. I did OK as a batsman but my bowling in the one hundred plus degrees was sadly lacking in pace. We returned to the car and left with the knowledge that I had taught a large number of Indian boys how to say G'day. The next hold up involved some animal that had been run over by a bus, what it was I couldn't recognise by the time we passed it, with a dozen vultures picking at what was left of the poor creature on the side of the road amongst all the dust and dirt.

Needless to say on arrival at the Taj Mahal it was easy to see why it's listed as one of the wonders of the world. It is a wonderful edifice and I cannot praise it enough and as I sat beside the artificial ponds that lead one to the main building. Again it's the title of this book as I sighed to myself "It's A Long Way From Ferryhill".

Some 17 years later when I saw the photograph of Diana, Princess of Wales, sitting on the very same bench that I rested on in those 100 degree temperatures that prevail around Agra I recalled my time there. But this journey was not yet over. The return road trip was uneventful apart from stopping at some roadside cafe where we ate on the roof under a moon that filled the sky and then returned exhausted to the hotel. Ten hours driving and two hours at the Taj Mahal but worth all the pain we had had to go through.

Although nothing untoward had happened between myself and the hostess some months later on the day we were moving into our apartment we had just bought the phone rang and my wife answered it. It's an American lady on the line. She had arranged a flight to Sydney hoping to meet up with me but she slammed down the phone when I told her it was my wife who had answered the phone. Well she had never asked if I was married.

Fortunately I was able to continue my journey the next evening as they were able to find a seat for me on the onward going flight but the excitement was not yet over.

On landing in Beirut around 11pm local time I realised that the plane was not taxiing to the terminal but was stationary on the tarmac with a few short messages over the intercom that Beirut passengers would be disembarking on the tarmac onto a coach to take them to the terminal. On glancing out of the windows we could see what looked like a miniature fireworks display going on some kilometres away, maybe a national day or something similar. Oh no!

Nothing as simple as that and here comes Cliff's next incredible adventure.

After some time a hostess came to me and asked if she could inspect my ticket. She took it away and then returned in ten minutes and reminded me that I was on a Free of Charge Ticket. Nothing's changed only the name. This meant that as they had to assist another airline that had some maintenance problems I had to relinquish my seat for a paying passenger. My first thoughts were that it's not too bad to give up first class and go down one or two levels but that wasn't what they meant. I was to be offloaded and they would do their best to retrieve my luggage and in the most polite way possible I was escorted down the stairs and into the back of a military open topped Jeep with three armed uniformed guards as my escort. Who knows what the other passengers thought was going on as I was driven hastily towards the terminal.

I then realised also it was not a fireworks display but the flashes and booms were coming from artillery barrages. I had landed in the middle of a civil war and the airport was the strategic area being fought for by all sides. Now I was in a quandary as to what to do. Pan Am flew in only once a day which meant it looked like my best plan would be to doss down in the airport and hope I could catch the next plane out ie. One days time. The Pan Am staff advised me that I could be there for some days as the civil war was causing havoc with their schedules, and yes they were hoping to get my luggage for me. I decided to have a tour of the airport and while walking past the Middle East Airlines check in department I saw there was a flight in twenty minutes leaving for Cairo. Thank you God I whispered to myself, out with the American Express card, a student's half price return ticket to Cairo, return flight open and off to the Land Of The Pharoahs I went, must say without any luggage, but didn't care, the artillery to me was getting louder and louder and Egypt seemed a lot safer place to be than in the middle of a Lebanese civil war.

The plane was reminiscent of train and coach journeys in third world countries with every seat taken, the aisles full of luggage and baggage, in fact everything apart from the chickens or goats.

Landing in Cairo airport at 2am is an experience I'll never forget or ever hope to repeat with people milling all over the terminal shouting and screaming at anyone who would listen. In most cases one would find the hotel wall where you can normally push a button on what looks like your style of accommodation and they would advise how to get there recommending either taxis or airport shuttle buses. Nothing like that. Panic starts to creep in, if panic ever creeps, and as I join the immigration and customs queue all my bravado is drying up then a very well spoken guy, the plum in the mouth kind of speech, real pukka, with a moustache taken directly from the Lord Kitchener recruitment posters, engages me in conversation and he soon discovers I'm a lamb that has strayed into the wolf's lair. Turns out he's the Danish ambassador to Egypt and a few other neighbouring nations and his first favour is to loan me twenty Egyptian pounds as the visa fee, then offers me a lift in the diplomatic vehicle, I say vehicle because this was like something from Lawrence of Arabia with outriders to get us into town. He then very kindly gets his driver to take me to a recommended hotel, the Queen Victoria situated in the middle of the CMD, that's Central Market District as distinct from Central Business District, still crowded and busy considering the time it was, as it would be at rush hour anywhere else in the world. The exotic sounds that filled the air outside the hotel included donkeys braying, dogs barking, hawkers and cart drivers yelling at the top of their voices, no car horns but plenty of bells. The hotel itself was from bygone days with massive staircases and pillars, staff at every door to open it for you. The room was bigger than any house I've ever owned with a four poster, king size plus bed and furnishings that would have not looked out of place in any Victorian mansion. In the bar the air was circulated by carpet material suspended from the ceiling with men pulling on ropes to make them swish backwards and forwards to push the air around.

The next morning confirmed that there were no seats available on the evening's Pan Am flight so I decided to make the best of it and make my way to see the pyramids and the Sphinx. The easiest way there was to catch the local bus right outside the hotel costing about ten cents for the journey and share the experience of travelling with the locals as they went about their business. For people who have visited Cairo in recent years they have seen the miles and miles of four and five star hotels lining the motorway to the pyramids but at this time construction had only just begun on the motorway and the hotels. Noticeable at the time was the heavy construction machinery was not Caterpillar as one would expect but Russian and Czechoslovakian branded versions of Caterpillar. It's only a short trip till one reaches the outskirts of the city and there is the desert reaching out for kilometres reminding one of Beau Geste and hundreds of other foreign legion films. A short walk and there I was at the base of Giza where the three great pyramids of Cheop, Chefrens and Mykerinos are situated, as well as the great Sphinx, that got badly abused by the bored soldiers of the Napoleon army. Having nothing better to do they practised shooting at the poor Sphinx' nose! Next step was the guided tour into the innards of a Cheop's pyramid with narrow tunnels and a feeling of claustrophobia as we descended and then opened out into a massive burial chamber.

After lunch I hired a camel that was so well trained it took me around the Giza plateau stopping at certain points of interest where it would kneel down to let me dismount then wait for me to do a short inspection then wherever I was it would find me to make me re-mount and off to the next point. He had a timetable and schedule that he kept better than any Sydney Buses drivers could ever do. The next day brought no joy regarding an ongoing flight out of Beirut but I was now feeling a lot more relaxed in the surroundings so a meal in the town square was on the cards that evening and the next morning it was off to the Egyptian Museum of Antiquities only a short walk from the hotel and worth every Egyptian pound I paid for the experience. The mummies of Tutankhamun and Ramases along with twenty or more other mummies plus all the treasures that hadn't been pillaged over the centuries. Spent the whole day there soaking it in and the only things missing were Peter Cushing and Christopher Lee from the curse of the mummies Hammer films that I had enjoyed over the years.

Back at the hotel got the news that I could catch a plane out of Beirut the next night. At this point I was ambivalent as to whether that was good or bad news, but booked a flight back to Beirut and then decided I should see the Son et Lumiere spectacular at the Sphinx that evening. Took the bus and on alighting was approached by the owner of a stable of Arabian horses offering me the hire for the evening of a horse. Duly accepted and off I went like Lawrence of Arabia into the darkness that is the Sahara and as the horse galloped along I thought of the word serendipity and how it's a word difficult to define but this was one of those moments. As the horse slowed down and snorted a little, bearing in mind he was in total control of the pace as I had absolutely nothing to do with direction or speed, out of the pitch black darkness appeared a small boy with a tray around his neck just like the old fashioned cinema usherettes offering me a Coca-Cola or ice cream. Couldn't resist the charm of it all so bought one of each.

On returning the horse to its owner, or more truthfully the horse returned me to the staging yard, it was time for the light and sound show which was only spoilt by the fact they repeated everything in English and French, very much like IOC speeches.

On checking out the next morning another pleasant surprise, the bill had been paid by the Danish Charge D'Affaires. Never got an opportunity to thank them but have loved Danish butter and cheeses since then.

Nothing exciting for the next part of the trip as it appeared there was a lull in the Lebanese civil war but I did get a surprise when disembarking at Istanbul to stretch my legs during a re-fuelling stop and as I walked through the transit lounge there behind a rope cordon was about a dozen pieces of luggage and you wouldn't believe it but included my sole piece of luggage. Over the rope I went retrieved my bag and back on the plane to London.

Thank you. Only five more wonders of the world left to see...............

CHAPTER 53!

A Presidential Pardon!

Then there was the time in 2011 when I met a political hero of mine as I was walking along a street in Sydney. I had been to a monthly networking lunch that was hosted by Capital Partners, a company involved with fund raising for companies listing on the ASX. I can remember what time of year it was as it was a very hot day in November and the cold beer had been flowing in the Harbourview Hotel the venue for the monthly get-togethers, officially networking but mainly an excuse for a bunch of businessmen to waste an afternoon in the pub with lots of beer and deep fried food that we could feel hardening our arteries as we bit on it. The hotel is situated in perhaps the oldest part of European settlement of Australia the Rocks. On Sydney Harbour with views through to the heads and located under the Harbour Bridge. As we ate, drank and tried to make deals over beer, wine and terribly deep fried unhealthy food that none of our wives ever allowed us to eat at home we could almost touch the people finishing their Harbour Bridge climb, one of Sydney's most famous and worthwhile tourist attractions. Something I had done myself years ago when producing a children's television show "Nine'll Fix It", a direct copy of an English television show featuring the now infamous Jimmy Saville, "Jim'll" Fix It. We used to fix up the wishes that we wanted to shoot and deemed interesting, and then found kids to take part as if the wish was theirs. We dummied up a letter requesting a climb to the top of the Harbour Bridge was an ambition and on approaching the department of main roads we were knocked back on the basis that only people over eighteen were allowed on the gantries and stairs. We solved the problem by using my girlfriend of the time who was nineteen but small enough and looked as if she could be thirteen or fourteen and off we went. Segment went to air and we were busted in the paper the next afternoon when a journalist we knew pointed out her age and the fact that she was the girlfriend of the producer. The headline was 'Nine really did fix it!'

Because it was a hot day the lunch went longer than usual and needless to say sobriety was a victim so about 4pm I decided it was time to de-camp and try to catch a bus home to the North Shore. Tentatively climbing down the staircase the whole three floors from the roof garden to the ground floor and with a slight lurch I left the Harbourview and made my way along Carrington St. then down the Argyle steps, sidestepping the crowds of tourists and buskers and into the main thoroughfare of Sydney, George St.

Past the Orient Hotel, nodding to all the tourists, helped with directions for a Japanese family, hope they made it to where they were going. Not tempted at all by all the pubs I was walking past and sweating profusely with the exercise. Not dressed for the day, I was wearing a suit and tie and as I walked past the Four Seasons hotel along with all the milling crowd when coming towards me were two men chatting amiably and noticeable by their genuine Ralph Lauren Polo shirts, especially the one in pink with cream trousers. Warranting a second look I realised it was President Bill Clinton accompanied by what could have been a security guard and no-one else. How wonderful is this city I thought, that a former President of the U.S.A. could be walking casually along the main street of Sydney with no-one taking any notice of him. Let me re-phrase that, no-one but me! I approached him, held out my hand and welcomed him to Australia, he clasped my hand with both his hands and asked how I was, and how happy he was to meet me. He made me feel like we were old friends. Quite a diplomat. Not tongue tied at all I asked if he would like a beer, my shout, that's Australian for I'll pay, at the Brooklyn, about 30 metres away, he politely declined and suggested I'd probably had enough and should take it easy.

How many people can say they have been RSA'd (That's Responsible Service of Alcohol for non-Australians) by a President of the U.S.A. I cherish the memory. It was all over in a few seconds and as I kept on walking I was asking other pedestrians if they had noticed who I had just been talking to. No-one had noticed.

The sting in the tale of this story is that feeling so self-important telling Lisa, my wife, who only believed me when she saw Bill Clinton on the TV news that night wearing the pink polo shirt I'd talked about, I then called my sister Joyce in Cairns to have a little brag. She said is that all and she then emailed me a picture of her husband Ron selling an Australian bush hat to Bill and Hilary Clinton three years earlier in Port Douglas a major tourist resort in Queensland.

I never got a picture.

Topped again.

CHAPTER 54

There's No Place Like Lome!

There was the time in 2009 when I was a guest of the government of Togo. For the uninformed it's a small republic in West Africa formerly a French colony with its capital Lome. Officially the Togolese Republic is a country bordered by Ghana to the west, Benin to the east and Burkina Faso to the north

I often wondered why my partner Colin Archer seemed to make the business trips to modern places like Shanghai, Singapore, Hong Kong, Beijing etc. while I drew the short straw for the West African republics. It was put down to the fact that I spoke French but somehow Col and his addiction to airline food trumped me on destinations. The invitation was extended to us by the President of Togo Faure Gnassingbe to assist them with their prime industry and the basis of their economy, their wealth of phosphates all over the nation. We had a client very interested in phosphates as the base ingredient for fertilisers and with access to top government officials and the President himself opportunity was knocking. Arrangements were made with dates and schedules in place. All that was required now was the transfer of funds from Togo to cover expenses. Note here, when travelling overseas, and especially into the third world, do not let anyone else book the flight tickets. Why? Because if there is any dispute when in their country they will have the prerogative to cancel the flight and cause undue stress. In this case the funds arrived on the Thursday with the flights from Sydney to Paris then on to Lome scheduled for the Sunday. Then to meet up with our client in Lome on the Tuesday as he was flying in from Cape Town.

Here's where it all started to go wrong! Went into the Flight Centre in Hunter St. in the city, booked the flights and presented my credit card to pay the $14,000 for the business class flights. The agent informed me that they would not accept credit card payments for flights leaving so soon after payment so would I mind going to my bank and withdrawing cash to pay the account. Of course I minded but it looked like I had no option as I was running to a very tight schedule so off to the bank I set off. HSBC bank was two blocks away but on the way there's another travel agent STA so in I went and made the bookings, saved $1800 on the fares and they accepted Visa. Serves Flight Centre right I thought, missing out on $14000, should send their share price into a downward spiral. Went home feeling rather smug and prepared for the journey.

Sunday morning came, Lisa drove me to Sydney airport to catch my Air France flight. Made our farewells then off to business class check in I strolled.

Much to my chagrin on trying to check in it turned out someone had cancelled my tickets and I was not booked on any flight. Tried to contact STA, yes, forgetting it was a Sunday morning, no-one to assist me, Air France flight booked out. Panic! You better believe it.

Where there's a will there's always a way. Off to the Qantas desk. Yes they can get me on a flight to London leaving in one hour, over the counter goes the much abused Visa card and I'm booked economy to London. I'll worry about the next stage later.

Arrived Heathrow early Monday morning that is late afternoon Sydney time and was able to contact STA who rang me back with the news that Flight Centre, on my not returning to their office had cancelled my flights and the STA booking had somehow been enmeshed in the system but I was assured that the Paris- Lome - Paris flights were confirmed and they would seek to get things back to steady ground. The original flight schedule had good connections with no hotel stop overs necessary but now I had to negotiate London to Paris and overnight accommodation in Paris. Please imagine how mentally and physically exhausted I am at this stage, but can't keep a President waiting, especially one who has signed a cheque to get me there.

Off to St. Pancras. On to Eurostar. Very good but very expensive on a walk up basis and a few hours later I'm at Gare de Nord. Which fortunately is on the Metro line that takes passengers to Charles De Gaulle airport. Remembered a small hotel Lisa and I had stayed in just off the Boulevard San Michel and fortunately they had a broom closet available at extortionate rates for one night but I didn't care at this time.

The next morning left in good time to catch the train to the airport and on arrival at Charles De Gaulle was met with the news that our departure gate was one of a dozen that had been waterlogged during the night and could we be patient while alternatives were being worked out. Well nothing could faze me now. I could take this and anything else life threw at me all in my stride.

Is there anything worse when travelling than crowded airports overflowing with masses of people uninformed on what is happening? If so I can't think of anything. Children laughing. OK! Children yelling and crying incessantly. Not OK. Parents screaming. Not OK. Self-appointed leaders of these masses demanding from airline staff information at the top of their self-important voices. It's just as bad in French as it is in English. In the midst of all this was an oasis of calm, me, as I ate my croissant with strong coffee. This was nothing within the scheme of things and what I'd had to negotiate the past two days.

Eventually some kind of order was restored and we made our way to the appointed departure gates.

We are now checking in on a Paris to Togo flight with family re-unions obviously at the back of passengers minds each check in seemed to take forever as arguments abounded as to excess charges for both checked in and on board baggage with the airline winning every time. This paragraph will resonate later when we arrived in Lome.

I would say an uneventful flight if it didn't remind me of train journeys taken in China at Chinese New Year or bus journeys in Bolivia.

Was able to practise my French with the young couple beside me who were so interested in Australia and possible emigration. Arrived in Lome. Just like any airport in West Africa, crowded, noisy, and technically back in the 19th century as far as systems for customs and immigration apply. In my case I was greeted by a government official who guided me to the VIP arrival lounge where my passport was duly stamped and all paperwork completed. My new best friend Stanislous went to recover my luggage, one bag that acted as a suit press, remember I'm meeting the President, a suit a requisite item of clothing, and as a suitcase. Half an hour went by, no Stanislous. Another half hour then he appeared with the Air France representative, yes, you guessed it, no baggage. But it had been found at Charles De Gaulle and will be on the next flight. When you may ask. Thursday. Only two flights a week Paris-Lome and return. Hang on that's the flight I'm booked on to return to Paris.

Could things get worse?

CHAPTER 55!

To Go or Not Togo!

At Lome airport could things get worse? Of course they could and being me I knew it just would. Driven to the hotel with police outriders accompanying us and passing through what appeared to be one small village after another I checked in, without any baggage, and pondered my situation. I had appointments arranged with a number of government ministers including the President and I was going to create a great impression wearing Levis, Nikes and an AC/DC T-shirt.

Slept quite well considering my circumstances and the next morning was pleased to meet up with Mark Sumich from Globe Minerals Ltd who had flown in from Cape Town to meet up with me as his company were very interested in the phosphate deposits. Over breakfast we discussed our itinerary and to my relief found out he had an extra suit with him and he was very close to my build so one problem was solved. The first day we spent travelling around the hinterland exploring the current phosphate mines and the infrastructure already in place. It was pointed out to me that anywhere in Togo if you dropped a salted peanut the soil was so fertile you would have a peanut shrub in a couple of weeks.

Despite this we realised their phosphate and fertiliser industry were still locked in the past and needed a total overhaul to increase their production. We calculated it was working at about eight per cent capacity with kilometres of conveyer belts to be replaced along with modernisation of the treatment plant which was situated on the beach and pouring thousands of litres of waste into the ocean not more than fifty metres from the shore. It was a horrible yellow colour and we knew that if an Australian company took over the project the Australian public would be up in arms if any pictures of this environmental vandalism would surface.

That night we formulated a business plan that would involve closing down the whole phosphate industry for twelve months thus allowing us to modernise all equipment and systems. It was also on the table that we would guarantee the current revenues to the government while this process was ongoing.

Armed with our business plan we were looking forward to locking horns with the government departments and ministers and after fitting my borrowed suit, shirt, tie and shoes off we went to the first appointment of the day at the Ministry of Trade.

In my travels through many countries in the world I have come across the best and worst of timekeepers but this one took the cake.

We sat outside in the reception area for over three hours after we had been announced and during that three hours not one person came and spoke to us or offered an explanation or an apology. Not even a cup of tea. Eventually we were ushered into the inner sanctum where, without any apology for the tardiness, we were able to state our case and were promised serious consideration of our plan and would hopefully have a memorandum of understanding before we departed in two days time. We then spent some time with officials supplying corporate details and outlines of the model we were proposing.

The rest of the day involved meetings with other government officials including industry and agriculture and we felt we had the deal in the bag. The best news came when we were advised we had an appointment arranged with the President Faure Gnassingbe for the following morning. Things certainly were looking a little bit better.

It was at this time that we discovered we couldn't use our debit cards on the ATMs in Togo as they were only set up for credit cards. Now who carries around their credit card pin numbers for cash withdrawals I ask you?

Well no one in our group.

Fortunately I had withdrawn a few hundred euros when passing through Paris so I became the paymaster for everyone.

That evening we had dinner with the equivalent of the Attorney General, a generous lady who had studied in Paris and was very European in her outlook and she pointed out that we were in a good position as there was still a colonial hangover and the Togolese were suspicious of French and European investments as they always seemed to come with lots of strings attached. Fortunately I speak French, not fluently, but passable. We were given tips on protocol and a brief history on how the current President came to power and we were prepared.

The next day arrived and we were driven to the Presidential palace, termed loosely, and were led into the President's suite where we shook hands, were welcomed, hoped we could do business together and then shown the door.

Oh well it's a story to tell the office on my return.

On checking out of the hotel the next day I tried to pay for my extras with my Visa card. Declined! I had no idea why but fortunately I had just enough euros to cover the charges and luckily the hotel had a courtesy bus to take us to the airport free of charge. On the way to the airport we received a call to advise us the memorandum of understanding would be emailed to me in the next twenty four hours.

I reminded myself that my luggage was coming in on the plane from Paris so instead of Departures I had to wait in Arrivals where to my relief out came my suitcase on the carousel. Quickly I grabbed it and ran to departures to check in. Got there just in time.

Paris here I come then home to Sydney.

First task on arriving at Charles De Gaulle airport was to find an ATM machine to get some cash so I could afford the train fare to Gare De Nord then the metro to St. Michel.

Not having access to my Visa credit card I decided I'd better get moving back to Sydney so I found out where the airline office was and headed there. As I was standing at the desk about to confirm a flight for that evening I received two phone calls within minutes of each other. First one introduced themselves from HSBC, my bank in Sydney, asking me if I had tried to use my credit card in Lome, Togo. My positive reply elicited an apology but then chastisement for not informing the bank before I left that I was going to be in West Africa, the world's centre for credit card fraud. My card was now active. However now feeling exhausted I decided I was going to catch the earliest flight available, and as they were about to process my credit card for the plane ticket when my phone rang again. It was our son Durham who lives in London and as we were talking he asked where I was. On hearing I was in Paris he told me he was in Marseilles so he said he'd catch a train and meet me in Paris.

Something good came out of this as without realising it we were in Paris on the Sunday when the Tour De France finishes with its round the streets and the victory laps up and down the Champs Elysees. These are accidents to savour being in Paris with your son as one appreciates just what the tour is.

We sat in a restaurant eating and drinking beer on the Champs Elysees thinking how lucky we were and then Durham uttered the immortal line "It's a Long Way from Ferryhill."

Incidentally we didn't get the phosphate deal it went to an Israeli group and the latest news is that nothing has been done to date. In fact we have been invited back all these years later to pick up where we left off.

CHAPTER 56!

The Killing Fields!

Having visited two of the world's seven wonders that I had put on my bucket list that there were five more to go. The third came about on a business trip in 2013 when I was invited to Cambodia by a group purporting to be representatives of the government with influential friends in the communist political hierarchy. Their story was that they had exploration and mining rights to a small mountain inland with huge deposits of gold and copper. They were looking for partners to invest around five million dollars to complete the exploration and begin production. We flew into Siem Reap via Singapore where we were met at the airport by our hosts and driven for around three hours from the city passing through the rice paddies for kilometre after kilometre providing us with the whole feeling generated by the film The Killing Fields. With our driver and host telling us the stories of what had happened in each village as we passed through them. It's only when you hear first-hand the reports of people that experienced the horror does the cruelty of mankind sink in and we realise how fortunate we are living in our western cocoon. Khmers rouges was the name given to the followers of the Communist Party of Kampuchea in Cambodia.

On arrival in the village we were to use as our base the younger of the hosts took us for dinner at a street side restaurant which he said was owned and managed by his mother. As the evening wore on it became evident that she was not his birth mother but rather she had adopted him during the civil strife. The story went that he was in the village acting as an interpreter for the United Nations and as the Khmer Rouge were approaching the UN people called for a helicopter to evacuate themselves and their local guides and interpreters. Only one helicopter came and they were told another was on the way so stay close to the mustering point and wait. Which they did and it proved fatal to most of those left. He watched from the long grass as the Khmer Rouge forces entered the village and were shooting people indiscriminately in the road. He took refuge in the restaurant where the owner through an apron on him and told him he was now a waiter and her eldest son. The troops pillaged the village but fortunately the restaurant was used by the officers as a base and canteen so he survived by learning how to wait tables at a very quick pace. From that day on he had called the lady his mother and she him her son.

The next day was to be the day we visited the mining site. So up at the crack of dawn we climbed into the four wheel drive and off we went. It was my assumption that the mine site would only be outside the village so I was prepared for a thirty minute ride. As we left the town and were approaching the jungle area we noticed quite a lot of trucks going in the opposite direction loaded up with tonnes of timber as though there was a sawmill somewhere ahead of us. It was explained that these were trucks loaded with illicit timber as there were forestry regulations in place banning the felling of trees. Four hours later after we had left sealed roads and were now in jungle territory with only tyre tracks acting as the road. We were met by our bodyguards, heavily armed military types on motor bikes. They went front and back of our vehicle and I was afraid to ask why they were necessary. Every few kilometres we passed groups of young men with felled trees and diesel powered band saws working on the timber. As we approached they would make a run to hide in the under growth, then as soon as we were past they came back out and continued as if nothing had happened. I suggested at the time the authorities should mark the trees they needed cutting down to clear the road as one's backside took a lot of punishment on these tracks and I couldn't see Gina Rhinehart Australia's giant mining magnate making the journey no matter how big the deposits were.

We eventually reached the mine site and I was completely unprepared for what they considered an exploration team and equipment. Six young men, from Vietnam we were told, had hoisted a sheet of canvas and this was their camp site. Third World doesn't explain it adequately but our hosts tried to convince us this was normal mining practice. I was going to mention that I had researched the Cambodian Mining Act that was a direct copy of the Australian protocol but thought better of it till I was back in Siem Reap and closer to civilisation. After checking a few samples and taking a number of pictures it was back to our village to discuss terms and conditions. It was agreed that night that we would return to Siem Reap and we would draw up a heads of agreement the next day then it would be back to Sydney.

On our return to Siem Reap the plan was for the Cambodians to prepare the documents and we would sign in the afternoon. Having a few hours to myself I decided to visit the Angkor Wat historical park. There is no way anyone can prepare themselves for the magnitude of Angkor Wat.

The tourist brochures merely highlight the entry point but behind the facade are dozens of smaller temples with wonderful artworks, murals and intricate tiled floors. It is no wonder the United Nations have taken responsibility of preserving he temples as Angkor Wat certainly deserves it's place alongside the other six Wonders of the World. The whole area is now under United Nations protection and there is a massive maintenance crew continually acting to preserve the site.

As we were leaving the park I mentioned to my driver "It's A Long Way from Ferryhill".

As a wrap up to this episode worth noting that the deal fell through as the Cambodians were unable to provide any proof of ownership, any exploration or mining licences from the government and as a final nail in the coffin wanted one million American dollars within the next seven days deposited in a Singapore bank.

Hello! I may be a small town boy from Ferryhill but not that simple.

CHAPTER 57

Little Britain and Goodluck!

After suffering the serious heart attack I began a new stage in my life which involved giving up smoking, eating healthily, enrolling in Fitness First and making gym visits a habit rather than a chore. The lifestyle change seemed to work and a year afterwards the doctors were saying I was in better shape than I had been before the heart attack. The advice given by the medical staff at the time was not to take it easy but rather to make an effort to keep on working and playing as if nothing had happened, along the lines that if I'd run marathons before the heart attack it should be a goal to run them again rather than becoming a 'coronary cripple'. I took their advice and for years never had any health problems. I had even joined a Fitness First gym in Sydney's CBD which saw me exercising every lunchtime instead of actually lunching. In 2012 our company Phoenix Green Capital were invited to Nigeria to advise on infrastructure projects along with mining and agribusiness opportunities. It would be our task for the next year or two to encourage investors to invest in Nigeria and in particular it's massive oil industry which was being severely mismanaged and corrupted. To get to Nigeria from Australia it's more convenient to fly into London first then fly to Lagos and return the same way. As it was at the time our son Durham was working in London, as most young Australians do for a while, so it seemed a good idea to treat his mother to the trip so she could catch up with him and his girlfriend. It was also a co-incidence that my older brother, Barry, would be celebrating his seventieth birthday on the day we were due to fly into Heathrow so bearing cash presents from our two sisters living in Australia and ourselves we thought we'd surprise him by ringing from Heathrow to let him know we would be there to celebrate with him.

Oh the well laid plans of mice and men! On calling from the airport his daughter, our niece, another Lisa Atkinson, answered the phone and told us he wasn't at home but was with his eldest son in London. It seemed the obvious thing to ask for their number or Barry's mobile number and the response that one number she didn't know and that he didn't have a mobile phone didn't quite ring true.

However he was due to be back in Clyffe Pypard, the village in the Cotswolds where they were living, the coming Friday. Taking her at her word and having three days before I was to fly to Lagos we decided to visit my other sister Anne and her husband Stuart in Peterlee, County Durham.

On the Friday we drove back south to find Clyffe Pypard, and trust me it's not easy. Tucked somewhere in the nooks and crannies of the Cotswolds somewhere near Swindon it took us most of the day to find it and when we did it was like something out of the television series Little Britain.

Picture a very tired couple who had flown from the other side of the world to visit a brother, they had driven for over six hours down country lanes being held up by horses and carts, shepherds with their sheep etc. etc. I must say in defence of the district the scenery is beautiful but it can lose some of its lustre after days of travelling.

The couple knock on the door. The door opens.

Answered by our niece, another Lisa Atkinson. She looks at us and says that Barry's not here and slams the door in our face without another word.

We were so shocked we couldn't do anything else but laugh it was so bizarre having spent so much time trying to get there to be met by this Little Britain scenario. So back to London we went and I had to prepare to leave for Lagos the next day. My business partner Colin had arrived in London and we have one more appointment in London with major financiers before leaving for Lagos in the afternoon.

An uneventful flight, but being our first time in Nigeria we were totally unprepared for what Lagos airport had to offer.

On leaving the terminal we are greeted by our hosts who guide us to our ground transport and then as we begin the drive out of the car park it is impossible to put in words the sight that greets you. What looks like a crowd of around forty thousand people are milling around seemingly with nothing to occupy them. It took hours to get to the hotel which again surprised us as massive steel gates were opened by machine gun carrying security guards then quickly closed behind us. With razor wire on top of six metre walls it resembled a prison and we were instructed not to leave without our security guards at any time for any purpose.

The next couple of days involved a lot of driving to construction sites and mining towns on the outskirts of Lagos and then a long drive south to the coast and the Lekki Free Trade Zone. All quite impressive and especially as we had armed guards driving both ahead and behind us at all times.

Only major thing to report was the driver had only one cassette in the SUV and so we learnt all of Kenny Rogers' lyrics over the next three days.

The third day saw us fly to the capital Abuja, where we were to meet the power brokers, politicians and government officers. A whole day was spent meeting ministers and advisers and then we were told the President Jonathan Goodluck had asked to meet up with us. To us this means they really mean business and so off we went. Security was unbelievable as we entered the Presidential compound and after about an hours wait in an ante room we were ushered into the President's office where we all shook hands made small talk and posed for a few photographs. The whole process took less than five minutes and the reason for us being in Nigeria was never discussed with the President but his Chief of Staff talked with us for about an hour and we felt things were on track. Our hosts informed us that we had to meet the former disgraced president as without his approval nothing would happen. So after a four hour drive we arrived at his compound and the surprising thing was the long line of people waiting to see him seeking his favour.

We were due to fly out the Sunday morning to London and I'd worked out that my football team, Sunderland, were playing at West Ham that same afternoon. Upton Park is on the Piccadilly line direct from Heathrow and I'd calculated all going to plan I'd make it for the second half so I contacted my son to try to find Barry so we could meet at the game.

Nothing goes according to plan in Nigeria. The British Airways flight from Abuja to London was scheduled to depart at eight am and on arriving at the airport we were advised the plane had not left London yet and at best we would be leaving around eight pm. Having checked out of the hotel we were driven back to our host's house and given the run of the place with the house servants plying us with food and drink all day.

Eventually we left for London later that evening and if the flight to Nigeria was uneventful not so the return flight. About thirty minutes after take-off I had major stomach cramps and started to feel nauseous just like I had when feeling the heart attack coming on some years ago. I stood up to try to make the toilet and next thing I knew I was flat on my face in the aisle. I'd collapsed, again like all those years ago. All I could think of at the time was how people would laugh on learning I'd died on a flight from Abuja, which most people had never heard of, to London, the irony of it. However the next thought became more important as I felt the total urge to get to the bathroom before there was another major event and it wasn't going to be pleasant. The airline staff were fussing around and above me, telling me to lie still and I kept telling them they had better get me to the toilet or they would regret it. Eventually I won the argument and they deferred to their better judgement for the comfort of the other passengers. After about thirty minutes in the toilet I exited not feeling too good and in fact thinking death would have been preferable. I was probably about five kilograms lighter than when I went into the toilet.

The stewards tried to make me comfortable, failed, but I eventually arrived at Heathrow feeling the worst I'd ever felt but thought I could make it to Earls Court where we were staying in London, on the train and after having to disembark at four different stations along the Piccadilly line I eventually made the hotel where our son on seeing me took me immediately to the Chelsea Westminster hospital. For the next twenty four hours I was poked, prodded, drained, sampled and any other action that hospital doctors can manage to dream up. Eventually I was put on a drip and some kind of normalcy prevailed.

On checking out and on my return to Australia we were telling the story to an English girl who had been a nurse at Chelsea Westminster she told us they would have been hoping I'd died as they were the teaching hospital in Britain for exotic diseases and in particular ones picked up in Africa. Sorry to disappoint them but after my second flirtation with death I became totally obsessive about foods I eat when abroad, and that includes England.

Postscript to the Nigerian expedition is that over the following weeks we were able to convince major investment groups in Australia, Europe, United States and China that Nigeria was the next frontier and had commitments of over half a billion Euros then Boko Haram the Muslim terrorist group upped their activities and the investors moved on to safer territories.

CHAPTER 58!

Out Of Africa!

Then there was the time in 1976 when I was asked by the African Queen nightclub at St. Leonards if I could get them an international act for their opening in three weeks time. In anybody's language that's a pretty steep order but I said I'd do my best. I contacted everyone I knew in America and the U.K. with little success it being such short notice but I kept on trying phoning all night until I decided to give my old friend John Hall a call. I had known John through my advertising days when he was promotions manager of RCA here in Australia and he was now holding down the same position in RCA London. As we were talking on the phone he asked if I could be interested in R & J Stone who were with him in his office. Would I? Of course they were currently number one on all the charts around the world including Australia with their hit We Do It. He put Russel on the phone and we struck a deal there and then. The usual package seven shows over seven nights, air fares for three, an apartment for the duration, a rent a car, and of course an agreed financial arrangement.

How lucky am I? I thought, but it now got down to the details including clearance from Actors Equity and the Musicians Union, not a problem. But arranging working visas could be a worry so after discussing my dilemma with our contact in the immigration department it appeared the only solution was for me to actually fly to London with the clearance papers, remember no emails in those days, and so I began to make my travel arrangements. More good luck when my phone rang and it was Lyle McCabe, who I didn't know at the time but he was producing the television quiz programme Celebrity Squares and could he book the Stones for a day of recording. Lyle later in life turned out to be my boss when I went into television production with McCabe Collins a couple of years later. Of course they are available, for a suitable fee. I then made contact with South African Airways to talk a deal which would involve sponsorship of the whole tour with television commercials thrown in. Things couldn't get better I was now holding from the airline eight round the world business class tickets worth about $48k at the time. Four to use on the promotion and four more to use in the future. The up fronts paid by the nightclub and I was off to London to seal the deal and arrange visas.

I left on the Thursday with all meetings arranged for the Monday then we were to fly back together on the Friday ready for a week of promotion before the next Saturday opening.

I had decided seeing I was flying South African Airways and first stop was Johannesburg I'd grab the opportunity to visit my brother and his family who had lived there for about seven years and I hadn't seen them in that time. In fact I'd never met his three children. As I wasn't due in London till the Monday everything appeared to fit.

It was here I made the mistake of thinking South Africa would be just like Australia being former British colonies surely the mindset and the infrastructure would Johannesburg like Sydney without a harbour. Was I in for a surprise? I had their address but I hadn't the time to let them know I was on my way but I thought all I would have to do would be to catch a train from Jan Smuts airport to the suburban station and then catch a taxi to Barry's address in Honeydew and what a surprise that would be for his family. I was travelling very light as I was only going to be away for a few days. I was dressed in a T-shirt and jeans with a light cotton bomber jacket. There was a small haversack with a change of socks and underpants that would see me through the journey. Arrived in Johannesburg in the afternoon and my first experience of South Africa came at customs where they confiscated my book and magazines. I can remember the officer pulling out a large folder with dozens of pages having the names of banned publications. I then tried to call my brother at his home but got no reply or an invitation to leave a message on an answering machine so off to the railway station I went.

On the station platform I had my first hint of what apartheid meant when noticing the 'whites only' benches and drinking fountains. We'd heard about it in Australia even to the point of a major South African rugby tour facing unprecedented demonstrations all over Australia leading to the cancellation of a scheduled cricket tour. Hearing about it a few thousand kilometres away is one thing but the actuality still comes as a shock. As the train pulled in I saw that the coloured passengers all entered the rear carriages and the few whites used the leading cars. I can still remember the feeling of discomfort as I travelled on that train to Honeydew.

On alighting from the train at Honeydew the first thing I noticed was how much the temperature had fallen and how quickly the sky had darkened. I was later to find out that was because Johannesburg is built on a massive plateau way above sea level and when the sun sets below the reef it's dark and cold within minutes.

Nothing to worry about, just find the taxi rank and I should be at Barry's place within minutes. Not so fast! I then realised this was not a proper railway station with ticket offices, guards and all the other attachments I was used to in Sydney. No the station was only a concrete platform that had steps on each side giving you no option but to cross the track either east or west.

I made my selection and with no other ideas I began to walk along the road hoping I'd come to a telephone box or a shopping precinct, in fact anything, even a house would provide some comfort. By now I was freezing cold and with no street lighting I was beginning to fear the worst that someone may find the frozen corpse of an Australian backpacker in the middle of a South African side road.

Life moves in mysterious ways and just as I was on the brink of sitting down and giving up I came across a guy, black, and his girlfriend trying to push start their broken down car. I asked if he needed a hand. The guy nearly wet his pants at the sound of my voice coming out of the blackness and I could sense his fear at the fact that I was white and hence potentially dangerous. I reassured him by telling him I was from Australia and I was totally lost so with the girlfriend in the driving seat ready to clutch start him and I gave the car a good push, the engine roared into life and in his gratitude asked me where I was heading. I told him Honeydew and he had no idea where it was. Thinking I may have got off at the wrong platform I didn't have a clue as to my next move. They offered me a lift which I thankfully accepted and after driving a few kilometres following the railway line I noticed a red light on the other side of the railway tracks which to my delight looked like a pub. I thanked my new found friends and clambered down the scrub over the lines and back up and presented myself at the door of the public house. There was no-one in the public bar so I wandered around looking for a sign of life then on hearing voices coming from another room, and even better they had English accents, I opened the door to the cocktail bar where there was a barman and two customers having a friendly chat. My teeth were chattering with the cold so I asked for a brandy. Much to my surprise the barman informed me he couldn't serve me. Why? Because I wasn't wearing a tie! Has the world gone mad I thought and out I came describing my misadventures since leaving Sydney that morning in a tone that I don't usually have but it served the purpose as the barman turned around and pulled a tie, already knotted, from a peg on the shelf and placed it around my neck then served me the brandy.

After settling down and realising it was now around eleven o clock at night it appeared I had no way of finding my brother's house as even these guys hadn't heard of the suburb Honeydew so I asked if the pub had a room for the night. No such luck it wasn't a residential hotel but the two customers offered to drive me to what they called a transient workers hotel a few kilometres away. They drove me to the hotel, which seemed to be in the middle of nowhere, and when the dropped me off at the front door I gave them a bottle of duty free scotch I had bought for my brother but this was a more deserving couple of guys. Off they went and I walked up the three steps to the front door which was lit up but on trying the door Oh No! it was locked. No-one at reception and no way around the back or telephone number to ring if late arriving. Not that that would have helped as I didn't have a phone or any means of finding one. I knocked and knocked. Then I knocked harder and was shouting through the gap in the doors until eventually the cleaning lady appeared carrying her bucket and mop and I asked her to let me in. No, no she waved her hand and shook her head. I was getting nowhere and it was looking more and more I was going to have to sleep on the porch in minus ten degree temperatures. I got angrier and angrier and even realising that the lady was only following instructions I started to shout at her in a manner that only Afrikaans can muster and she jumped to the door and let me in. I apologised profusely but I could see she was afraid of me. I still feel shame to this day and I hope nobody minds that I'm not putting in here the words I used to gain admission. I grabbed a key from behind the reception desk and helped myself to a room for the night.

The next morning I went downstairs, introduced myself to reception, paid for the room then went into the cafeteria for breakfast. The guys from last night were correct it was a hotel for transient workers, mainly European tradesmen working for the local mining companies.

One English guy sat at my table and it turned out he knew where Honeydew was. Apparently it was a new development with Macmansions everywhere and also a gated community which was the first time I had heard those expressions. He offered to drive me to my brother's place which I gladly accepted his offer and on arrival I gave him the other bottle of duty free scotch.

To say Barry and Christine were surprised doesn't quite catch the moment and after advising them I was only there for one day and in fact I was leaving that evening for London I never even got the chance to meet his children as they took me to the airport before they got home from horse riding practise after school. To his dying day my brother insisted to all who would listen that I was definitely a drug dealer or something criminally similar because of my many travel destinations over the years. But this story still has a lot to go on with.

On the Monday I met with John, R & J at RCA head office where we introduced ourselves to each other, signed agreement then made our way to Western Union to pick up cash deposit and on to Australia House in The Strand. Met with the immigration officer for Australia with the paperwork I had carried with me from Sydney. Passports produced and stamped accordingly then off to lunch courtesy of RCA. Having a day to spare I rang my middle sister Anne who was the only one of the Atkinson brood still living in England and I made arrangements to catch a train to Durham where she and her husband Stuart met me. It's good to catch up with family members one hasn't seen for some years.

Back to London and off to Heathrow where I met Mr. and Mrs. Stone with their musical director at the South African Airways check in desk. They check in before me and I tell them I'll meet them in the lounge after I check in. Not quite what I expected as I plonked my United Kingdom passport on the desk only to be told that I didn't have a visa to re-enter Australia and the airline couldn't let me board as the rules were that I would become the responsibility of the airline if I wasn't allowed to disembark and they would then have to return me to England.

How had this happened? Turns out Australia for decades had allowed British subjects to travel freely without visas in and out of the country and in the few days I had been away the new system requiring visas for British subjects had been gazetted and was now law.

I was stuck. Made sure Russell and Joanne were advised of my position and using an airline internal phone system told them to go ahead and I'll have someone to meet them in Sydney on arrival. Then on to the Piccadilly line to try and reach The Strand before Australia House closed for the weekend.

Didn't make it!

Stuck in London till at the earliest Monday or Tuesday.

I then made the decision to fly to Johannesburg on the Saturday in the mistaken belief that being half way there would be better than hanging around in London and I could apply for the visa in Johannesburg. Another mistake. I'd forgotten the capital of South Africa is not Johannesburg it is Pretoria a fair trip out from Johannesburg. I checked into an airport hotel feeling a little stupid at these snap decisions I had been making and decided I'd try again with the airline staff the next morning and see if I could charm my way on to a flight.

I turned up at the check in desk and was given the same story as the London staff had given me. The lady handed me a brochure from Australian Department of Immigration explaining the new visa rules.

I sat down and started to read the brochure which listed the new rules and then listed the exceptions to the new rules which included diplomats, overseas members of parliament, guests of the Australian Government and also passengers in transit who could stay no longer than forty eight hours in Australia. On flashed the light bulb and back to the desk I went, bought a single ticket from Sydney to Auckland New Zealand on a flight leaving the day after my arrival in Sydney. The lady behind the desk started to laugh as I put down my credit card to pay for the ticket and when I enquired as to why she was laughing she told me I had just given her the perfect plan for any others who were caught like me. Glad I was of some assistance.

At immigration in Sydney I was given the treatment. Held for a few hours pleading my innocence and they were threatening to keep me in detention till the Auckland flight left. The suddenly I was out of there and I soon knew why.

To my surprise I was met by a media scrum who had heard of my dilemna as R & J Stone in all their interviews on television, radio and press had been having a good laugh at my expense retelling the story of my travel disruptions. I was a bit of a joke until I told them how I had beaten the system so I went from being a joke to being a smart arse.

The post script to quite a successful venture came a couple of months later when I went to arrange a couple of tickets to London from the deal done with South African Airways only to find Boris, the owner of the African Queen, had used them to bring some of his family from Yugoslavia for a holiday in Australia. The fracas with customs came back to haunt me some forty years later when I had forgotten to renew my visa when visiting Cambodia and they pulled out the old file with press clippings etc. and after another grilling session let me in again but with the warning that next time I wouldn't be allowed in and that's why I'm now applying for Australian citizenship. I'm too old to carry on being a subject of her majesty.

CHAPTER 59

One Step Ahead!

Having one's own television production company, appropriately called The Production Factory because of the sheer volume of product we were producing. This included television commercials, corporate and sales videos, music videos and eventually we tried our hand at producing television programmes. This is where I learnt that there's only one thing worse than being behind the times and that's being ahead of them. Our first venture was in cooking when we approached Margaret Chen the owner of Noble House Chinese restaurant in the Central Business District of Sydney. Noble House was regarded as one of the best Chinese restaurants in Australia at the time. This was years before Jamie Oliver, Nigella Lawson or any of the other celebrity chefs or cooking competition programmes.

We produced a pilot thirty minute programme that gave basic tips on cooking Chinese food at home and then actually cooked a stir fry dish on camera. While our hostess/chef visited her family in China we went into post production and offered the pilot to SBS television who were quite enthusiastic about the project and we would tie up details on Margaret's return. Unfortunately for all involved and especially Margaret's family she died in a plane crash while flying in China and never returned to Sydney.

Our next tentative step into programme production was based on health and fitness including correct dieting and exercise. We had a medical doctor, George Fishman as advisor on medical items, Rosemary Stanton dietician, and Garry Eggar as our fitness guru. We kept it light hearted with the odd serious insight including eating disorders and drug abuse. We were very proud of the production so imagine our disappointment when all networks knocked us back saying television was for entertainment not reality. Looking at what television offers now we were so far ahead of our time but we picked ourselves up dusted ourselves off and tried again this time working on something everyone had an interest in, money.

At this time television in Australia was in turmoil with stations and networks changing ownership on what appeared to be a weekly basis. I had made friends with the finance editor of the Daily Telegraph, Sydney's leading newspaper, Roger Scott while working on a pop music video of a Penthouse pet in Bellevue Hill. Suffice to say it was not a hit. However over a barbecue in his back garden we came up with the idea of a forty five minute weekly television series dealing with all aspects of money. We would include stock market reports, international investments, household spending, travel, dining out and in fact having no limits on what we would comment on as money is involved with every aspect of life. We decided on Dollars and Sense as a title and set about finding the right talent for the regular segments we would include. Thanks to Roger we enlisted journalists who could present and write their own material and as everyone knows all print journalists are looking for the television opportunity to present itself. We made arrangements with Steve Cosser who owned Broadcom, a production house making a bid to take over the Ten network, to use his studio and facilities free of charge with Broadcom having first right of refusal when the pilot was in the bag. It was also good fortune that his son and our son both attended Cranbrook School in the same year so we had been on nodding terms at school functions. Only one problem to solve. We need a host. Someone with the gravitas to talk on stocks and shares but also with a sense of humour that would endear him to the general public as were including domestic and leisure spending. We tried a few people with little success then Roger suggested we talk with a man who had been running a number of financial advice magazines but his company had closed the publication and he was looking for something to do. It was arranged that we would meet at the Point Piper Motor Yacht club the coming Saturday afternoon by the pool with all kids and family invited. Saturday came and Roger introduced me to David Koch, a successful financial journalist. He hadn't done television before but he came across as a genuine person and I agreed to him doing the pilot episode.

We furnished him with a rundown on what was to be included in the episode with some brief notes on what was involved and looked forward to the next Thursday afternoon when we had the studio and crew booked for Dollars and Sense.

Lights, Camera, Action, as they say in the movies, and we were underway. Opening titles with music and jingle underneath cut to David and never in my life had I come across a person destined to be on television as was David Koch. He was the most naturally talented person for television and it was plain to see from the looks on the faces of the crew and the other journalists. He looked right down the barrel of the cameras and into people's living rooms as though he belonged there as an old friend. Not being used to such professionalism from a novice I had to invent some faults in the presentation for a few more takes so I could look like I was earning my money as a director. A natural and it's very pleasing to see his current success as a major television presenter on one of Australia's major networks.

What happened to Dollars and Sense?

After shopping it around and receiving excellent feedback from the commercial networks we really believed we had a chance with it and imagine our disappointment when Broadcom and Max Walsh announced their own money based series on the Ten Network.

Our final hurrah in trying to get a television series came about through a nightclub operator, Leon Nacson, who had always wanted to get into television and had big ambitions for his younger brother, Angie, who was a disc jockey in Leon's clubs. The idea was to buy the time between midnight and six am on Friday and Saturday nights playing pop video clips with interviews and entertainment news and weekend gig guides. He would arrange a sales team who would space farm the commercial space to other clubs and concert promoters. It was to be called 2Mid-Dawn as a play on words to suggest radio with pictures. The first guests were to be the Penthouse Pet previously referred to and a quite famous actor Jack Thompson, currently best known for living in a polygamous state with two sisters and his nude centrefold in Cleo magazine. On taking his seat for the interview and the crew were setting up he pulled out a cigarette and I offered him a light from my disposable Bic lighter. He took the lighter from me, placed it on the desk then reached into the pocket in his denim shirt, pulled out a gold Dunhill lighter, proceeded to light his cigarette then returned it to his pocket and then picked up my Bic and gently handed it back to me with a smile and a thank you.

Never realised that one flame is better than others.

Again no success. By the time we had our pilot finished John Collins, an established television producer, had purchased the time to show horror movies from midnight to dawn so we were trumped again.

However there is another example of being one step ahead that I pride myself on spotting. There was a very small clothing company in Kingsgrove, a suburb of Sydney, Beach Fashions. The owner was a Greek gentleman who had approached us about whether he could afford a television advertising campaign and we put together a test package of fifteen thousand dollars of which five thousand would be for production of the commercial and the other ten thousand to buy fringe time television exposure. I set about writing and storyboarding the commercial and having a good time auditioning the swimsuit models we needed for the commercial. One slight bit of nepotism here as I booked my girlfriend Lisa first then went looking for others. Lisa suggested I call her agent, Peter Chadwick as he had a good stable of bikini models. On calling him he suggested that I could use one of his top models Elle Macpherson who was quite well known at the time and I said I'd put it to the client, Beach Fashions, to see his reaction. He also told me that she had just finished a photo shoot for Sports Illustrated magazine and there was a chance she would be on the cover of the annual swimwear edition.

I asked the cost and when told ten thousand dollars for a half day shoot and the commercial to be used for six months only, it appeared to be a bargain to me. He also offered a five year exclusive swimwear commercial deal that could involve a range of Elle Macpherson costumes for eighty thousand dollars a year. A lot of money in those days I know. However the success of Bendon, Intimates and The Body and other Elle Macpherson sponsorships make it look like peanuts now. The client deferred on both offers and the rest is history.

However as a postscript she was replaced for the commercial by another swimsuit model who went on to win fame and fortune, Jodhi Meares, soon to become Jodhi Packer. To complete this story of missed opportunities I was recently standing on the platform at Kingsgrove railway station heading back into the city when I noticed the back of the building which had housed Beach Fashions. The paintwork was peeling and falling, half the letters were missing and it had a very run down look about it.

Oh what might have been!

CHAPTER 60!

It's A Small World!

During the years of The Production Factory and our long standing relationship with K-Tel we were introduced to the surfing community who had recently formed the Professional Surfers association and had sponsors who wanted to raise the profile of the sport and the professional surfers involved. We were introduced to Graham Cassidy, the association's president who in turn introduced us to Roy Norris their promotions and advertising manager. Roy was one of those characters that filled a room as they walked in. Always new ideas, always new people with him, always talking and always enthusiastic on whatever he was involved with. Through Roy we met the world's leading surfers including five time World Champion, Mark Richards, a quiet gentleman the complete antithesis of Roy but obviously the best of friends. We produced a number of commercials for them including surfboards, boogie boards, roof racks etc. We also did a number of promotional videos which led us into producing mini documentaries on Pacific Island holiday spots. How good is this? Three weeks sampling every island in Fiji and getting paid for it. We were then hired by the major travel agents for Bali holidays and were looking forward to another three weeks of Paradise. Co-incidentally on the Sunday before our scheduled Thursday departure Australia's leading current affairs television programme, Sixty Minutes, did a story on the poor state of medical facilities available for tourists in Bali. The Indonesian government complained and it nearly caused an international incident because of the effect it could have on the tourist industry. Didn't think it would be causing us any problems as we were going there to promote Bali as a great holiday destination so imagine our surprise when at the check in desk of Garuda airlines we were told we were not allowed on board with our equipment as Indonesia had put a blanket ban on all television crews from Australia. Very disappointed we turned around and headed back to our Balmain office and on arrival were surprised to find journalists camped on our doorstep looking for quotes on our misadventure. We told what had occurred then left it at that thinking it was a storm in a teacup and we would probably be able to make the trip in a couple of weeks time. Not quite! On the drive to the office the next day outside every newsagent was the banners proclaiming Indonesian government bans on television crews with my picture displayed large as life. We had made all the front pages so it came as no surprise when we lost the contract for the job. We still maintained good relations with the surfing fraternity and Roy kept us entertained with all his stories and world altering plans. He turned up one day with a new friend, a panel beater from Five Dock. Very affable and pleasant company and a little star struck by mixing with people in the television industry. He was always offering to do favours like driving the crew around and I began to wonder whenever did he have the time to make a living at his trade. I soon found out. It was Lisa's eighteenth birthday and we were having a party in the basement of the office and I had a surprise for her in that I had bought her a small BMW car as a present. He took it back to his workshop and gave it the full detailing and it arrived at the party looking like a brand new car. He also brought something else, small packets of white powder that seemed to have mood changing effects on whichever people decided to snort it up their nose. Things are becoming clearer now, especially the permanent upbeat moods of Roy his new best friend. Later in the evening I was taken aside and told he had a great idea for me. At the time I drove a red Mercedes 450SL convertible sports car and his offer was that he knew some people who were looking to do an insurance scam on a 500SL, yes red in colour. The deal was for five thousand dollars the car would be stolen from the apartment's car park, taken to the panel beating shop where my car would be waiting to have all the plates changed including VIN numbers and no-one would notice the difference and I would have a brand new car worth around a hundred thousand dollars for the paltry sum of five thousand dollars. Needless to say I declined the offer. From then on I became a little wary of the company I was keeping.

It was at this time that I was approached by my client at K-Tel, Bob, who wanted me to arrange a licensing deal for some product that he and his immediate superior had put together but they couldn't offer it to K-Tel as employees so would I be willing to assist in a small subterfuge. Also worth noting neither was I able to make the offer as a service provider. I was given the master tapes of the product and told to deliver them to Maurie Nowytarger, the proprietor of Mission Records and a solicitor, who had done some licensing deals with K-Tel in the past. Their office was in the harbourside suburb of Woolloomooloo and was actually a very large warehouse with the open office on the mezzanine level. On the warehouse floor were three classic cars, a Bentley, an Aston Martin and some American classic. They were half covered with tarpaulins and dust and dirt was everywhere obviously being kept in storage. He already had a contract ready for me to sign giving him the rights to manufacture and distribute recordings of the tapes I was supplying with a royalty payable to me of fifty cents per copy. It slowly started to seep in what the deal was. I was enough arms length from K-Tel to license my product to Mission for fifty cents who would then license it to K-Tel, my client Bob having the say so on what was acceptable for K-Tel for fifty five cents. When royalty payments were made Murray would get his fifty five, pass fifty to me then I would pass forty cents on to Bob and partner. Simple! Contract signed and pocketed.

I was going down the stairs and who should I bump into coming in? The panel beater. Someone from another part of my life completely unconnected. We exchanged pleasantries and went our separate ways.

It was around this time we were looking to place our son in a pre-school kindergarten which was very difficult at the time due to shortage of spaces and also very expensive. We found Thumbelinas in Edgecliff but were told no vacancies and as desperation set in what a surprise to find out Roy Norris's fiancée Carol, was a teacher at Thumbelina. Problem solved!

The next event in this saga occurred some weeks later when K-Tel had made the first royalty payment so it was decided we would meet for lunch that day at La Grillade a very show business restaurant in Crows Nest. Over lunch cheques changed hands and we were full of bon hommie and a little red wine when Claude the owner of La Grillade came to the table with a phone call for Maurie. On taking the call Maurie politely made his excuses as he had to leave for something very important. Out of the restaurant he went and through the window we could see him climbing into his classic gull wing Mercedes sports car then driving away. As lunch was coming to a close someone noticed he had left his briefcase.

Claude picked it up saying he'd keep it behind the bar for Maurie to pick up later, however he couldn't resist undoing the clips and opening it on the table in front of all of us. Shock horror. In the briefcase were neat bundles of cash amounting to thousands of dollars and about twenty small gold ingots, but no-one wanted to inspect any further. The briefcase was closed a lot quicker than it was opened and we all swore each other to secrecy that none of us had seen anything. Just at that moment a gull winged Mercedes pulled up in a screeching halt outside the window and a very flustered Maurie came charging into the restaurant looking for his briefcase which had been placed exactly where he had left it. He departed quickly and we all had another drink to calm our nerves.

Things started to move very quickly as we entered the eighties. Roy got married to his fiancée, Carol, in a very expensive wedding at the Regent hotel with about five hundred guests and most of Dire Straits acting as the wedding band. Probably the biggest, most expensive wedding I've ever been to. Off they went on their honeymoon in Fiji.

On his return we got a call from him asking us to go with him and his wife to Kinselas to see Renee Geyer and Doug Parkinson and to meet him at the Oxford Motel in Oxford Street where they were staying. Sounded a little strange as they rented a house in Vaucluse just down the street from us.

We met them in the bar of the motel and when we asked what was happening and why they weren't at home we were informed that he was fearing for his life as he had hidden thirty thousand dollars cash in his garage before leaving for their honeymoon and on their return they discovered it had been stolen and it was owed to some very nasty people hence they were staying at this motel and were leaving the next day for places unknown and maybe in a few years time they'd contact us again. A little scary for us so we enjoyed the dinner and show said our goodbyes and we never saw them again. I always had it in mind he had returned to Wollongong which was where he grew up. The next we heard on Roy was that he disappeared in September 2004 leaving behind his wife and three children. It was rumoured he faked his own suicide or his past had caught up with him. We probably will never know.

The next event in my slight brush with criminal elements was in 1990 when Maurie Nowytarger was sentenced with his partner in crime, disgraced police detective Roger Rogerson, to four years in jail for conspiracy to pervert the course of justice using the sale of a restored Bentley to launder cash payments thought to be bribes or drug takings. It turned out our panel beater had been delivering invoices, and getting paid for restoration work that never took place. It was only with hindsight that I tried to connect some dots and wondered how I had become so close to these people through different avenues.

Met PB through Roy Norris, PB involved with Maurie Nowytarger, who I have met through K-Tel people and as told previously seen in Buona Gusto restaurant with Roger Rogerson after being invited to join their table after a late lunch. With all the comings and goings over the years I often thought maybe if there had been some police surveillance on these people they may have jumped to the conclusion I was a master criminal pulling the strings like a puppet master. But it does show that it's a small world, especially in the one I seem to move in.

CHAPTER 61!

Nice Bag Of Fruit!

Then there was the time recent when some friends of my wife had invited us to dinner at their house one Saturday night. Some background may be necessary here as they are a gay married couple, very wealthy and living in a beautiful mansion in one of the inner suburbs of Sydney, Glebe. The house itself worth some $9 million and the reason for the dinner was that the seller of another property had recently accepted their bid for a $20 million iconic Sydney mansion. We were regulars at their soirees and the guests were always entertaining and the couple themselves had no airs and graces being a very down to earth couple. The events were always fully catered with only the best beer and wines, even the annual Xmas parties they held for the neighbours' children with bouncing castles, circus clowns and jazz bands. But this dinner was for the inner circle of twelve that could be seated at their dining table. I hadn't given the event much thought and on that particular Saturday Lisa had gone to her showroom and I was working at home. Around two o clock Lisa called and I heard the panic in her voice as she told me she had forgotten it was to be a black tie formal dinner so get out the tuxedo, bow tie, dress shirt etc. Having not been to a formal function for some months it was no surprise to find on taking the dinner suit out of its bag a few white patches of what could have been anything, living or dead. Tried to brush them off, no luck. As most of us know given notice of a formal occasion we would have checked out the suit and send it to the dry cleaners. Tried the dress shirt, a few too many kilos since last worn had been added making fastening the buttons impossible. Only five hours to go, not an option. Shouldn't be a problem, just hire one. Called up a few hire companies.

Bad news it's a Saturday, the day of most weddings, balls etc. No-one could guarantee having a suit my size available and if they did it was going to cost over two hundred dollars to hire. I rang Lisa back with the news that I would wear my charcoal grey business suit with a bow tie and hope no-one would notice. That idea received short shrift and I was told to get out and hire an outfit, after all these were very good friends and everyone would be dressed up to the nines. I tried again, no luck and I was running out of time. I rang Lisa again explaining my dilemma and she came up with a brilliant idea. Worth noting here that Lisa runs a very successful furnishings company that specialises in rescuing old, classical pieces that have been discarded by others. She re-upholsters and paints them so a lot of her time is spent in op shops looking for furnishings she can work on. Her instructions were to get off my backside and get to the St. Vincents charity shop in Lane Cove, she had seen lots of men's suits hanging up for sale. So off I went. The shop was pretty full with people and certainly changed my ideas on what charity shops looked like. Very elegant décor, friendly staff and items displayed as well as most department stores. Down the back was the men's section and within five minutes I had a dinner jacket with the fashionable pointed lapels, much better than my rolled ones, a perfect fit and I did feel a little like Sean Connery or maybe Daniel Craig as I preened myself in the mirror. I now needed trousers to match. Should be simple, after all in the words of the song black is black. Not so. I was now finding out there are many shades of black and many textures of material so I couldn't find matching trousers. I did however find a brand new dress shirt with the black studs fitted in. Again a perfect fit in neck, chest and sleeves with the French cuffs.

Nearly there. Up to the cashier. Jacket - twenty dollars thank you, shirt six dollars-thanks again. Where could I find a pair of trousers? Try our Chatswood store just a few kilometres away.

Fifteen minute later I'm in Chatswood and with my new dinner jacket in hand I now work on my colour matching skills. After a few minutes Lady Luck smiles on me and I find again the perfect colour and perfectly fitting trousers. Feeling good I decide to invest in a new bow tie while I'm here. Up to the cashier. Trousers- yes sir that'll be eight dollars- thank you, bow tie four dollars-thanks again. I'm now the proud owner of a new formal outfit modern in design, expensive in looks and a perfect fit. The grand total of thirty eight dollars making me feel very pleased with myself. Couldn't find any dress shoes, but I had a decent pair at home anyway. Could life get any better? Off home to see Lisa already dressing, doing hair, and as ladies tend to do, panic over everything and applying make-up. I had achieved my result right on the deadline as I only had an hour before we were due at the other side of Sydney.

Had my shower, dressed myself, although Lisa had to tie the bow. She won't let me wear the clip-ons. There we were as is usual before the time of departure adding final touches in front of the mirror, bearing in mind Lisa had not seen the final result of my shopping expedition, bragging about how it had only cost me thirty eight dollars, and now for the first time the revelation of the full outfit. What did she think as I fastened the jacket button, then puffed out my chest, put my hands into the trouser pockets, and as she maintained her admiring looks I felt something in the pocket.

You wouldn't believe it in a hundred years - yes I had spent thirty eight dollars but even better still when I pulled my hand out of the pocket there was ninety dollars left there by the previous owner.

I would have loved to have told the story over the dinner table that night but Lisa swore me to secrecy about going into charity shops.

Might be a job opportunity for somebody to go into charity shops, not necessarily to buy anything, but more to search the pockets of all the jackets and trousers that are on the racks.

CHAPTER 62!

I'm Ready For My Close Up!

Having been on the fringes of show business for so many years my interest was piqued in 2013 when I saw an article in the newspaper discussing a seniors acting classes course being sponsored by the Sydney City Council. The article referred to a lady who had never acted in her life beforehand but after taking a few of the drama classes she had secured parts in television commercials and programmes. The classes were being held in a community centre in Potts Point and were strictly for people over sixty. The next Tuesday came around and I took the plunge. Don't know what my expectations were but on arrival found a very small group of 'oldies' being directed by Susie Dougherty, a well-known actress from the television drama Home and Away. It was slightly embarrassing initially as she led us through, what appeared to be, a number of breathing exercises and body stretches making funny faces and disgusting noises. If nothing else it levelled the playing field as we all looked quite silly to each other so barriers were down.

We were then led through a number of practise scripts in pairs and some of the more experienced delivered monologues. I was hooked. I liked the people and I liked the openness of the group as at the coffee break the conversation turned to what we were all doing there and why had we joined this disparate group. One lady actually wanted to be famous, another had a morbid fear of public speaking, two had been actors in former lives, but the main reason seemed to be to have some company to help them get away from the loneliness after losing husbands and wives.

Myself I was just curious.

A few weeks into the course Suzie suggested I should get an agent but I wasn't too interested but said I'd consider it. As what usually happens to me fate takes me by the hand and leads me into unchartered waters. As it was the fortieth anniversary of the opening of Sydney Opera House I was approached by a journalist who had heard my story to recount it for a major feature on the Opera House. The article appeared with a photograph of myself gracing the sails of the Opera House and on the day it appeared I received a phone call from a friend, Martin Bedford someone I hadn't seen or heard from in thirty five years and it turned out he was now a quite well known theatrical agent. We chatted for a while bringing each other up to date on what was happening in our lives and I happened to mention that I was involved in a seniors acting class. Thought nothing more of it then a couple of weeks later he called me again and asked if I was interested in acting because there was an opening in a movie production, The Unforgotten, being directed in Australia with no-one less than Angelina Jolie and he had sent my picture to them and they wanted to see me the next morning at Fox Studios in Moore Park. Who could resist this? The next day ten o clock on the dot I was at the studio gates where I announced myself to the security guards and a few minutes later a young lady arrived in a golf buggy which she used to take me around the old showgrounds to have pictures taken, measurements for wardrobes taken, dressed in a number of suits and shirts. Clothes hung on hangers with my name and photograph attached then round to make-up and hairdressers where most of my curls were hacked off to give me a look that was around in nineteen thirty six. Turns out the movie is a true story of an Italian migrant to America runs in the nineteen thirty six Olympics in Berlin then joins the American forces. A true story of heroism. It's reasonable to assume I was not to be the star or even have an important role to play but I liked the attention anyway. All I had to do now was wait for the call that would take me into the life one thinks of as Hollywood.

When the call came about two weeks later it was for me to be at Sydney Central Station at two o clock in the morning where transport would be provided to get myself and others to the Camden Showgrounds, a two hour drive out to the south west of Sydney. Yes that was the first shock, two o clock in the morning, but off I went and found two coaches there to transport actors and crew members numbering about eighty. On arrival at our destination the sun was about to rise and we were herded into make-up and wardrobe then mustered into a dining marquee where breakfast was served. It was all action stations as the sun appeared in the sky and off we went to the set in the showground which was now dressed up to be a Californian college athletics racing track. I was picked out and sent to the props department where I had a camera thrust at me, the old kind with the flash bulb and disc, and told I was playing the part of Sports Photographer Number One and I was to be featured in a number of shots at the beginning and end of the races.

Not too arduous I thought and obviously not too important a part to play that the director herself would need to pay me any individual attention.

There was take after take with me having to take shots on my knees then getting up asking for more photos, running alongside trying to get the magic shot. Absolutely exhausting especially as the temperature kept rising into the low thirties. The day was one of repetition with each segment being shot over and over again without setting eyes on our famous director till late in the afternoon when she approached our coterie of photographers and asked if I was available the next day. Yes, one of the most famous people on the planet had opened up a conversation with me. Needless to say I was quite pleased with the attention and while I was talking with her, her mobile phone rang and she turned away to speak then after putting it back in her pocket remarked that it was her husband who had just landed at Sydney airport. Husband! Good grief I was now almost best friends with Mr. and Mrs. Brad Pitt. I would like to point out that she had no airs and graces, was very down to earth, non-patronising and very professional at her job as director. I thought I could curry some favour with her when she asked me to take a number of pictures as the star crossed the finishing line. The director and the cameraman were now focused on me and I went into my routine. No-one had told me but I realised that these old flash cameras could only take one shot with the flash then the globe had to be changed. So after 'Action' I took the first photo then turned the camera so it was not in shot and I pretended to replace the globe even to the point of licking my fingers as if the hot globe had stung me. Madam director called 'Cut' and came to me asking what I was doing. After I explained she thanked me for thinking of it and congratulated me for acting on it. We were now best friends and having Angelina Jolie making such a fuss of me was creating some murmurs among the rest of the minor players, all in good jest, and I was booked again for the next day for close ups.

So watch out for me in the movie Unbroken.

I'm now in the movies.

Must start writing my acceptance speech for the Oscars.

The second day came and went with more of the same along with me being teased mercilessly by the other actors about the attention I was getting and considering it was my first days on a major film production. Oh well! Plucked out of obscurity then thrown back into it after two days and that was when I thought my acting career had ground to a halt. But there's more! A week or so later I was invited on to a new feature movie starring Adrien Brody, him from The Pianist and Sam Neill of Jurassic Park fame, called Backtrack, a horror thriller to be shot again in Sydney. First call was on New Year's Eve where myself and seven others spent the whole day performing in front of the green screen in preparation for special effects. We were to play fatal casualties of a train crash but somehow we never crossed the Styx and remained in limbo for the next thirty years. Our scenes involved us in an all night shoot on the platform seven at Sydney Central Station boarding the train that was taking us to our death. We also worked the next night all through the night at Warragamba a small area outside of Sydney where the train wreckage had been constructed in the old lion park and the irony of this was that we were now all dead on the train and as it was working through the night we kept falling asleep only for them to keep waking us up then telling us to play dead.

CHAPTER 63!

Flying Blind!

It's now September 2014 and our funding of infrastructure projects in Africa and Asia are motoring along and Colin our chairman is in Ghana putting finishing touches to a deal where we would be financing a housing project of four thousand affordable homes with the support of the Ghanaian government when he decided it was getting close to completing the details of the deal and I would have to be there next week to supervise contracts etc. Not a problem so I began making my travel plans when later that same day I received an email from our Cameroon associate that they needed me in Yaounde also the next week. This is getting better the countries are neighbours so I can kill two birds with one stone.

Then a sharp reminder from Lisa that we hadn't seen our son for nearly two years saw me booking for the two of us to London and back and I would leave her in London while I explored West Africa and then pick her up on the way back.

Everything falling into place. We'll stop over for two nights in Bangkok just to break up the twenty five hours travelling time and then off to London.

Lisa settled in the apartment off I went on the train to Heathrow to catch my plane to Accra via Amsterdam.

Arrived to check in at the KLM desk only to be informed that three others and myself had been dumped off the plane due to overbooking and they would fly us there tomorrow.

Tomorrow's no good I'm meeting minister of public works at ten in the morning tomorrow. I left the other three arguing with the service desk and headed to terminal five where I was counting on getting a seat with British Airways that afternoon.

Fortunately there was a seat available and the mystery of airline ticket pricing became a bigger mystery when I was told it was a thousand euros cheaper to book a return ticket to Accra than if I was to book a one way. I booked the return shaking my head and wondering about it all and I now had a return ticket Accra to London in my possession that I had absolutely no intention of using.

Such is life!

Accra and Ghana went well. We met all the people we had to meet and business was completed so while Colin headed back to Sydney I boarded another plane to Yaounde the capital of Cameroon.

Once again went through the rituals of meeting government ministers and heads of departments and received mandates to seek out investors and construction companies to facilitate two billion dollars worth of infrastructure projects so it was now time to make my departure and leave for London to meet up with Lisa and head back to Bangkok and then home to Sydney. I must be either the most unlucky or the most cavalier plane passenger in the world as news came through that the pilots of Air France were going on strike and there was no chance of me catching my flight to Paris and then on to London. After a gruelling three hours in a non air conditioned Air France office in Yaounde the lady behind the desk said she could pull a favour from a friend at Air Cameroon and I had to be at the airport at ten o' clock that evening and ask for Jean Paul and he would get me on a flight to Paris.

Not exactly filled with confidence I did as I was told and without a ticket or boarding pass I was given a seat at the back and with some relief landed in Paris the next morning.

Sill had to get to London and my Air France ticket of no use took the opportunity of catching the Eurostar first class at Air France's expense.

It was a relief to get back to civilisation and much to my pleasant surprise on my return to Sydney I was refunded six thousand dollars by Air France for mishaps that had cost me less than a thousand dollars.

CHAPTER 64!

Short Takes!

A SECRET AGENT!

Then there was the time in 1982 when I answered the phone and it turned out to be from the jail at Long Bay, the main prison for the state of New South Wales in the southern suburbs of Sydney. It turned out to be from a former employee who had been a roadie and he had found himself on remand for some drugs misdemeanour. He wanted to meet up with me to discuss a good business proposition he had. Difficult to imagine what it could be considering his current place of residence but he said it was all above board and could I get out to visit him the coming Sunday afternoon, Oh and please bring a carton of cigarettes. Sunday arrives and I try to psyche myself for my first ever visit to Her Majesty's Correctional Centre but on arrival found the experience not intimidating at all and in fact was more like a barbecue for families in very pleasant surroundings, open air, with timber benches and tables and people generally appearing to have a good time. On sitting down with the guy I was visiting he explained the proposal. It turned out that in the training centre they had a fully professional printing press capable of printing anything and everything. It was owned by the State government and printed most of the government's publications. He offered to do all my poster and flyer printing at half the cost outside the prison were charging and they could arrange delivery by state government trucks. Also if he could deliver my business he could get moved to the printing shop which was one of the better jobs available. Sounded like a good proposition and he told me he would introduce me to the prisoner in charge of the press. What a surprise when it turned out to be Harry M. Miller the famous entrepreneur and infamous fraudster serving ten months for his dealings in the Computicket failure.

He joined us at our table and barely remembered me as we hadn't met since the Opera House days and he explained how he was in charge of the printing press and he was looking for cash jobs to keep the machines in work. Sounded good to me so we shook hands and I agreed to provide artwork for any upcoming promotions that needed posters or flyers.

It was only a short few weeks after that meeting and I hadn't the need at the time for printing, that on picking up the daily newspaper I read that Harry M. had been moved out of that part of the prison that was considered the soft option and was in danger of losing his good behaviour time off for illegally using Her majesty's printing press to print catalogues, flyers and tickets for his own annual cattle auction.

He may have had a memory lapse as on reading his book 'Confessions of a Not So Secret Agent', he denies any involvement with misuse of the printing press.

IT STOPS A NATION!

In nineteen sixty nine I had recently arrived in Australia and was teaching mathematics at Birrong Boys High School. I can remember the first time I came along an event that stops a nation on the first Tuesday in November. I was teaching a class of fifth formers in the last period of the day when I turned around from the blackboard to see transistor radios being pulled out of school bags and switched on without a care in the world that this was in fact a maths lesson. I put on my most stern voice and told them to put everything away that was not related to calculus and I was howled down by every boy in the class. This was starting to get out of hand and I didn't have a clue as to what was going on. I was noisily informed that it was the Melbourne Cup. So what! The boys pleaded with me so much I decided to seek advice from an Australian teacher. So I walked outside and looked through the window of the class next door and you could have knocked me down with a feather as I saw George Jackson, head of mathematics department writing names of horses on the blackboard, organising a sweepstake and placing a small TV set on his desk for his class to watch the race. Over and out for the day. I went back tail between my legs and sat at the back of the classroom till it was over. I do remember the winner, Rain Lover, and on looking up the result the next day I realised if I'd known about it I would have backed it simply because the owner was also called Clifford.

One year later I was stopped in the street at Bondi by a television crew and asked if I had a story about the Melbourne cup – Did I ever!

FRANKLY I DON'T GIVE A DAMN!

Then there was the time when we had just opened our television production company The Production Factory in Saint Leonards on Sydney's lower north shore. We had rented some office space and purchased some low band tape editing machines primarily to perform off-line editing of the commercials which would save hundreds of dollars when we went into the expensive on-line suites to put together the finished product. This was the early days of VHS and Beta and video stores were not yet in the marketplace. However a friend of mine came to me one day and asked if I could make a copy of a movie for him. Not a problem so out came his copy of Gone with The Wind. He provided me with a tape and we made a copy for him. Later I made a copy for myself. Well shiver me timbers I guess that makes us pirates. Never thought any more about it till a few weeks later a young lady comes into the office and asks if we have any movies for sale. She was looking for movies as she was planning a hen's night for a friend and they were looking at having a night in watching movies. Of course we didn't have any movies until Tracey, our receptionist, reminded me about the copy of Gone with the Wind. Could she have it? Of course! How much? Nothing just replace the VHS tape. She offered to pay the ten dollars it was worth and I took it and that was that or so I thought. I should have got suspicious when she asked for a signed receipt which I duly provided.

The incident was forgotten until about two months later she returned looking for more movies due to the great success of the hen's night. We didn't have any but Tracey, God bless her, happened to pipe up that she had a copy of the Goodbye Girl in her bag. A ten dollar exchange took place and office duties resumed but only for a few minutes. She returned with six guys that looked like something out of an FBI movie. They were flashing their identity cards and one handed me a document that turned out to be a search warrant suggesting that we were running a video piracy business and they could confiscate any materials or equipment they needed to make a criminal case against us. Imagine their disappointment when they burst past reception into a room that could hardly fit them in, never mind a major duplication suite. Their search took all of two minutes. No movies or equipment to be found. A sort of apology and a few red faces especially on the lady federal policewoman. As they were leaving I apologised to them for not letting them know that they were a day late as Eliot Ness and the Untouchables had beaten them by one day taking everything away with them.

It didn't get a laugh.

THE TIME LORDS!

Then there was the time in 1979 when Bryan Nichols of J and B Records called me and invited me to lunch at La Grillade the show business haunt in Crows Nest. It was a surprise when I arrived there to find Bryan, Bob James and the one and only Evil Knievel. Lunch was enjoyable with Evil telling some really tall tales and one couldn't help but be charmed by him. I had no idea what Bryan was doing with him as the only things they had in common was a sense of humour and a tendency to brag about their money and possessions. Bryan was not usually so gregarious but it appeared he needed to keep up in the boasting stakes. This led to Evil taking off his Rolex wristwatch and announcing that this was one of a kind especially crafted by Rolex for him personally and he handed it over to be passed around and inspected. When Bryan was looking at the watch a large grin appeared on his face and he took his own watch off his wrist, passed it to Evil and announced it was exactly the same model Rolex he had paid eleven thousand dollars for. Evil looked at it and grinning like a Cheshire cat he put Bryan's eleven thousand dollar Rolex on the table, picked up the pepper pot and proceeded to smash the watch into pieces. He then handed the pieces to Bryan remarking that as he had said his Rolex was one of a kind.

The rich are different.

A PRIME SUSPECT!

Then there was the time in London in the eighties when Bob and I were making our annual pilgrimage to the Midem music convention in Cannes, France. As usual we spent some time in the U.K. to visit family and look or any business opportunities that presented themselves. At the time we had had a number of financially successful years and as is Bob's wont he insisted on flying business or first class and staying at the top hotels. In fact our nest stop after London was going to be to New York flying Concorde then Los Angeles and back to Sydney. We were booked in the Park Lane Hotel in exclusive Mayfair and Bob decided we were going to eat that night in the caviar and vodka bar that was in the Ritz hotel just a few minutes walk from our hotel. How indulgent I thought but agreed anyway. In the restaurant Bob ordered what could best be described as a tasters plate with a sample of about a dozen different caviars washed down with various vodkas.

It turned out we could only eat about half of what we had bought for around $900 and my immediate thought was to get a doggy bag to take the rest back to the hotel. Bob, being a bit of a snob, thought I was being cheap and we would be embarrassed by asking the question. What a surprise we got when the waiter said of course, they had special take-away packages and they would deliver it to our hotel that same night. Score one for me. In the afternoon of the next day we had a meeting with a film production group who had released a documentary called Executions and they were looking for an Australian New Zealand distributor for the movie. It was quite controversial and the normal distributors had passed on it. The meeting was in the cocktail bar of our hotel and as we reached an agreement on the distribution the barman came over to our table and mentioned that he had our caviar in the fridge behind the bar and would we like it served as a mid-afternoon snack. Everyone at our table was suitably impressed by our gesture to share it so out it came on the best crockery in the hotel and they had provided the crackers and we invested in a bottle of vodka. I use the word investment wisely, as for what we were charged I usually spend only with our stockbroker. There was another couple in the bar discussing business it appeared to us and the lady came over and asked if they would mind them joining us to help us with the caviar.

Who can say no to any lady who looks and talks exactly like Helen Mirren? Of course they can join us.

We bought the distribution rights to Executions but hit a storm of controversy when we went to market it. The media jumped on us saying we were appealing to sadists and lowlifes and this was before they had seen it and if so they would have realised it was a serious documentary which showed how once governments have the right to execution it then moves on to tyranny eg. Nazi Germany and the Spanish Inquisition

We barely made our money back but it was serious lesson I learnt about the media as I was featured on every current affairs television programme along with press and radio criticisms.

HOWAY THE LADS!

Then there was the time in 2002 when Lisa and I were in Britain for a nephew's wedding and a school reunion which were four weeks apart so we had decided to go 'flash packing' which is the equivalent of back packing for better-off older travellers. Using Ryan Air and Easyjet we were able to fly London - Paris- Rome - Barcelona – Venice - London – Ferryhill in the in between weeks costing us about four hundred dollars for the two of us and arriving back in time for the reunion. On the Sunday after the reunion my brother Barry had made it up to the North East and we were having lunch in a small pub in Sedgefield, Tony Blair territory, when I noticed in the paper that Middlesborough, Barry's team, were playing Everton in an FA cup round at the new Riverside Stadium that same afternoon. I asked him he'd like to go and he jumped at the chance so in a purposely designed manner to impress him I called up the stadium and asked for Mark Schwarzer the Middlesborough and Australian goalkeeper who I had met a few times while working with Soccer Australia. He wasn't there but the switchboard said they'd pass on the message when he arrived. Barry thought I was full of bull and said so. So we carried on with lunch and when my phone rang and it was Mark he nearly choked on his Sunday roast beef. We arranged for two tickets in the corporate area and admission to the player's lounge. Barry was flabbergasted when I told him we were going to the match. I kept the VIP parts to myself. One small problem Barry hadn't brought a suit with him but fortunately Stuart, our brother in law, was about the same size so back to their house to get dressed for the occasion. Mark had done well by us. No schlepping about looking for car parking, our names were on the gate so in we went, picked up our passes and were escorted into the inner sanctum of corporate boxes and players lounges. Our second lunch of the day. Everything laid on was too good to leave untouched and the added bonus of Paul Gascoigne playing for Everton.

The game came and went nothing spectacular to report apart from a three nil loss to Middlesborough but then back into the corporate area, drink a few beers and wine then it's time to leave. As we left the lounge who was coming down the corridor going to the lounge? It was Alan Hansen and Gary Lineker, two very famous football internationals now commentating for the BBC. As we neared them I stuck out my right hand and as Hansen grabbed it I asked him how he was and introduced my brother to both of them. We then carried on walking with Barry so gob smacked he couldn't talk till we reached the car. He was so impressed that I knew all these people I couldn't spoil it for him by telling him I didn't know them it's just knowing that if you're confident enough to walk up to anyone in the world as though you know them the great majority will be too well mannered to deny your acquaintance. He believed to his dying day that I knew all these players.

Another football story involves Graeme Souness former captain of Liverpool and Scotland who I met when he was doing a speaking tour of Australia arranged by his business partner, Matt Guildea, a good friend of mine. Graeme had just been sacked by Liverpool and had come through a divorce and was taking an extended honeymoon with his new wife Karen. Lisa and I enjoyed their company over dinner a few times and when they left there was the usual exchange of phone numbers and to make sure to get in touch whenever in England.

Time passed and eventually I had some business in England which allowed me a few days off to spend in the North East catching up with some relatives so I took Lisa and Durham our eight year old son along for the ride. We checked into the only Ferryhill hotel, The Manor House, met the family and enjoyed a couple of days rest. I then realised that as this was Saturday the match of the day was Newcastle against Manchester United on Sunday. So I dug out the Souness's telephone number and rang from the hotel's public phone and spoke to Karen who let me know that Graeme was playing golf but he'd call me on his return so I gave the hotel's number to ring back on. Lisa and Durham had decided to go shopping in Newcastle so I decided to join the locals in the public bar and have a few beers. Telling them I was expecting a call about tickets to the game. Their attitude was there was no chance I could get tickets, it was completely sold out. There were a couple of old school friends I hadn't seen for decades so I was holding court for a while telling stories of world travel. Later in the afternoon the hotel phone rang and the barman answered it then asked if there was a Cliff Atkinson in the bar. I showed myself then totally on purpose asked him who it was on the phone. 'Graeme Souness' was the response. The whole bar went silent as I took the call then came back with the news I had got two tickets for the game and admission to the Platinum Lounge. Graeme would arrange it with his friend, Kevin Keegan, the manager of Newcastle. Was I then king of the kids? My stories of being involved with football as a job elevated me to almost celebrity status with free beer now flowing my way. There's something that needs to be said at this point. I am not a Newcastle supporter and never have been. I have supported Sunderland, Newcastle's arch rivals, all my life.

The next morning after staying in the bar through the Saturday night karaoke saw me feeling a bit fragile but never going to miss out on the occasion we decided as we were leaving for Australia on the Monday, Lisa would catch the train back to London while Durham and I would catch the train after the match and meet her at the Heathrow Airport Hilton in the evening. I then decided to call a friend from my student days, Harry Ashby, who was an ardent Newcastle supporter, who on answering when I mentioned the match told me he couldn't help as he was on a waiting list for a season ticket and didn't have any way of getting a ticket for himself.

He was shell shocked when I told him I was inviting him, so to meet me at Newcastle airport where I was returning our rent a car.

When he picked us up I told him I had two tickets and he swiftly counted there were three of us and offered to give up the idea. No way could I get three of us in. Just watch.

On arrival at St. James Park we walked up to the guest's ticket box office and I asked for the three tickets as arranged with Mr.Souness and Mr. Keegan. The lady was very polite and said she only had two but if we didn't mind the security guard would escort us to the player's lounge.

Did we mind? Of course not. So up in the lift we went, escorted into the player's lounge and told to help ourselves to the food and drink provided. The very first thing I noticed was the players themselves from both teams chatting away to each other and the second was Cantona, the famous French player who became better known for his two legged jump over the fence at a supporter who was heckling him, and Beardsley, an English international, discussing their betting sheets they were filling in.

We trust not on this game we're about to play. It was some years later that I realised where the television series Footballer's Wives came from. The player's lounge could have been backstage at a Rolling Stones concert. Groupies everywhere, standing room only. About half an hour before kick off the players started to head towards the dressing rooms and then to our complete surprise in walked Kevin Keegan with our three passes. I think he thought Graeme Souness would have been there but he was polite anyway and to see the look on Harry's face as I introduced him was worth the whole trip.

I should tell here that Harry was a bit of a personality in the North East of England having been English amateur golf champion in 1972 and 1973 and had joined the pro circuit with Nick Faldo. I had once caddied for him when he won the Durham County championship. He was now head of prisoner education for the north of England and had been for a number of years so he was well up in the contacts ledger so at half time when we were in the Platinum Lounge he was welcomed by dozens of corporate types asking him how he'd obtained tickets for the game and I well remember his response.

"Typical of Newcastle" he said,

"A bloody Sunderland supporter from Australia can get tickets before me who has been on a season ticket waiting list for two years."

STRICTLY ADULTS ONLY

During the Production Factory years we had many strange requests including weddings, will readings, travel guides alongside our staples which included television commercials and pop videos.

As this was the time that video was becoming popular among the masses with the advent of the VCR and home video cameras it was almost compulsory to have a video of any product you were selling.

Perhaps the strangest job we took on was in Kings Cross the red light district of Sydney with its strip clubs and sex shows and we took a telephone call from a gentleman who told us he was opening a new club in the Cross and he needed a ten minute video to be playing outside his front door to attract customers with samples of what was going on inside. Sounded an easy job and quote was accepted and two days later we arrived at the premises on Darlinghurst Road.

On arrival we had no idea of what the job entailed but we soon found out. The proprietor, a middle aged gentleman who wouldn't have looked out of place as a school headmaster led us upstairs to the performance areas and the first shoot to be in the sultan's room.

A large room decorated like something out of Arabian Nights with beautiful furnishings and masses of large scatter cushions all over the floor and erotic paintings on the walls inspired by the Kama Sutra.

The main feature in the middle of the room was a stainless steel pole from floor to ceiling and it soon became the major prop in the video production.

We called action not knowing what to expect and the music started, very Middle Eastern belly dancing kind of music, and in came the performer dressed like Jeannie from the I Dream of Jeannie television show. Small bra top and harem pants. Not that they were on for very long as she stripped down to naked and proceeded to perform what is now known as a pole dance.

The music stopped after a few minutes I called 'cut' and the young lady gathered up her costume and left the room.

We were then guided along the passage way with our equipment into another room which was described as the wigwam and yes, it was decorated like the fantasy world of Hiawatha with nods to all Red Indian icons.

Buffalo hides everywhere and the ubiquitous steel pole in the centre of the room. On action in came two young ladies with wearing the skimpiest squaw costumes and on the sound of the drums began an erotic dance with them pretending to be lesbian lovers.

At this Fitz on camera and Dennis on audio were thanking me for hiring them for such interesting documentaries and could they join the Production Factory full time.

But the job had to be finished and tough as the assignment was somebody had to do it.

Finally we were escorted into the third and last room which was like a school classroom with a couple of desks and all the usual props like maps and blackboard dressing the set.

Yes indeed in came two girls dressed in school uniforms looking like runaways from Saint Trinians, short skirts, white socks, school ties and blouses.

Before we started shooting one of the girls pointed out that usually they had a male dancer with them dressed as a schoolteacher with a cane but he hadn't turned up so how could they perform without him. Us three guys looked at each other, then Fitz and I fixed our gazes on Dennis and after much persuasion, not, he volunteered to venture into the lion's den, sorry classroom.

The girls produced a cane, a mortar board hat and a teacher's black gown and Dennis was ready. Or was he?

The music started and the pseudo erotic dance began with the girls mercilessly teasing Dennis as only erotic dancers can and then they began to involve Dennis by making him stand and rubbing themselves against him. The act started to become a bit more adult as they started to strip the clothes off Dennis and themselves till they were stark naked and he down to his trousers. They then made him lie down and were squirming all over him and it was obvious to all he was reacting to what was going on as one of them took off his belt and was starting to open his trouser flies and I called 'cut'. The girls immediately stopped what they were doing and matter of factly stood up, gathered their clothes and thanked Dennis as they left the classroom.

Poor Dennis. There he was lying semi naked on the floor, unable to move for whatever reason, and he started to mutter a few nasty names aimed at me under his breath.

He never forgave me for the unkindest cut of all and I often had a laugh to myself as I passed the club and saw the video playing on the twenty six inch screen for a few years.

A NORMAL LIFE

I was only wondering what makes a 'normal' life and whether my own fell into that category. Sometime ago I had my 69th birthday in Yaounde in the Cameroon Republic after a successful business week discussing with the President of Cameroon his country's infrastructure needs. The opulence of the presidential palace is in sharp contrast to the rest of the country. The next morning I was invited to a reception for the return of the Cameroon national football team after the African Nations Cup. I was flattered as most of the players wanted to shake my hand and it turned out someone had falsely said I was an ex-footballer. Not true! There's no ex! I still play for North Sydney's over 45's. Not bad seeing at my age. They had been bundled out early. It was intended that I would be driven 600kms to Douala that same afternoon to catch my return flight to Sydney via Johannesburg normally a 24 hour straight through flight via Perth. The reception went too long and I had to race to catch a plane to Douala. Rushing is a strange description for any driving in any African city traffic. Without going into too many details the flight schedule went completely awry and after a world discovery tour taking in, Libreville in Gabon, Nairobi in Kenya, Addis Ababa in Ethiopia, Johannesburg in South Africa then Perth and finally Sydney where my Lisa picked me up at the airport and told me I had called her three days ago when at Douala airport ready to board. A couple of days de-briefing and following up on the trip and then it was Sunday and a football game for Bantry Bay kick off 8am.

A good win and I scored a goal. A few beers and sausage sandwiches after the game, I know it's only ten o clock in the morning, but this is Australia. From the match I went directly to the film studios where I am cast as a lawyer in an American TV series. Luckily I watch Law and Order. Filming took the rest of the day and into the evening. Next day Monday, and I have an appointment with the heart specialist at Royal North Shore Hospital for a routine check-up following my heart attack in 1998. Worth noting the referral was made in June 2014 and the first available time was February 16th 2015. I was feeling very fit and well, no problems, meet specialist at 11am and at 11.10am, told I have a heart rate of 28bpm, 'Is that good?' I asked. That's nearly a third of what it should be. The next 48 hours are a blur as by 12.30pm I'm in a hospital bed with needles and other things sticking in me, doctors and nurses fussing over me and asking me about my symptoms and registering their surprise at the fact I didn't have any. Told I would be having an operation the following afternoon I settled in only to be woken up at 7am with the news there had been two cancellations and I was on the table at 7.30am. Next thing I know I wake up to be told I've had a pacemaker inserted and my heart rate is now normal at 68bpm. A few more checks through the day and then told everything went perfectly. Slept that night and was woken up to a couple more checks then told I could go home. Got showered, left RNSH and caught the bus home outside the main doors.

P.S. Can't praise the staff at RNSH enough they were magnificent.

Normal life is very good. Playing football on Saturday then on Monday off to Laos and Myanmar to help build major concrete plants for dam constructions.

It certainly is A Long Way From Ferryhill.

Looking back on my life to date I have seen many places and met many people both likable and dislikable and in looking forward to my next stage in life I hope I can accomplish only a part of what has gone before. In travelling to many undeveloped countries I have seen noses pressed up against the window panes from a different angle and I can assure you there is no pleasure in being on the other side seeing the poverty that prevails in many countries, in fact it makes me very sad to see it having known it.

Atkinson Grandparents I never knew. Dad is baby in arms.

Barry and Clifford Redcar beach 1950

Clifford with first bike Circa 1954

Our parent's wedding.

Our parents at my first wedding.

1983 First Sydney marathon. Last Clifford marathon.

Nearly famous film director. 'It's the glamour'.

Lisa and Cliff's wedding 1993.

Durham, my best man, wants the ring.

Back lane of 1, Surtees Tce. Ferryhill

Lisa and Cliff with one of the world's richest women
Gina Rinehart at 2017 Australian mining awards.

First time in 30 years the Atkinson brood in one place.
From l-r Anne, Barry, Sheila, Clifford, Joyce.

Still playing football for North Sydney at 73 years old

Celebrating being number one crowd pulling
promoter in first year of SOH

Breaking the parallel import cartel reducing price of music by 60%.

Printed in the United States
___ Bloomington?

Printed in the United States
By Bookmasters